WHAT MAKES GREAT PRODUCTS GREAT?

A PRODUCT MANAGEMENT BOOTCAMP

The How-To Guide To Discover Best Practices,
Answer Hard Questions and Build Better Products

Jeff Callan

tyghtwyre
Published by Tyghtwyre

Copyright © 2023 by Jeff Callan

All rights reserved. No part of this book may be reproduced or used in any manner without the prior written permission of the copyright owner, except for the use of brief quotations in a book, blog or book review. Thank you for buying an authorized copy of this book and for complying with all copyright laws.

While the publisher and author have made best efforts in creating this book, there are no representations or warranties with regard to the completeness or accuracy of the contents of this book. No warranty is made, implied or otherwise, that the information contained herein is suitable for any particular purpose. Specifically, the ideas, strategies and tactics included here may not be appropriate for your particular situation. You should discuss any planned actions with a knowledgeable professional when possible. Execution is everything. Neither the publisher nor author shall be liable for any damages arising from the use of this book.

The author has made every effort to provide current information as of the publishing of this edition of the book. QR codes are provided throughout the book which may include links to updates and revisions. The author and publisher assume no responsibility for any errors or omissions or for any third-party content referenced herein. In the event that you feel that something requires a correction, please contact the publisher or author so that it can be updated in future editions.

Hardcover ISBN: 979-8-9884309-2-6
Paperback ISBN: 979-8-9884309-1-9
Kindle/E-book ISBN: 979-8-9884309-0-2
First edition, August 2023
Library of Congress Control Number: 2023912295

Edited by Laurie Ellinghausen Callan
Cover art, book layout, templates and diagrams by Jeff Callan
Cover photograph by wayhomestudioo,
under license from Envato Elements (License Code: GY9XTR5ZVA)

Printed by Kindle Direct Publishing
Published by Tyghtwyre LLC in Overland Park, Kansas

www.tyghtwyre.com
www.whatmakesgreatproductsgreat.com

To my wife, Laurie, my first reader and trusted editor who inspires me every day with her integrity, intelligence, beauty and passion for excellence. Without her support, this book wouldn't exist.

To my guys, Reggie and Myles, great writing companions who teach me important product lessons from a cat's perspective.

TABLE of CONTENTS

CHAPTER 1: Things Could Be So Much Better... OMG. Does My Product Suck? 1

CHAPTER 2: Products Are Everywhere!........................ 5

CHAPTER 3: Product Problems Are Company Problems 20

CHAPTER 4: Twelve Things Your Product Team Should STOP Doing Today 29

CHAPTER 5: Are You Too Busy "Getting Stuff Done" To Think About Strategy? 46

CHAPTER 6: Even A GOAT Needs A Plan. Where's Yours? 59

CHAPTER 7: Telling Your Product's Story To People With Short Attention Spans – The Power Of An Elevator Pitch 71

CHAPTER 8: The Four Whys - If Your Competition Reads This First, They'll Probably Take Your Customers Too 80

CHAPTER 9: There's A Story in Your Product's Data – Do You Know What It Is? 94

CHAPTER 10: The Tour De France And What You Need to Know About Business Processes 127

CHAPTER 11: What Is The Product Life-Cycle? Or, How To Kill Your Product (Or Maybe Not) 141

CHAPTER 12: Creating A Feedback-Rich Product Environment ... 153

CHAPTER 13: What Is A North Star And Why Is It Important? ... 171

CHAPTER 14: Your Product Plan - The Bridge Between Vision And Execution 180

CHAPTER 15: Getting To The Bottom Line - Building A Strong Business Case For Your Product 198

CHAPTER 16: Writing Effective Product Requirements - It's Not Rocket Science 208

CHAPTER 17: Why Product Roadmaps Matter For Your Business (And How To Create One).. 227

CHAPTER 18: Prioritization – Essential And Not As Hard As You Think 240

CHAPTER 19: The Real MVP = Minimum Viable Prototype....... 253

CHAPTER 20: How To Know If You're Winning - Choosing The Right KPIs For Your Product 265

CHAPTER 21: Going Beyond Product-Market Fit 279

CHAPTER 22: Achieving Long-Term Product-Business Strategy Alignment.. 292

CHAPTER 23: Van Halen And (Not The) WHO – How To Use A Checklist For Your Next Product Launch 303

CHAPTER 24: What Makes Great Products Great? The Magic Of A Customer Journey 318

CHAPTER 25: Getting More Productive by Taking Control of Your Time and Fighting Interruption Culture.............. 339

CHAPTER 26: The Art of Innovation – What You Need to Know to Get and Stay Ahead 354

CHAPTER 27: How To Build A Product-Focused Culture 383

Community, Future Chapters and Downloads 415
Acknowledgements 416
About The Author 422
Author's Recommended Reading List 423
Index 426

CHAPTER 1:
Things Could Be So Much Better...
OMG. Does My Product Suck?

It all starts with an "oh no!" moment when you realize you just might be in a little bit over your head. How'd you end up here? Maybe somebody on your team quit unexpectedly. Or maybe you simply underestimated the resources that you needed to deliver this product. It doesn't really matter today. Either way, you're not making that deadline. Even worse, you personally are working harder than ever – doing multiple jobs now trying to fill the gaps, triaging battle-scarred egos and fighting the inevitable fires that spread easily when you're short-staffed.

No one else in the organization really understands your situation. They've got their own fires to put out. But you can bet that everyone will notice the minute you miss your date. Marketing and PR is all lined up around those dates. The sales team is revved up and pitching the new features and customers are delaying purchases to make sure they get the new stuff.

Now, you're alone and you're in trouble. If you're prone to panic attacks, you're deep into one now. Deep breaths in. Count to four. Deep breaths out....

Is it time to compromise on the 1.0 version of the product and start cutting features and scaling back expectations? The minute you do that, you're on a steep and slippery slope. But there'll be less to notice by cutting a feature here or there than there will be if you miss that date. After all, the marketing team and your C-suite executives aren't actually going to **USE** the product. They just talk about it. Besides, you can always get the missing stuff into the next release. Right? So, you make the compromise, de-scope the features and push the pause button on the pressure cooker you've been living in.

Ultimately, you manage to hit your launch date, but the product's not everything that you or the actual paying customers expected. Sales are not quite hitting projections. Is it the fact that you don't have that key feature that you scoped out? Is it the sales team? Let's say it's sales. Whatever you do, just don't blink.

The support team is getting slammed with tickets on the new release too. Maybe it wasn't the best idea to cut back on some of the testing, but you had to get the product shipped, right? You'll have to triage the bugs that should have been caught by your team and not a customer. More communications. More follow-ups. More (lots more) emails.

You haven't been home for dinner at a decent time for months. You're living on coffee and adrenaline. Even your dog is pissed off at you.

When things aren't going right from a product standpoint and you're the one in charge, it can have a tremendous impact on all aspects of your life. Maybe it means that you're working seventy hours a week. Maybe you don't get to spend as much time at home with your family. Maybe the stress of it all gets to you and impacts your physical health. Maybe you haven't had a weekend off for six months. Or maybe you have weekends, but you hate Sunday nights because you know that you gotta get up first thing on Monday and go back to the job that's killing you.

What the hell happened here? Doesn't there have to be a better way? What are you missing that other people have figured out?

But see, the thing is you're not alone. Others have been here. Others have figured this out. You've survived a hundred percent of your "oh no!" moments so far, and you can survive this batch too if you can learn to identify the problems and figure out the solutions. There's still a chance that you can be the hero in this story and this book will show you how. There's a lot of experience on these pages.

Learn from the mistakes that people have made. Copy their successes and avoid their failures.

Your product doesn't have to suck. Or suck the life out of *you*.

You can do this.

This book is for you if...

...you're an aspiring product manager who wants to learn but you don't have a ton of product management implementation experience or the time to acquire it. You wonder, "Am I doing this right?" and feel like you're always learning everything the hard way.
...you're an experienced product manager, a product management leader, a startup founder or someone who wants to build great products and scale a business but you're slipping dates and missing on your metrics or shipping broken products on time and hoping no one notices. You've got pressure from investors or the C-suite to deliver quick results and everyone's expecting great things to happen with never-enough resources and unrealistic timelines.
...you're a business executive, product marketing person or a C-suite leader who doesn't fully understand what product managers do, but you sense that things might be askew in that part of the business and you might need to troubleshoot it.

If any of that sounds like you, you're going to get a better understanding of product management essentials from reading this book. You'll find techniques and strategies that will lead to better, more consistent product launches and significantly improved products in the market. You'll learn how to manage your time and set priorities. Your team and organization will find confidence knowing that they've got an actual product methodology in place to deliver consistent results and the metrics in place to know when they're going off target.

In this book, I've included stories about products that succeeded and others that completely failed. There will be exercises to help you learn more about yourself, your products and your organization. You'll find examples and templates for key deliverables that are essential parts of a product manager's day-to-day existence.

The subject matter for the book loosely aligns to three key areas for product management. First, we'll help you understand what's broken or not working optimally in the products you have in the market now and make recommendations on things you can do to fix them. Second, we'll define best practices for product management organizations with a detailed, easy-to-understand breakdown of the tricks and techniques you can use to be an effective product manager. Third, the book will make recommendations on how to implement and execute on those techniques and build a solid product-focused culture that delivers well-prioritized features and products on time and with consistent quality.

One last important point before we get going – while the book has a beginning, middle and end, you can really read it in any order. If a chapter doesn't feel relevant to your work situation, skip it and go back to the Table of Contents and pick out one that's calling to you. I won't mind.

If you're a product person (or aspire to be one), you're in the right place. I'm glad you're here. Let's begin.

CHAPTER 2:
Products Are Everywhere!

In March 2003, my buddy Jason Delker and I were zipping down I-35 through central Texas on our way back from Austin's South By Southwest music conference. Delk's a product guy too. One of the best. I'm not sure exactly how many patents he's on, but I know it's in the 100s and counting. The trip back from SXSW is always a bit of a downer after the dizzy rush of seeing forty or so bands in over four days playing in small clubs on Sixth Street. The drive back to Kansas City is nine hours and it can feel like ninety. The only way to do this trip is to hit triple digits as much as possible across Oklahoma when the traffic thins out.

But we hadn't hit the OK-TEX border yet and the traffic's a lot thicker between Austin and Dallas. We were buzzing about a then up-and-coming band we'd seen called The Black Keys as we drove past an interstate-facing storefront that had a twenty-five-foot-tall fiberglass dude in a cowboy hat standing in front. Arms extended, he was inviting passersby to look, stop and visit the store.

I don't know what inspired me that day. Maybe the boredom of the drive was starting to settle in. But I started riffing about the idea that back in the sixties, there was a "Big F*ckin' Guy" salesman that was going door-to-door to businesses across Texas trying to sell everyone a BFG that was going to stand out in front of their store along the newly minted interstate and get people's attention.

The BFG salesperson, I imagined, worked for a BFG business that designed and made the BFGs. Somewhere a BFG product manager was coming up with ideas for new versions of the BFG. And there was a warehouse full of BFGs that the sales guy needed to clear out and they were priced to move. Delk and I were dying laughing at the idea that any of this would actually exist.

Maybe you had to be there.

But I was thinking about that day as I was doing the research for this book. I found out that the BFGs had a name. They're called "muffler men." There's a Wikipedia page that lists the location of over one hundred of 'em. Roadside America (roadsideamerica.com) has a map with even more of them identified. Some of these muffler men are famous enough to have their own websites including Chicken Boy in Los Angeles (chickenboy.com) and Gemini Giant on Route 66 in Wilmington, Illinois (geminigiant.com).

Turns out the reality is that I wasn't far off when I was riffing with Delk across Texas. Back in the sixties, there was a business called International Fiberglass in Venice, California. The first muffler man was actually a custom-built Paul Bunyan that was built for the Paul Bunyan Restaurant on Route 66 in Flagstaff, Arizona. Instead of a muffler, he was holding Paul Bunyan's ax. Once the fiberglass molds were made, it was relatively easy to make alternative versions holding things like mufflers, hot dogs, golf clubs and rockets. The muffler men sold for between $1000 and $3000 each and a business was born.

As novel as muffler men are, it's easy to forget that the fiberglass giants were designed to solve a business problem. The USA was becoming an automobile-centered driving culture. We were going coast-to-coast on new interstates and highways. Businesses were trying to catch the attention of the cars that were zipping past their establishments. Having a twenty-five-foot BFG standing outside your business was a sure bet to catch people's eyes as they drove by.

Eventually, the market for BFGs tapered off. International Fiberglass was sold in 1976 and the huge molds used to create the plastic goliaths were destroyed. Over time, the remaining muffler men have been changed to become spacemen, football players, women in bikinis, aliens, pirates, and so on. Today, they're still standing tall, selling tires, hamburgers, ice cream, chips and salsa, and of course, mufflers. And although you can't buy a new muffler man, as often happens, they've been replaced by a cheaper and more high-tech version.

The tube man.

Also known as an air dancer, you've probably seen those whippy guys trying to get your attention as you drive past a new business's grand opening. They're giant twenty-foot-tall inflatable stick figures, usually with waving arms and a silly googly-eyed face. They solve the same problem as a BFG, but they're cheaper (under $200), lighter to transport, and easier to set up or take down. They also have the added feature of movement to help mesmerize the passing motorists.

As it turns out, even though I was joking about the idea of BFG salespeople and BFG product managers, it brings home the reality that products are everywhere you look. The decisions made by someone in the role of a product manager, even if they don't have that specific title, impact every aspect of our lives. And product management lessons, just like products, are also everywhere you look.

Defining The Role of Product Management

In this chapter, we're going to get a better understanding of what a product manager does and the key skills that they need to be successful in the job. So, what exactly is product management? The definition according to Wikipedia is:

"Product management is the business process of planning, developing, launching, and managing a product or service. It includes the entire lifecycle of a product, from ideation to development to go to market. Product managers are responsible for ensuring that a product meets the needs of its target market and contributes to the business strategy, while managing a product or products at all stages of the product lifecycle."

That's a pretty reasonable definition. When I try to explain to people what a product manager does, I ask them to picture a person sitting in a swivel chair. The person in the chair talks to a potential customer, someone like my mom, and figures out what types of problems or pain points she might have that could be solved to create a market opportunity. Then they swivel in their chairs to talk to engineers, designers, and developers to generate a solution for the pain point. Next, they swivel to talk to marketing and sales to figure out how to communicate the value of this new solution back to my mom. Along the way, they're swiveling and having conversations with other departments like legal (to create terms and conditions), customer support (to understand and fix any product defects), manufacturing, research, design, operations, finance, IT, and so on. The product manager is the hub of the wheel, the subject matter expert, and the primary decision-maker for their product. They're the communication hub that keeps all the other teams in the loop and they drive action with those teams as it relates to their product.

What product management ISN'T is project management, although this is often confused by people who have done neither. Project management is all about timelines, scope, and deliverables. In comparison, product management is about vision, strategy, execution, and results. Project management is focused on the delivery of a specific set of requirements on a specific timeline. Product management is focused on figuring out what those requirements should be so that they meet customer needs and can be sold profitably. Project management gets something built. Product managers make sure that the thing getting built is the right thing. They are complementary positions that can and should collaborate, but not the same job.

Product Management Wheel

Different companies may define their product management role differently. Some companies might consider the product manager to be more of a product owner role focused on product requirements and user stories in an Agile/Scrum development shop. Unfortunately, those shops are probably focused more on generating features than creating cohesive and strategic products. Frequently, larger companies will see the product manager in more of a product marketing role. This tends to be focused on revenue generation, but often falls short of really accounting for the product costs and efficiencies that ultimately drive profitability. Sometimes the product manager is really more of a channel manager or a vendor manager because the company isn't building their own solutions. At the end of the day, if it works for the organization, I'm not here to say they're doing it wrong. But I think that they could be doing it better by adopting a more traditional product management role where the PM sits in the swivel chair and collaborates across multiple teams to manage these areas with a cohesive single product vision and a well-formed strategy. We'll talk about this a lot more later in the book.

The Eleven Core Skills of a Product Manager

To be a successful product manager, you need to have a wide range of skills in your toolkit. From the ability to communicate both verbally and in writing to strong interpersonal skills, problem solving, and technical understanding, product managers need to wear many hats. Let's take a closer look at each of these eleven key skills.

1. *Communication* - One of the most important skills for any product manager is the ability to communicate both verbally and in writing. This includes being able to clearly articulate your vision for the product, its features and benefits, and how it fits into the overall company strategy. It also means being able to effectively communicate with cross-functional teams such as engineering, design, sales, marketing, and support. Strong communication skills are essential for any product manager who wants to be successful.

2. *Interpersonal Skills* - To be an effective product manager, you need strong people skills. You have to build relationships with people inside and outside of the company. It also means being able to influence people without having direct authority over them. Additionally, interpersonal skills are important for managing conflict and handling the difficult conversations that inevitably arise when you're moving fast as a team and building things.

3. *Problem Solving* - Another key skill that all product managers need is problem solving. You'll need to be able to identify problems early on and then quickly produce creative solutions that work within the constraints of the situation. Additionally, problem-solving skills are important for troubleshooting issues that arise during development or after launch.

4. *Technical Understanding* - A successful product manager often needs a strong technical understanding. Not always, but this is increasingly important. At a minimum, you'll be expected to understand how the product works under the hood as well as being familiar with common technical terms and jargon.

Additionally, technical understanding is important for collaborating closely with engineers during development and for debugging issues that arise after launch.

5. *Marketing Expertise* - Marketing ability is another key skill that all product managers need, such as understanding core principles such as market segmentation, target markets, positioning, and messaging. Additionally, marketing expertise is important for developing go-to-market strategies and launch plans that get results.

6. *Business Acumen* - In addition to marketing expertise, product managers also need a strong business acumen. You'll want to understand basic financial concepts such as profit and loss (P&L), return on investment (ROI), and cost of goods sold (COGS). Additionally, business acumen is important for evaluating opportunities, making decisions about features and pricing, and developing business cases for new products or features.

7. *Setting Priorities* - Another important skill for product managers is the ability to set priorities. A product manager makes decisions and needs to have a good reason for those choices. Understand the company's overall strategy and objectives and then align your work with those goals. Additionally, setting priorities is important for deciding which features to build and when to release them.

8. *Attention to Detail* - In addition to setting priorities, paying attention to detail is another important skill for product managers. This includes being able to keep track of all the

moving parts of a project and making sure that nothing falls through the cracks. Additionally, paying attention to detail is important for catching errors and ensuring that the final product meets all quality standards.

9. *Project Management* - Wait. Didn't I just say that a product manager and a project manager aren't the same? Yeah, well, a lot of times as a product manager, you won't have the luxury of having a dedicated project management resource and you'll have to do it yourself. Stuff still needs to get delivered on time, so project management is another key skill that product managers need to be able to step into as a subset of their overall role. This includes being able to effectively manage *all* aspects of a project, from start to finish. Additionally, project management skills are important for working with cross-functional teams, managing budgets, and ensuring that projects are delivered on time and within scope.

10. *Strategic Thinking* - Strategic thinking is another key skill that product managers need. This includes being able to see the big picture and think long-term when making decisions about the product. Additionally, strategic thinking is important for aligning the product with the company's overall business goals and objectives.

11. *Time Management* - Last but not least, time management is an important skill for product managers. This includes being able to juggle multiple projects at the same time and prioritize tasks to meet deadlines. Additionally, time management skills are important for dealing with unexpected delays or disruptions and for staying calm under pressure.

As you can see from this list of key skills, there's a lot that goes into being a successful product manager. Sometimes the search for a great product manager hire can feel a bit like unicorn hunting. But I swear they exist and even if you can't find one, hopefully you can develop some of the skills by reading about them in this book. Or maybe you're not convinced yet that product managers are important and their work is everywhere you look? If not, please indulge me for another page.

No. Really. They're Everywhere.

Take a look around the room you're in now. Somewhere in there, you'll probably find a light bulb. A simple light bulb. But is it fluorescent? LED? Halogen? Incandescent?

There are a variety of light bulbs on the market today, and each has its advantages and disadvantages. Incandescent bulbs are the traditional type of light bulb, but they are not very energy-efficient. Compact fluorescent lamps (CFLs) are more energy-efficient than incandescent bulbs, but they contain mercury and can take longer to reach full brightness. Light-emitting diodes (LEDs) are the most energy-efficient type of light bulb, but they are also the most expensive.

Light bulbs can also have a range of colors just to define white light – soft white, bright white, cool white, outdoors. A single LED can produce a range of colors on demand. The amount of light needed, measured in lumens, also matters. You might need 1500 lumen in your living room, but as much as 10,000 lumen in a kitchen. Concerned about energy efficiency? Wattage for standard indoor bulbs can range from four watts for a low-light LED to 100 watts for the brightest incandescent standard bulbs.

There's a light switch on the wall and it's got a light switch cover. Plastic, wood, or metal? Dimmer switch? One switch or two or even three or four? A slider or rotating knob? Paired with an electrical outlet or USB connection? Alexa-controlled smart switch? White, off-white, cream, or some other color?

All of these options were created to meet your anticipated lighting needs in terms of cost, style, amount of light, and so on. Someone had to do the work to figure out the ways you might want to use light in your house.

Everywhere you look someone's made decisions on what to make and why. Someone's taken an idea and turned it into a commodity that can be sold profitably at scale. And even if those people didn't have the title of product manager, they were filling the same role of determining a potential customer's needs and figuring out a solution that could be developed and sold for a profit.

Products are everywhere.

Once you see the world this way, it's really hard to see it any other way. When I go to see a live concert, of course I'm there to see the band. But I notice the equipment that they use and the production elements that go into the on-stage performance. Video, lighting, sound, stage design – all of it pairs with the music to create a full sensory audience experience. That's the product a ticket holder buys. Sometimes, like with the Electric Daisy Carnival in Las Vegas, the experience is a blaze of lights, colors and sounds. Other times, say at a Bruce Springsteen and the E Street Band show, the stage is spare, everyone's wearing black, and the show is focused on The Boss himself.

But even inside the arena itself, there are other subtle experience details that someone had to work out. For example, at the T-Mobile Center here in Kansas City, when you go to a concert and the lights are down and the music's getting loud, there are these almost unnoticeable pinpoint lights coming down from the ceiling of the arena. They illuminate just the path for the steps so that people can safely go up and down during the show in an otherwise darkened venue. Somehow, they've managed to figure out how to illuminate ONLY those paths, the steps, and not have the light bleed into or disrupt the view from the audience.

How did they do that? Someone had to figure out exactly how much light they could create and then what kind of distribution pattern to use from the ceiling so that it wouldn't spread out and diffuse into the audience. But you also don't want people falling down steps or tumbling into rows of seats, especially after they've had a couple of adult beverages. That's a pretty specific problem to solve and they nailed it.

Nearly every aspect of modern life has been impacted by product management decisions. There are all kinds of modern-day muffler men being created to get your attention or solve your problems. But they don't always get it right. Sometimes products suck and when they miss the mark, it can impact an entire company. We'll talk about that in the next chapter.

TL;DR
- Muffler men were created in the sixties by a company called International Fiberglass to solve a business problem – businesses needed a way to catch people's attention as they drove by.
- There is no one authoritative definition of product management, but it generally refers to the process of planning, developing, launching, and managing a product or service.
- Product managers are responsible for ensuring that a product meets the needs of its target market and contributes to the business strategy while managing stakeholders and all phases of the product's life-cycle.
- To be a successful product manager requires eleven core skills: communication, interpersonal skills, problem solving, technical understanding, marketing expertise, business acumen, setting priorities, paying attention to detail, project management, strategic thinking, and time management.

CHAPTER EXERCISES:
1. Take a few minutes and make a list of some of the products in the room you're sitting in right now. Think about some of the choices that the people making the product decisions must have made when they designed the product.
2. Look at the stakeholder groups mentioned in the Product Management wheel diagram. How do these functions map over to your company or organization? Are there other groups you'd add? Groups you'd remove? Maybe there are some groups that have a different name but cover the same functions?

3. Rate yourself on each of the core skills by putting a check mark in the appropriate box:

Core Skill	Strong	Average	Need Improvement
Communication			
Interpersonal Skills			
Problem Solving			
Technical Understanding			
Marketing Expertise			
Business Acumen			
Setting Priorities			
Attention to Detail			
Project Management			
Strategic Thinking			
Time Management			

CHAPTER NOTES:

Because I tend to read a lot and synthesize my ideas across all the reading, I wanted to share some of my research notes and links so you can engage with some of the great websites, blogs, books and videos that helped me write a better book. These QR codes included at the end of each chapter will lead to a set of chapter notes including clickable links that will take you directly to the content. My hope is that the codes will make it as frictionless as possible for you to take a look. I'd love to hear your feedback on this idea – good or bad.

CHAPTER 3:
Product Problems Are Company Problems

In 1996, the FDA approved a product called Olestra, a fat substitute that added no calories to foods and could be used in cooking, frying, and baking. Procter & Gamble had been working on versions of the product since it was originally discovered almost 30 years earlier in 1968. The key selling point of Olestra was that this fat was not absorbed by the body and was deemed safe for human consumption.

By 1998, Frito-Lay launched their WOW Chips using P&G's Olestra and they exploded onto the scene. The snack became the best-selling new product in the USA with almost $400 million in sales.

But just two years later, sales had fallen to $200 million. Why such a substantial drop in a product that had launched so successfully? Well, the FDA issued a warning that Olestra consumption might cause some unpleasant side effects, including diarrhea and abdominal cramping. They may have also used the term "anal leakage" at one point. Evidently, these side effects had snuck up on a few people, much to their mortified surprise.

Or maybe it was more than a few people. The FDA received more than 20,000 consumer complaints about the product, which was more than they had ever received for all other food additives combined. Turned out that Olestra was reasonably safe to consume in small amounts, but excessive consumption could cause gastrointestinal fireworks. Of course, Lay's iconic slogan at the time was "Betcha Can't Eat Just One."

WOW, indeed.

Olestra is a clear example of how a product problem can ripple and rumble its way through the rest of an organization. Procter & Gamble was getting impassioned feedback from the market that this product was causing some volatile issues with customers. Sales dropped in half, but you could hardly blame the sales teams for the rapid contraction in the market after the initial eruption in sales. It's not the marketing team's fault either. Were they supposed to change the slogan to "Betcha Can't Eat Just One, But You Better Not Eat a Whole Bag Either"?

As a side note, Olestra hasn't entirely been flushed away. In the 2000's it made a comeback as an industrial lubricant and paints additive under the brand name Sefose. Because all the best food additives double as industrial lube...

In this section, we're going to explore the impact of product issues on an organization and better understand why the investment made in your products is so important. So, while we're kinda on the subject of food, think about a time you waited forever at a restaurant. You walk into a place and nobody's there to seat you or take your order. People are standing around. It just doesn't feel like the business is running smoothly and you can sense the bad energy the minute you walk in the door.

Most of the time when you're waiting forever, it's because there's a problem in the kitchen. When the kitchen slows, the rest of the business suffers. Keeping the food flowing is essential to a smoothly running restaurant. Food is their product and when there's no product coming out of the kitchen, everything else breaks down. Servers are standing around. People who were working on the service side shift to the kitchen to help out and service slows down. Tables aren't getting turned over and the wait time to even get seated spirals up. But it's not a service problem; it's a food problem that shows up in the service. This can be worsened when you have complex menus with lots of different items to make. It can put a strain on the kitchen to execute.

Compare that to your favorite hole-in-the-wall joint. A lot of times they have very simple menus – a handful of items that they crank out easily. Maybe they don't do a lot, but what they do, they do very well and very efficiently. My favorite chicken in Kansas City (or the rest of the world, for that matter) comes from a little place called El Pollo Rey. They have three things on the menu – half a grilled chicken, whole grilled chicken, and buffalo chicken wings. And you don't get the wings, which likely start out frozen, because the main event is the fresh chicken smoking on the grill. The smell is amazing. You'll probably sniff it on your clothes the rest of the day, which is a bonus in my book. Every meal is served with fresh tortillas, salsa and beans. That's it. Nothing else. And there's a line out the door to get this wood-fired, no-frills experience.

If you went to a fancy restaurant with great service but the food sucked, how many times would you go back? Getting bad food with a smile is not exactly a winning recipe for a successful bistro. A product problem is a business problem. The investment that your company makes in your product is the single most important investment that your business makes.

Think about it.

If you're not solving customer problems, then how do you expect to get customers? How many businesses can last long with not enough customers? Venture-funded startups aside, not many.

Bad Product = No Customers = No Company

In Mike Michalowicz's book *Fix This Next*, he talks about The Business Hierarchy of Needs. Compare this to Maslow's hierarchy of needs that you might have learned about in school, which says that humans have certain types of needs and that these start with basic needs for survival (food, water) and safety (shelter). Once these basic needs are met, people move up the hierarchy to the need for love and belongingness. Eventually, they reach the highest levels where things like esteem and self-actualization exist. It becomes difficult, if not impossible, to reach the highest needs if you're still trying to survive each day.

In a model that Michalowicz calls the Business Hierarchy, he starts at the bottom of his pyramid with Sales, going through Profit, Order, Impact, and Legacy at the highest level. To sustain your business, you have to have sales and cash flow before you can worry about profit and efficiency. So, if you have a product that falls short, you'll have too few customers and eventually, no company. And that's why the investment in getting your product right is the most important one your company can make.

If a bad product hits the streets, it'll leave a stain on everything it touches. It can take years to overcome the brand impact of a single bad product release, driving significant expense in the form of brand marketing to clean up your company's reputation afterward.

A second area that'll require a clean up – your social media and online reviews. These days, when someone's considering any purchase of significance, they go online. They do their research to try to understand what people who have had a similar interest, problem, or need have done. They're gonna "Google it" and see all the Yelp or Amazon reviews. The blog posts. The tweets. The YouTube videos.

If your online presence sucks, that creates a real drag on your ability to get new customers.

Going a step far beyond a few bad reviews, legal liability lawsuits from a bad product can put a company in a deep financial hole if not completely shut down the business. Even worse, defective products can cause injury or loss of life. For example, back in the 1970s, Ford was trying to respond to the growing threat of Japanese competition in the US small car market. They rushed the Ford Pinto to market and the results were tragic.

Ford Motor Company introduced the Pinto in 1971 as a compact car that would compete with foreign manufacturers such as Volkswagen, Honda, and Toyota. The product took just twenty-five months to get to market, compared to the typical forty-three months in the auto industry at the time.

But rushing the car to market caused significant design and testing issues. Most notably, there was a rear-mounted fuel tank that could explode when the car was rear-ended, causing horrible fiery accidents. In 1978, criminal charges of reckless homicide were filed against Ford after a Pinto exploded, killing three girls. Ultimately, more than a hundred lawsuits were brought against Ford, with more than $100 million in damages and settlements. The Pinto story is often cited as an example of corporate negligence, and it continues to be a cautionary tale in business ethics to this day.

But even if your product issues are much less severe than the Ford Pinto, they can drive unwanted costs into your business. Product returns will drive up inventory handling and processing costs, not to mention the fact that you're giving back money you worked hard to earn. If you have to provide replacements, you're incurring those costs again.

Moreover, any business that sells products knows that product support can be a significant cost. If people can't figure out how to use your product due to poor design, bad or missing documentation, or an actual defect, someone's going to have to talk to that customer unless you're ok with losing them. A bad product can produce a spike, or worse, a long-term increase in customer support calls resulting in bigger teams of people handling the call volume, and higher overall labor costs as a percentage of your product's price.

On top of that, a warranty may be needed as your company competes for customers, but if you have to repair your product under warranty, you'll be eating those costs. Just the cost of shipping the product back and forth can add up quickly. In addition, the cost of labor to repair the product can also be significant. In some cases, the cost of parts may also be a factor. As a result, product repairs under warranty can drive unwanted costs into a business. Underestimating these costs can impact pricing and put your product's business case underwater if the issues are severe enough. As a result, businesses must be diligent in watching their repair costs and making sure that they are not eating into their profits.

There's more. If you have established resellers or other external sales channels, you could get dropped if your partners are spending too much of their time dealing with the headaches that can come from a troublesome product. Excessive amounts of customer refunds can even get you kicked off the payment platforms used to collect your revenue because that's frequently seen as an indicator of fraudulent activity.

One further impact is that product problems result in a lack of repeat customers. The customer acquisition costs you incur to gain a customer can be a significant upfront investment and getting a customer to buy more than once is a critical sustaining element for most businesses. When a customer receives a defective product or can't get through your onboarding process, they are immediately overcome with buyer's remorse and likely feel that they wasted their money. If you're lucky, the issues are minor and if your product still provides some value, they might give you a second chance and buy again. But if the customer experience is poor and they never stick around long enough to discover your product's value, how likely are they to buy a second time even if you've improved the product?

Deaths and physical injuries aside, maybe the worst impact for a company with a bad product is that over time, a history of underwhelming products can lead to poor company morale, increased employee turnover, and negative company culture. People know when they're selling crap. If your job all day long every day is to try to sell that crap, you're not going to feel very good about yourself. You're not going to feel great about the people that you work with either. Ultimately, you're going to try to find a more positive work environment with better products that are more aligned with your values and personal identity. This results in the best people with higher work standards moving on and taking their experience and accumulated knowledge with them, leaving mediocrity behind along with the costs of onboarding and training someone to take their place. Once you land in this death spiral, lifting the company out can be a Sisyphean job that challenges even the strongest of leaders.

In sum, product defects can have a significant negative impact on a business, both in terms of costs and reputation. Consequently, businesses need to take measures to prevent or mitigate product defects. By doing so, they can minimize the unwanted costs associated with defective products. If you're seeing issues in sales, marketing, support, or HR, any of those problems might have a product problem as their root cause.

And that's why the investment your company makes in your products is so important.

TL;DR

- The investment in getting your product right is the most important one your company can make.
- If you're not solving customer problems, then how do you expect to get customers?
- If a business wants to sustain itself, it needs sales and cash flow before worrying about profit and efficiency.
- Product problems often result in a lack of repeat customers which then affects revenue, resources, company morale and turnover rates.
- A bad product can take years to recover from in terms of brand reputation and online presence. It can also lead to legal liability lawsuits, increased customer support costs, warranty expenses, etc.
- Legal liability lawsuits from a bad product can put a company in a deep financial hole if not completely shut down the business.
- Product returns will drive up inventory handling and processing costs, not to mention the fact that you're giving back money you worked hard to earn.
- If people can't figure out how to use your product due to poor design, bad or missing documentation, or an actual defect, someone's going to have to help that customer or you'll lose them.

CHAPTER EXERCISES:

1. Which of these problems have you seen in your organization?
   - [ ] Low sales
   - [ ] Poor online presence/bad reviews
   - [ ] Losing customers during onboarding
   - [ ] Poor product design
   - [ ] High product returns
   - [ ] High support costs
   - [ ] Lack of repeat customers
   - [ ] Low company morale
   - [ ] High employee turnover
   - [ ] Lawsuits over product issues

2. For any of the problems you saw, can you identify a connection to your organization's products and processes and suggest possible ways to reduce or eliminate the issue?

CHAPTER NOTES:

CHAPTER 4: Twelve Things Your Product Team Should STOP Doing Today

"The definition of insanity is doing the same thing over and over again and expecting different results." – attributed to Albert Einstein

"If you do the same thing over and over and get a different result, you need better quality control." – Me

We've all heard the saying "the definition of insanity is doing the same thing over and over again and expecting different results." But what if the results we're expecting are different from what we're actually getting? As a product manager, it's important to stay aware of the traps and routines that can lead your team astray. When things are going well, it's easy to become complacent and take your eye off the ball. Complacency breeds mediocrity, and before you know it, your team is coasting along without making any real progress.

Complacency is often the first step on the road to bad habits. When we become too comfortable, we stop pushing ourselves to improve. We start doing things the easy way instead of the right way. We become stuck in our ways and resistant to change. And that's when bad habits start to form.

Bad habits are destructive to both our personal and professional lives. They can hold us back from reaching our full potential and achieving our goals. And once they're established, they can be very difficult to break. That's why it's so important to avoid them in the first place. So how do we do that? By staying vigilant and constantly striving for improvement, even when things are going well.

One of the biggest dangers of complacency is that it leads to a false sense of security. When we're comfortable, we tend to let our guard down. We stop paying attention to detail and become sloppy in our work. We round off the corners and grab for shortcuts that we wouldn't normally take. And that's when mistakes and bad habits happen. Avoid this trap by constantly challenging your team to do better and refusing to settle for mediocrity.

Stop Doing These Things Now

Take a look at the twelve items on this list below. Do any of them sound familiar? If you or your team are doing any of the things on this list, you need to stop now! Hiring the wrong people, fighting fires, creating features instead of products, and designing problems without customer feedback are all common traps that product teams fall into. By avoiding these mistakes and focusing on best practices again, you'll be able to create an improved work environment for your team and better products that your users will love.

Here are twelve things that your product team should stop doing NOW:

- Hiring the wrong people
- Fighting fires
- Building features instead of products
- Designing/solving problems without customer feedback
- Ignoring the user experience
- Doing things just because that's the way we've always done them
- Working in silos
- Reacting to the loudest voice in the room
- Ignoring the data
- Focusing on technology and not use cases
- Working without an actual written plan and goals
- Not differentiating between product management and project management

1. Hiring the wrong people

Probably the single biggest mistake you can make is hiring the wrong people. If you miss badly on a hire, you're not just impacting the position you hired. It can hurt your entire product team. Inserting a single disruptive team member into a high-performing team can end up not just lowering the team's overall performance into the disruptor's lane, but it can slow the entire team down. The team may not be able to work together effectively, and problems with team communication and collaboration will reduce overall productivity across the team. Worse, it can have an impact on team morale and employee retention and drive your better performers away. If you have a team that doesn't like each other and doesn't work well together, take a hard look at the person making those hiring decisions. If that's you, well, grab a mirror.

If you feel like you're making bad hires, a little self-analysis is in order. Do you have a blind spot? Are you making the same kind of mistake over and over? Maybe you could have other peers or members of the team also participate in the process to get a broader set of viewpoints and eliminate some personal biases you might be introducing. Ask yourself why you think that the people have failed in the roles and think about how you might better screen by asking the right questions to identify these traits going forward.

Carefully consider each candidate during the hiring process. Make sure that you are hiring people who have the eleven skills outlined in Chapter 2, which outlines the experience necessary to be successful in product management. But while getting the right skill set is important, it is equally important to ensure that the team is cohesive and has good communication with the new person. Maybe that means hiring someone based on team fit and chemistry and not just looking at who has the best resume on paper. Way too many hiring managers make the mistake of hiring based just on skill set or experience without considering how the person's going to fit with the rest of the team. Don't make this mistake. The best individual people might not fit together as a cohesive team. Assembling a high-performing team means that you're constantly optimizing the performance of the entire team and not just the individual roles.

2. Fighting fires

If your workplace always feels like barely manageable chaos, that's a message that shouldn't be ignored. Constantly fighting internal product fires leads to frustration because your team can't hit its goals. If the team is always reacting to problems, they may not have time to focus on executing against your priorities or planning and strategizing for the future.

To avoid these negative consequences, it's important to focus on fire prevention. This means being proactive and addressing potential problems before they become actual fires. You might need to say "No" more often to protect your ability to say "Yes" to the important things. Set priorities and don't get distracted by shiny objects that glimmer during your work day. Additionally, it's important to have a plan in place for how to deal with fires when they do occur.

Sometimes the right strategy could be to just let the fire burn, especially if you think the damage is going to be minor and it'll burn itself out. Keep working on the top priorities, especially if doing that actually reduces the number of future fires you'll have to deal with. It can be hard to watch things burn and our instinct is to stop what we're doing, jump in and put out the fire. But your priorities are there for a reason. Work your plan. Ask yourself why these fires are happening and FIX THAT, so you have fewer fires in the first place.

By taking these steps, you can avoid constantly fighting fires and help the product development team be successful.

3. Building features instead of products

This one happens too much and it's painful to see if you're a true product leader. Typically, it occurs when non-product people (C-suite, Marketing, Sales) are making the product decisions and setting the product strategy instead of a product manager. They send the "product" team a stack of feature requests to generate short-term market energy without concern about how that fits with the product. To be sure, company leaders, marketing and sales are all stakeholders that have valuable feedback any product manager should collect. And frequently, the company's leadership will have more insight and experience than a freshly-minted junior product manager, which sometimes leads to product teams turning into feature teams.

What's the difference? Feature teams are focused more on execution and output, while product teams are more focused on strategy and outcomes. Feature teams are often focused more on the role of product owner and less on the role of product manager. Product teams are collaborative and empowered to be innovative while feature teams are just there to deliver on other people's ideas.

Ask yourself, "Does my team own our product roadmap?" Not the backlog – the roadmap. If the answer's "No," you're probably working on a feature team. Product teams are empowered to deliver solutions. If you have accountability without authority, you're probably working on a feature team. If you're focused more on the "when" (project work) than the "why," "what" and "how" (product work), you're probably working on a feature team.

If your team is focused on building features instead of products, they may miss important opportunities to create value for the company. Additionally, if the team is only focused on short-term goals, they may not be able to make long-term decisions that are in the best interest of the product.

If your product team is more focused on churning out features instead of understanding customer needs and the benefits of the product, likely, you're at risk of building things that customers don't value. This can lead to a lot of wasted effort and frustration on both sides. It can also lead to losing your best people because they want to work on building creative and challenging solutions that require them to be fully engaged in their work and that doesn't always happen in a feature factory.

To avoid these negative consequences, it is important to focus on empowering your product teams to make decisions with an emphasis on creating value for the customer. This means understanding their needs and solving their problems instead of just spitting out features from a company to-do list. Additionally, it is important to focus on long-term goals so that you can make decisions that will benefit the product in the future. By taking these steps, you can help the team be successful and create a product that is valuable for the customer.

Understand your customer's needs and build strategic products that meet those needs. Demonstrate leadership and develop trust from your executives by showing them that you know your customers better than they do and show your ability to prioritize work, think strategically and deliver customer value. This will not only save you time and energy, but it'll also make your customers (and product team) much happier and lead to long-term business success.

4. Designing products without customer feedback

If you're designing a product and trying to solve customer problems without getting feedback from customers, you're not likely to be successful in the long run. Your product may end up over-baked or under-baked – too complicated or not meeting the needs of your target market. Without customer feedback, it's difficult to assess what features are most important to include in your product. It might be an educated guess, but it's still just guessing.

Make sure to get feedback from customers at every stage of product development to create a successful product. You might end up building features that no one wants or needs, and your product will suffer as a result. Extra features might sound like a bonus, but they can clutter a product and confuse your users if you're not careful (see #5). They'll also be a waste of resources and potentially slow your time to market. It's essential to get feedback from customers throughout the product development process to build a successful product.

5. Ignoring the user experience

Product managers have a lot of responsibility when it comes to building products. They need to make sure that the products they create are engaging and interesting for users. If a product is boring or difficult to use, people will quickly lose interest and move on to something else. Research suggests that the average installed Android app loses 77% of its Daily Average Users in the first 3 days after installation. Clearly, these users are not getting what they need from those apps.

A significant difference between a product's user experience and getting customer feedback on a product (see #4 above) lies in how the information is gathered. User experience focuses on how users actually interact with a product, while customer feedback looks to capture user opinion and sentiment from surveys and interviews.

User experience requires collecting data from actual user interactions, such as tracking mouse clicks, page views, or time spent using the product. This data can then be analyzed to identify areas of improvement and help inform product design decisions.

Customer feedback relies more on direct input from customers in the form of surveys and interviews. These offer valuable insight into what people like or dislike about a product, as well as any potential pain points that may not be evident through user experience testing alone. By using both user experience data and customer feedback companies can create an overall better product experience for their users.

Designing a product with the user experience in mind is essential. Neglecting this can lead to confusion and difficulty of use, wasting resources and damaging your brand reputation through bad reviews and word-of-mouth advertising. A successful product should be simple to use, meet customers' needs and provide a positive experience. Ask your customers what they want but also watch how they use your product. Once you've done that, you should be able to crisply deliver a product experience that engages users and keeps them coming back.

6. Doing things "the way we've always done them"

Product teams should constantly strive for innovation and improvement. Questioning the status quo and using accumulated experience can lead to more efficient processes, shorter cycle times, reduced product costs and new revenue sources. It is important to also stay on top of industry trends, find new opportunities and be able to adapt to change in order to remain competitive. Doing what has been done before won't get you far. Companies that are innovative and embrace change will thrive in their respective industries.

By constantly questioning the status quo and looking for ways to improve, we can create better products and streamline our processes. If we can't justify why we're doing something, then it may be time to change the way we're doing it. As we gain experience doing certain tasks, hopefully we get better at it. With that experience, we start to see opportunities for more improvement. Should we just ignore our experience and our gained mastery over a task to keep doing things the same way forever into infinity?

Innovation is essential for product teams to maintain a competitive advantage. This process of innovation allows product teams to stay ahead of the curve and keep a competitive edge. Additionally, by maintaining a competitive advantage, product teams can attract and retain customers, reducing product churn. Refining your process by taking advantage of your experience can increase efficiency, shorten cycle times and reduce your product costs. Finally, this process also allows product teams to come up with new ideas that could generate more revenue. More revenue and lower cost deliver a fatter bottom line.

7. Teams working in silos instead of collaborating

Effective product teams thrive on collaboration, not isolation. Working in functional silos can lead to stagnation, duplication of efforts and missed opportunities. Open communication and knowledge sharing are essential for successful product development as it allows teams to use each other's strengths and create better outcomes. Collaboration brings out collective creativity, which leads to more innovative products and better user experience, helping companies stay competitive in their respective industries.

Don't get me wrong here. It's important to have clear roles and responsibilities and to know when to stay in your lane. But at the same time, make sure you know what's going on in each of the other lanes. When teams put their heads down and work in silos without proper collaboration, they are simultaneously more likely to duplicate efforts and have gaps in what gets done because they aren't communicating.

Cross-team communication is essential for product teams to break down a siloed culture. By communicating consistently with other functional groups and stakeholders (remember the swivel chair), product teams can get a better understanding of the overall product landscape internally and externally. Additionally, cross-team communication allows product teams to coordinate efforts and avoid duplication of work. Finally, the shared knowledge that comes with the engaged interaction of your team can help identify potential risks and problems early on. By being aware of these possible issues, product teams can take steps to avoid them much earlier in the development cycle, minimizing the cost and impact.

8. Reacting only to the loudest voices in the room

To be sure, sometimes the loudest voice understands the issues, strategy and priorities. But a lot of times, the loudest voice is just loud and focused only on their own perspective. By reacting to the loudest voice, product teams can lose sight of their strategies, goals and objectives. This can lead to short-term thinking and decision-making. Frequently, it leads to building features instead of building a cohesive product. Additionally, reacting to the loudest voice can lead to a lack of objectivity if they're focused only on achieving their own objectives without looking at them in the context of the bigger picture.

Sometimes the loudest voice can take the form of a high-value customer. Maybe they want you to prioritize a custom feature that really only drives value for them and not the rest of your customer base. It can be a challenge to say no in this situation, but taking resources from higher priority work that will drive more value for your entire community of users can have long-term effects that might not be so obvious in the moment.

When focusing on the loudest voice in the room instead of taking a more holistic view, you are effectively ignoring the needs and inputs of your other stakeholders. You're also creating a dynamic that can lead to chaos. As your other stakeholders start to figure out that they need to be louder to get their input considered, you may find that you're encouraging shouting matches instead of team collaboration.

9. Ignoring product data and analytics

As product teams increasingly rely on data to make decisions, ignoring the data available to them can have serious consequences. Data provides valuable insights into how users are using the product and what features they find most valuable. Working with your product's data is an essential part of the product development process as it helps product teams validate their assumptions and make informed decisions.

Without data, product teams are flying blind and risk missing out on key insights that could improve the product. You can't optimize your knowledge about your customers if you don't take advantage of the opportunity to review the data your product generates. And if you don't understand the importance of knowing your customer at this point, you must have skipped straight to this page in the book and missed the rest of this chapter.

Product teams need to be proactive about collecting data and then analyzing that data to find areas of opportunity and potential issues. Establish common themes and pain points that your potential customers have. Look for patterns and trends in how your users interact with the product. Compare your findings with market analysis and historical trends. Leverage your data to identify competitive areas where you can differentiate your product from others in the market.

Ignoring data can lead to making decisions based on assumptions instead of facts. Sure, intuition is important. But guessing about what your customer needs can waste both time and resources as it can lead to building features that users don't want or need.

10. Using technology for the sake of technology

When product teams get too caught up in using technology just for the sake of it, they can easily lose sight of their ultimate goal: delivering a great product that meets customer needs. This "hammer in search of a nail" approach can lead to all sorts of problems, from features that don't solve customer problems, to products that are difficult or impossible to use.

Sometimes, teams will try to wedge a hot technology into the product because they think it'll make it easier to market to customers or to find investors. I've seen this happen over and over, with the most recent iteration as I write this book focusing on AI/ChatGPT, blockchain, NFTs and web3 tech. I'm not suggesting that there aren't valuable applications for those technologies. But bolting on an NFT as part of a bottle of tequila doesn't make the tequila taste any better. That's a real pitch I saw. If you don't have a good handle on your user needs and how the tech provides a better solution, be careful.

Technology should always be used in service of the user experience, not the other way around. If your product team is ignoring the user experience in favor of technology, it's time to make a change.

11. Lacking a written plan and goals

A well-written plan is essential for any aspect of a business, but especially for the product team. A carefully crafted plan sets the tone for your business, establishes clear goals, and serves as a road map for your team. Without a plan, it's all too easy to get off track and lose sight of your goals.

If you don't have a plan, you don't know where you're trying to go. Worse, your TEAM doesn't know where you're trying to lead them. Because of this, everyone involved will be less effective. Your team may lose confidence in you. Your boss may lose confidence in you. With everyone else losing confidence in you, you might lose confidence in yourself too.

Setting goals is a critical part of planning. Goals give you something to aim for. A clearly stated goal can become a rallying point for your team and inspire better performance. Measuring progress towards your goals also lets you know if you're winning or losing. And it'll help keep everyone aligned and focused on the mission.

12. Not differentiating between product management and project management

Yeah, this again. Product management and project management are two different disciplines with different goals. Product managers wear many hats and often find themselves naturally doing a bit of both product management and project management. This can add to the role confusion when people outside your team are looking at the two disciplines.

Project management is about getting things done, while product management is about making sure that the things you're doing are the right things to get done. Product management is about understanding customer needs and building products that meet those needs. Product managers need to be able to see the big picture and understand how all the pieces fit together, while project managers need to be able to focus on the details and make sure that everything is moving forward according to plan. As a general rule, product managers focus on the long-term vision for a product, while project managers focus on the day-to-day execution of projects.

As a product manager, your primary focus should be on delivering the long-term vision for your product. Outcomes instead of output. If you're spending more time as a project lead than as a product manager, that's another sign that you're really leading a features team and not a product team. This isn't to suggest that product managers have no involvement in the daily activities of a product team. They do. But that's not ALL they do.

Ok. That's the list. Do any of those things sound familiar? It's not going to be easy to change bad habits. Old habits die hard, and it's natural to resist doing things differently—even if those changes are better for us in the long run. But like former President Barack Obama said:

"Change will not come if we wait for some other person or some other time. We are the ones we've been waiting for. We are the change that we seek."

We're often quick to point the finger when things go wrong. It's much easier to blame others—or outside circumstances—for our failings than it is to accept responsibility and take corrective action. Most people fall into bad work habits because they're too busy or there's too much inertia to overcome. But don't sit back and hope that someone else will come along and fix everything for you. Change starts from within. If you want things to be different, you need to be the one to make them different.

Of course, changing your behavior is never easy. But if you're serious about making a change, start changing the things that are within your control to change. Set the right example. Do things the right way, even if it's a little harder at first. Take responsibility and take charge today. Only then will real change start to occur.

TL;DR

- Hiring the wrong people can have a negative impact on team morale, productivity and employee retention. Self-analysis is important when making hiring decisions, as well as considering team fit and chemistry in addition to skill set.

- Constantly fighting internal product fires leads to frustration and prevents teams from executing against priorities or planning for the future. Fire prevention should be a focus by setting priorities, avoiding distractions, having a plan in place for dealing with fires when they occur and understanding why they are happening so that fewer fires have to be dealt with in the first place.
- Building features instead of products means missing out on important opportunities for value creation as well as making decisions that don't benefit long-term success or customer needs. Empower your teams to make decisions based on creating value for customers rather than churning out feature requests from other departments or stakeholders within an organization.
- Designing products without customer feedback results in an inadequate solution due to lack of insight into user needs; gathering data from user interactions (user experience) combined with direct input from customers (customer feedback) helps create an overall better product experience tailored specifically around users' wants/needs.
- A written plan with clear goals is necessary as it sets direction, serves as a road map, rallies team members together, measures progress towards objectives and keeps everyone aligned with mission objectives.

CHAPTER EXERCISES

1. Which of the twelve items in this chapter do you think your organization currently does? Check all that apply.
    [ ] Hiring the wrong people
    [ ] Fighting fires
    [ ] Building features instead of products
    [ ] Designing/solving problems without customer feedback
    [ ] Ignoring the user experience

[ ] Doing things just because that's the way we've always done them
[ ] Working in silos
[ ] Reacting to the loudest voice in the room
[ ] Ignoring the data
[ ] Focusing on technology and not use cases
[ ] Working without an actual written plan and goals
[ ] Not differentiating between product management and project management

2. For each of the items you just checked, can you think of one thing that's in your control that you could change to improve in that area? If there's nothing you can control personally, can you identify the person in your organization who could?
3. As the person responsible for hiring a new team member, what questions would you ask during the interview process to determine if a candidate is a good fit for your team in terms of chemistry and teamwork?

CHAPTER NOTES

CHAPTER 5: Are You Too Busy "Getting Stuff Done" To Think About Strategy?

Almost every leader wants to make more time for strategic thinking. In one survey of ten thousand senior leaders, 97% of them said that being strategic was the leadership behavior most important to their organization's success.

And yet, in another study, 96% of the leaders surveyed said that they lack the time for strategic thinking.

STOP. Let this sink in. These leaders know better, and yet there is clearly a disconnect between what they know and what's actually happening.

What gives? Why is it that so many leaders know they need to be more strategic, but can't seem to find the time to do it?

According to Dorie Clark's *Harvard Business Review* article "If Strategy Is So Important, Why Don't We Make Time For It?", the answer is that we have a false dichotomy between "thinking about strategy" and "doing the work." We think that if we're busy "getting stuff done," then we can't possibly have time to step back and think about our strategy. But this is a false dichotomy. We can, and should, be doing both simultaneously.

The problem is that we have a very narrow definition of what "strategy" is. We think of it as something that we do in the rarefied air of the executive suite, disconnected from the day-to-day work of the organization. But this is not what strategy is. Strategy is simply making choices about how we allocate our limited resources. It's about deciding what we're going to do, and what we're not going to do. And this is something that we can, and should, be doing at all levels of the organization.

In this chapter, we'll take a look at strategy and why it's so important to avoid the "No time for it" trap. We'll talk about saying "No" and learn a couple of prioritization techniques you might be able to use to clear enough time on your calendar.

So, time for a bit of self-reflection. Is your business a well-run machine purring along on all cylinders? Or would you describe your day-to-day as barely manageable chaos? Are you constantly fighting fires?

We've all heard the excuses: "I don't have time for that." "I'm too busy." "There's just not enough hours in the day." But the truth is, we all have the same twenty-four hours in a day. It's how we choose to spend that time that makes the difference.

The real issue is not a lack of time, but rather a lack of priorities. If your business is constantly fighting fires, it may be missing a key element: strategy. When you're constantly reacting to the latest crisis or putting out fires, it can be difficult to pause, step back and think strategically. But if you want to be successful in business, you need to make time for strategy.

What is strategy, exactly? Strategy is about making choices - deciding what actions to take (or not take) to achieve your desired goal. It's also about prioritizing which actions are most aligned with your goals and will have the biggest impact to help you achieve them. And it's about being intentional in everything you do, rather than just going through the motions or blindly following someone else's path.

Why is strategy so important? Because without a clear strategy, you'll just be racing along, reacting to whatever comes your way. You've probably heard the quote frequently attributed to baseball great Yogi Berra – "We don't know where we're going, but we're making good time!"

You're more likely to waste time and energy on things that don't matter, or that don't help you move closer to your goal. And while you might get lucky and stumble upon success from time to time, it won't be sustainable or repeatable. Having a strong strategy gives you direction and helps you stay focused on what's most important. It also allows you to make better use of limited resources. Strategy helps make sure you're working on the right things at the right time.

If you're always busy with the daily grind and have no time for strategy, take a moment to evaluate your decisions on how to allocate limited resources. What are you doing and, more importantly, what are you not doing? It's these strategic choices that every one of us needs to make, regardless of our organizational position.

Meet the Eisenhower Matrix

"If everything is important, then nothing is" - Patrick Lencioni

The Eisenhower Matrix is a simple tool that can help you make better choices about how to allocate your limited resources. It was developed by President Dwight D. Eisenhower, and it is based on the principle that "What is important is seldom urgent and what is urgent is seldom important."

The Eisenhower Matrix has four quadrants:

- Low urgency/Low importance = Delete
- High urgency/Low important = Delegate
- Low urgency/High importance = Decide/Schedule
- High urgency/High importance = Do

Again, if you find yourself too busy "getting stuff done" to think about strategy, ask yourself which quadrant your activities fall into.

Are they in the Low urgency/Low importance quadrant? If so, then it might be time to delete them from your to-do list. Are they in the High urgency/Low importance quadrant? If so, then you might want to consider delegating them to someone else.

Eisenhower Matrix

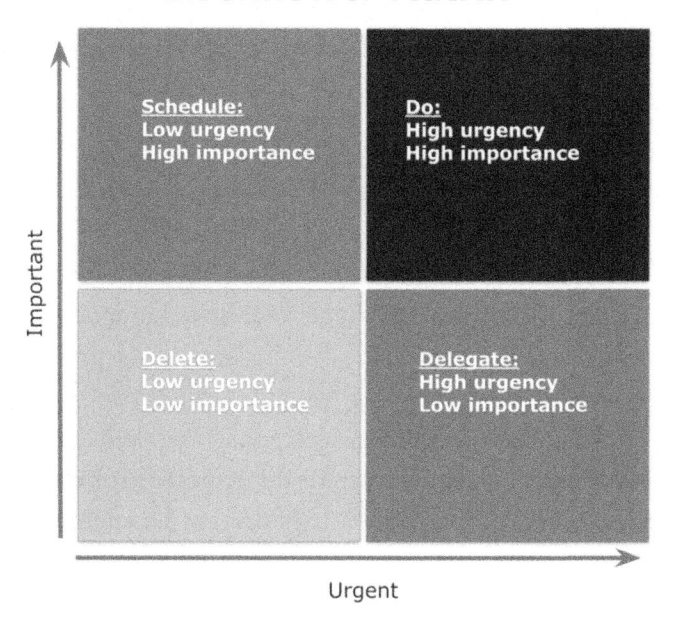

Schedule: Low urgency, High importance	**Do:** High urgency, High importance
Delete: Low urgency, Low importance	**Delegate:** High urgency, Low importance

(y-axis: Important; x-axis: Urgent)

It might feel good if you're constantly working in the "Do" quadrant, with the adrenalin rush of always working on High urgency/High importance things. But ask yourself if you could have handled the task when it was a lower-urgency item by doing a better job of scheduling your time and deleting or delegating the lower importance item. Don't wait for it to escalate into a crisis before you give it your attention.

One key to getting the time to think strategically is to make time to focus your attention on the activities that are in the Low urgency/High importance quadrant. These are the activities that will help you to achieve your long-term goals, and they should be given priority on your to-do list. If you're doing this right, you'll be spending most of your time in the "Schedule" quadrant taking care of things before they blow up, and only rarely dealing with the high urgency of "Do." By using the Eisenhower Matrix, you can ensure that you are making the best use of your limited resources, and you can make sure that your time is spent on truly important activities.

Optimize Resources: Aligning Priorities with Strategy

In today's business world, it's more important than ever to be strategic about the way you use your resources. Small businesses especially need to be mindful of how they allocate their time and energy, because they often don't have a lot of redundancy built into their operations. That's why it's so important to set priorities and align them with your overall strategy. Otherwise, you risk wasting valuable time and resources on projects that don't move the needle for your business. Of course, it can be difficult to think strategically when you're feeling the time pressures of your business ratcheting up. But if you make the effort to do so, it will pay off in the long run. By being thoughtful about your priorities and ensuring that they align with your strategy, you can make the most of your limited resources and ensure that your business is successful.

It's even more critical when you don't have a lot of time or energy to waste. If you don't have time to think strategically, do you have clear priorities? Attending to the loudest voice in the room is no way to prioritize work, but is that what's happening? If you're running around with your hair on fire trying to work on things that you don't even know are the most important things to do, please just stop. That's a recipe for disaster. You have to be clear about what's important and what's not. Otherwise, you'll just end up spinning your wheels and getting nowhere. Or you're making progress on all the wrong things while the important needle-moving stuff piles up in drifts around you.

Most people think of tactics as the "how" of getting things done – the actual steps and processes you take to achieve your goals. But tactics are only effective if they're aligned with your strategy – the "what" and "why" of your actions. In other words, tactics without strategy means you're just randomly working on stuff and hoping it'll somehow all work out in the end. But with a sound strategy in place, tactics become the basis for a focused plan of action that's much more likely to lead to success.

If you're feeling stretched thin and like you can't catch a break, take a step back and assess what's really important. Set some priorities and focus on the things that are going to make the biggest impact. It might not be easy, but it's essential for your business' success.

Focus on Saying "No"[1]: Prioritizing for Success

As any successful entrepreneur knows, priorities are everything. You can't do everything, and you shouldn't try to. If you want your business to succeed, you need to focus on the most important things and say "No" to everything else. One of the major limiting factors that restricts a business's growth is not having a strategy for saying "No" especially in companies living in the under $5M range. Think about it. Why are you busy doing things if you don't even know if the things you're working so hard to finish are actually aligned with the needs of the business? It can be hard to know what the most important things are, but that's where a good strategy comes in. By taking the time to plan out your priorities, you can make sure that everything you're working on is aligned with the needs of the business. And when you've got a clear strategy, it becomes much easier to say "No" to all of the other things that come up. You've only got so much bandwidth. Saying "No" protects your ability to say "Yes" to the real priorities.

Steve Jobs said, "People think focus means saying yes to the thing you've got to focus on. But that's not what it means at all. It means saying no to the hundred other good ideas that there are. You have to pick carefully. I'm actually as proud of the things we haven't done as the things I have done. Innovation is saying 'No' to 1,000 things."

So, if you want to be more successful, take a page from Steve Jobs' book and focus on saying "No." It might seem counterintuitive, but it's the only way to ensure that you're working on the most important things. And when you've got a clear strategy in place, it becomes much easier to do.

The bottom line is this: if you're too busy "getting stuff done" to think about strategy, you're doing it wrong. Prioritize the things that are truly important and say "No" to everything else. It's the only way to ensure that your business is successful.

The Vital Few and the Trivial Many

We are so busy these days, trying to do more and more and fit it all in. But is this the best way to run our businesses? According to the book *Essentialism*, the answer is a resounding no.

In his book, Greg McKeown makes the case that we would be much better off if we focus on doing less but doing it better. He argues that there are two types of things in the world: the vital few and the trivial many. And it's our job to focus on the vital few and say no to the trivial many.

According to McKeown, "We need to learn the slow 'yes' and the quick 'no.'" The slow yes and the quick no – that is, say "No," quickly to whatever you can. This eliminates the mental overhead of making that decision. Say "Yes" slowly to as much of the rest because once you do, you're committed.

Don't focus on getting more done. Focus on getting the RIGHT things done better and faster.

McKeown is not the only leader who espouses this philosophy. In Tim Ferriss's book *Tools of Titans*, he talks with LinkedIn co-founder Reid Hoffman about focusing on the 80/20 rule to identify the 20% of actions that will produce 80% of the results, and THEN doing the easiest thing on the high-value list.

For example, if you're trying to increase sales by 15%, focus on the 20% of activities that you think will produce 80% of that increase. And then, within those potential actions, knock out the easiest thing to do first. This way, you'll get a quick win on the board and gain some momentum to tackle the harder items on your list.

You have to get really good at saying "No" to things. This is hard for a lot of people, but if you want to make time for planning, you have to be okay with saying "No" to other things. "No" is a complete sentence. You don't need to explain yourself or make excuses. Just say "No" and move on. You can also try the "if/then" technique. For example, "If you want me to do X, then I can't do Y." This way, you're not saying "No" outright, but you're still setting a boundary.

Finally, don't be afraid to delegate. There are only so many hours in the day, and you can't do everything yourself. Delegate tasks to others on your team and trust them to get the job done. This will free up your time so that you can focus on planning.

Blocking Time and Task Batching

One of the most important things you can do for your business is to make time to plan. Unfortunately, this is often easier said than done. There are always going to be things competing for your attention, and it can be hard to say "No" but you're going to get better at that, right? If you want to make time for planning and if you want to be able to set priorities and work on achieving your goals, you have to be okay with saying "No" to other things.

Making time to plan can be as straightforward as just scheduling it. Make these blocks on your calendar sacred time and don't schedule over it with other meetings or sales calls. When you make time to plan, you're demonstrating your commitment to your business. This is vital if you want to be successful. The only way you're ever going to make time to plan is to make time to plan AND stick with it. If you absolutely must schedule over a planning session, reschedule it right then and there. Don't put this off for when you'll get around to it.

This is your business and your future we're talking about. Make it a priority.

Be aware that different businesses may have different planning rhythms. For example, you might want to align your efforts with a company-wide annual planning cycle that determines budgets and projects for the next year and syncs with the company's fiscal year. Or you might want some alignment with a go-to-market plan or a marketing or social media content calendar. Either way, the key is to schedule and prioritize the time to make it happen.

One way to make some time for planning is task batching. People don't effectively multi-task, but you can reduce switching costs by doing similar tasks together. By minimizing the number of times you have to switch gears throughout the day, you can increase your productivity and free up time for other things.

For example, if you're a solopreneur, you might want to batch your social media posts for the week on Monday morning. Or if you're a small business owner, you might want to batch your blog post writing all at once, one day out of the month, and get a few in the queue to post once a week on Wednesdays.

Task batching is a great way to save time and increase your productivity. But it's not the only way. You can also hire support where/when you can, use automation tools like social media schedulers (HootSuite), workflow tools (Zapier), chat bots, marketing automation, Shopify, and Calendly.

Don't try to do everything yourself. Delegate tasks to others on your team and trust them to get the job done. This will free up your time so that you can focus on planning.

Beware of The Planning Fallacy

When you're setting aside time for planning a project, if you haven't done similar work before or don't have historical data to review, it's important to be aware of something called the planning fallacy. This was originally proposed by Daniel Kahneman and Amos Tversky. Kahneman's also known for winning the 2002 Nobel Prize in Economic Sciences and wrote the classic *Thinking Fast and Slow*.

The planning fallacy is the idea that people are too optimistic when estimating the amount of time or resources needed to complete a project. This can lead to planning failures, as people often underestimate the difficulty of a task or the amount of time it will take to complete it. The planning fallacy is a common cognitive bias that can have serious implications for both individuals and organizations.

If you're planning a project, it's important to be aware of the planning fallacy and make sure you allow yourself enough time and resources to complete the task. Otherwise, you may find yourself in a situation where you've bitten off more than you can chew.

One way to avoid the planning fallacy is to use the premortem technique. This is a tool for imagining that a project has failed and then brainstorming all the reasons why it might have failed. By doing this, you can find potential problems before they occur and make sure you have a plan to deal with them. Other ways to avoid the planning fallacy include being realistic about the difficulty of a task and allowing for extra time and resources in your estimate. By being aware of the planning fallacy, you can make sure you don't fall victim to it and, instead, set yourself up for success.

Wrapping Up

"To attain knowledge, add things every day. To attain wisdom, subtract things every day." - Lao-Tzu

"If you don't have time to talk to me, you probably need to talk to me." - Me

The takeaway from this chapter is that if you don't have time to plan, you need to make time. Planning is essential to the success of any business venture and should be given priority. There are many ways to save time when planning, such as task batching and hiring support. You'll find even more time management tips in Chapter 25. However, it is also important to be aware of the potential pitfalls of planning, such as the planning fallacy. By being aware of these pitfalls, you can avoid them and set yourself up for success. Consistently setting aside time to plan is one of the most important things that any leader can do to change the trajectory of an organization.

TL;DR

- Almost every leader wants to make more time for strategic thinking, but many lack the time due to a false dichotomy between "thinking about strategy" and "doing the work."
- The Eisenhower Matrix is a tool that can improve resource allocation by helping distinguish between important/urgent tasks versus those that aren't so critical.
- Strategy is making choices about how we allocate our limited resources - deciding what we are going to do, and what we are not going to do. It should be done at all levels of an organization.
- Focus on saying "No" when necessary, in order to protect the ability to say "Yes" to true priorities.
- Performing actions without a strategy is just randomly working on stuff hoping it'll all work out in the end; having a sound strategy helps ensure tactics become focused plans likely leading to success instead.
- Greg McKeown's book *Essentialism* makes the case that businesses should focus on doing less but better, and to distinguish between the vital few and trivial many.
- Blocking out time in your schedule for planning is important, as is task batching similar activities together to reduce switching costs throughout the day.
- Get quick high-value wins by using the 80/20 rule to identify which 20% of tasks could produce 80% of results, then start with the easiest task first.
- Leaders must be aware of the potential pitfalls associated with inadequate planning – such as the planning fallacy, which occurs when people overestimate their ability to complete a task within a certain amount of resources or timeframe.

CHAPTER EXERCISES

1. Block off a weekly recurring hour on your schedule for strategic thinking and planning. You can always increase it in the future, but let's get at least one hour on your calendar today.
2. Take your current to-do list and use the Eisenhower Matrix to practice placing the items across the four quadrants.
3. Identify something you're doing right now where you probably should have said "No." Get ready for next time by thinking about the words you'll use when a similar request comes in.
4. What are some routine tasks that you could start batching together to gain some efficiency and reduce the overhead of task switching?

CHAPTER NOTES

CHAPTER 6: Even A GOAT Needs A Plan. Where's Yours?

As a lifelong Cincinnati Bengals fan (yeah... I know, I know... but maybe someday), it's hard to talk about the legendary San Francisco 49ers coach Bill Walsh or the long-time New England Patriots coach Bill Belichick. But drawing on their cases in this chapter, we'll start with a coach's perspective on planning, take a look at the different roles in the planning process as well as different types of plans that add value in the product space. We'll also highlight some important tips for putting together your plans.

Any NFL coach will tell you, game planning is essential to success on the gridiron. Each play is a self-contained unit, with specific assignments, formations, sequences, cadences, and timings that need to be executed perfectly. One missed block or timing cue can blow up the whole play. That's why Walsh, who won three Super Bowls in his eight years as the Niners' head coach, would game-plan the first twenty-five plays of the game. "You need to have a plan even for the worst-case scenario," he said. "It doesn't mean that it will always work; it doesn't mean that you will always be successful. But you will always be prepared and at your best."

Each week during the season, head coaches exemplify Walsh's advice when they come up with new game plans targeted at exploiting the specific weaknesses of their opponent. Sometimes those game plans are so effective that they become legendary. One such game plan is even enshrined in the Pro Football Hall of Fame.

Along with Walsh, Belichick is widely considered to be one of the best coaches in NFL history (aka GOAT or Greatest Of All Time). He has led the Patriots to six Super Bowl victories, and his teams have been known for their disciplined, well-executed play. Belichick is a master strategist, and his attention to detail and commitment to planning have made him one of the most successful coaches in NFL history.

But before Bill Belichick was the most successful head coach in NFL history with six championship rings, he won his first two rings (for a total of eight) as the defensive coordinator of the New York Giants. In Super Bowl XXV, the Giants took on the Buffalo Bills. These Bills were an explosive bunch who had scored ninety-five points in their two playoff games leading to the Super Bowl. The Bills' offense, which Belichick was tasked with stopping, had four future Hall of Famers in Jim Kelly, Thurman Thomas, Andre Reed, and James Lofton. The plan Belichick came up with would join those four in the Hall of Fame.

In the previous game for the AFC Championship, the Bills had scored a 51-3 victory over the then Los Angeles Raiders in what was the biggest margin of victory in any AFC Championship game. Meanwhile, the Giants got to the Super Bowl without scoring a single touchdown in the NFC Championship game, using five field goals, including one as the clock ran out, to edge the Niners 15 to 13. No one thought that the Giants stood a chance against the explosive Bills. The Bills were a seven-point favorite in Las Vegas.

Belichick planned to hold the high-power Bills' offense down by allowing them to GAIN yardage by running the ball – letting their running back Thurman Thomas get more than 100 yards. His players didn't want to do it. But Belichick knew that he could only stop either their running or passing game by stacking his defense against the pass, so he used only two linemen vs the typical three or four most teams have and used the rest to cover receivers. Remember back in Chapter 4 when we suggested that a strategy for fighting fires could be to let the smaller ones burn to stay focused on our higher priorities?

Belichick knew that he couldn't keep pace with the Bills' firepower. But by making it his number one priority to stop their high-powered passing game and assigning his limited resources to that goal, Belichick slowed down the game and kept the Bills within reach of the Giants' less-potent offense. This gave them a fighting chance to beat the heavily favored Bills. In the end, the Giants held the Bills' offense that had averaged 47.5 points in the prior two playoff games to just 19 points, winning the only Super Bowl decided by a single point, 20-19.

"The only sign we have in the locker room is from 'The Art Of War': Every battle is won before it is fought," Bill Belichick has said, referencing a quote by Sun Tzu.

Understanding Four Roles In The Planning Process

As an organization grows, a shareable plan becomes essential to coordinate work efforts and optimize results. Planning drives confidence and trust — and confidence and trust enable speed. Planning starts with leadership and focuses on strategy and execution. You can only ad-lib for so long.

An effective plan will help product managers, business executives and startup founders achieve their goals by providing a roadmap to success. A well-crafted plan can also help avoid duplication of effort by clarifying roles. Your plan keeps everyone on the same page and supplies a framework for measuring progress.

There are several important roles in the planning process. Here are a few of the most important:

1. Organizational Leader
2. Stakeholder
3. Plan Owner
4. Execution/Implementation Team

Organizational leaders are an essential part of the planning process. Frequently, they are the visionaries who see what could be and who are not afraid to dream big. But leaders are not just dreamers; they are also doers. They are the ones who drive people to act and who make things happen. This is why action-driven leaders are so important when it comes to planning. Without such leaders, there would be no one to develop the plans and no one to see them through to execution. These leaders are the key to making any plan a reality. So if you want your plans to succeed, start with leaders who have the vision and the drive to make them happen.

This doesn't mean that your leaders are always the best people to develop the plan's details though. Let them set the overall direction and vision for the organization. But often, they may not be the ones in the company who are familiar enough with the specifics of a particular technology or the details of a targeted marketing campaign. So, there's plenty of room for others to engage around the tactics and execution details required to make a plan into reality.

This includes your project's *stakeholders*. They'll bring important specifics and context for the plan based upon their view of the world. They may also control access to the resources you're hoping to use to deliver on the plan. Keeping them in the loop up front is always a good idea. Nobody likes to be surprised with a "we're doing what?" moment.

As a product leader, you're probably the *plan owner,* as planning is essential to ensure that your team can execute the vision and deliver results that meet or exceed everyone's expectations. Without a plan, it can be difficult to prioritize work and coordinate efforts across departments. A plan can also help you communicate your vision to stakeholders and get buy-in for your product roadmap.

It's also important to consider the people who will be players on your *implementation team*. Sometimes there will be overlap with your stakeholders, but often these folks will be a level down from the people you work with at the stakeholder level. They might not get the level of detail needed from their manager to execute the plan, so you'll want to make sure they have all the information they need to deliver excellence.

Business leaders know that, for their company to reach its full potential, some kind of plan must be in place. From solopreneurs and startups to global conglomerates, a well-crafted plan can ensure the best use of resources and personnel while ensuring the vision resonates with those involved in its execution — from raising capital as a startup to coordinating efforts between various branches within an established company. Without a plan in place, it can become difficult to decide where resources should be allocated, how efforts can build on each other or measure the progress toward goals – all key elements necessary for achieving success. A proper plan provides unparalleled guidance no matter the size of your business venture – setting direction so you never lose sight of what's important.

A 300-Year Plan

A lot of companies are lucky to plan the next 90 days, but Softbank's leader Masayoshi Son is famous for his 300-year plan. He has said that he wants Softbank to be around for 300 years, and he has made plans accordingly. His long-term plan focuses on the need for human connection. This is because he believes that, while many things may change significantly over the next 300 years, people will still have the basic social need to reduce their loneliness by connecting with other people.

In the short term, Son has focused on investing in companies that he believes will be leaders in enabling those human connections in the future. He has also made sure to build a strong team of executives who can carry out his vision. In the long term, Son has said that he wants Softbank to be a company that makes a positive impact on the world by helping solve global problems such as climate change and poverty. But the core of his business and personal strategy stays focused on enabling those basic human connections.

Even if you're focused on a timeframe that's less than the next 300 years, if you don't have a plan, it can be difficult to prioritize work and coordinate efforts across departments. A plan can help you focus on execution by supplying a roadmap for your team to follow. Without a plan, it can be easy to get sidetracked or bogged down in the details. Having a plan can help you stay focused on the task at hand and avoid getting caught up in distractions.

Not having a plan is like driving without a destination. If you don't have an end goal, how will you know when you're done? A plan gives your team a way to measure their progress and ensure that they are on track to meet your company's objectives.

If you're launching a product, it's important to coordinate with the development team, marketing, sales, legal, and customer support departments. A plan can help you do this by identifying the tasks that need to be completed and setting deadlines. Without a plan, it can be difficult to keep track of progress and ensure that everyone is on the same page.

A plan can also help you avoid potential problems before they arise. By planning for obstacles, you can develop contingency plans to keep your project on track. This can save you time and money in the long run by preventing problems from happening in the first place.

"To achieve great things, two things are needed; a plan, and not quite enough time." - Leonard Bernstein

If you want to be successful at shipping products, it all comes down to a careful balance of planning and taking decisive action. Too much time can breed complacency while too little can lead to rushed decisions; striking the right equilibrium is crucial. Having "not quite enough time" brings an urgency that lends the energy needed to get a project done. Without urgency, things tend to drift. A sense of urgency requires your team to focus and prioritize on staying on the critical path. To paraphrase the classic Rolling Stones' song, you might not get everything you want, but you'll get what you need.

Here's another dirty little secret found in most work environments and life in general. If you don't have a plan, you'll likely end up at the mercy of someone that does. You're either working your own plan or you're working on someone else's plan. This can be frustrating and can make it difficult to get your work done because someone else is getting the resources you need and filling up your to-do list with their own project's tasks. When it comes time to figure out a path forward, the person with a plan usually wins.

Other Types of Plans That Add Value for Products

There are many types of plans in the business world, some specific to lines of business or certain verticals. But some of the key types of plans can add value to your product are:

- Product Plan - A roadmap for your team to follow during the development process. It should include milestones and deadlines for each phase of development, as well as a list of features that need to be developed.

- Project Plan - Similar to the product plan, but it focuses on the implementation of a specific project. It should include a timeline, budget, and scope for the project.
- Business Plan - Outlines your company's goals and how you plan to achieve them. It should include information on your products or services, your target market, your marketing strategy, and your financial projections.
- Marketing Plan - Outlines your marketing strategies and tactics. It should include information on your target market, your positioning strategy, your messaging, and your media mix.

Ultimately, a plan is a communications vehicle, so make it clear and consistent. If you tap out a steady drumbeat of communication with your teams, you might be surprised to find that they've formed a parade behind you. That's real leadership.

A clear and consistent plan is essential for any team's success. It should be clear what the goals are and how you intend to achieve them. The Scrum backlog is a tool for developers to track their progress, but it is not a communications vehicle or a plan for anyone else. Be prepared to have different views based on your audience. For example, the C-suite may be more interested in the financial aspects of the plan, while marketing may be more interested in the messaging and branding. Build a plan for success, not to avoid failure. Linkage and alignment to business strategy are essential. There must be a clear connection between the plan, goal setting, KPIs (Key Performance Indicators), and OKRs (Objectives/Key Results). Without this linkage, it will be difficult to measure progress and decide whether or not the plan is working.

Eight Important Tips for Developing a Plan

Don't know where to start with putting together a plan? Try these eight tips to move forward:

1. *Define your goals:* What are you trying to achieve? Be as specific as possible.
2. *Do your research:* Understand your market and your competition. This will help you develop realistic goals and strategies.
3. *Make it actionable:* Your plan should be focused on things that can realistically be accomplished and maintained in a living document that you can refer to and update regularly.
4. *Get buy-in from stakeholders:* Get input from all of the relevant stakeholders before finalizing your plan. This will help ensure that everyone is on board with the plan and its objectives.
5. *Be prepared to pivot:* As your business grows and changes, so too should your plan. Be prepared to make changes as needed.
6. *Make a timeline:* When do you want to achieve your goals? Break down big goals into smaller milestones so you can track progress along the way.
7. *Create a budget:* How much money do you have to work with? What resources will you need?
8. *Put it in writing:* A written plan makes it easier to track progress and hold yourself accountable. It also makes it shareable, which helps to literally keep everyone on the same page.

When it comes to planning, there is no one-size-fits-all approach. Make sure your objectives are actionable, achievable, and aligned with business strategy. Be prepared to pivot as your business grows and changes. Put your plan in writing so it's easy to track progress and make changes as needed.

Planning can help drive organizational accountability. A good plan can also help boost your team's confidence and motivation. Finally, well-executed planning can establish trust. If you say you're going to deliver and then you actually do it, people might just start believing you.

TL;DR

- Planning is essential at all levels within an organization, from leadership setting direction and vision down through product managers coordinating work efforts across departments.
- There are four key roles in the product planning process: organizational leaders, stakeholders, a plan owner and the implementation team.
- A clear and consistent plan is essential for any team's success, outlining objectives that are actionable, achievable, and aligned with business strategy.
- A good balance of planning and taking decisive action is needed for success when shipping products. Having "not quite enough time" brings urgency that keeps teams focused on staying on track with the critical path tasks at hand.
- If you don't have a plan, you'll likely end up at the mercy of someone that does. When it comes time to figure out a path forward, the person with a plan usually wins.

- There are many types of plans in the business world, but some key ones relative to products include Product Plans, Project Plans, Business Plans and Marketing Plans.
- Eight important tips for developing a plan include defining goals; doing research; making it actionable; getting buy-in from stakeholders; being prepared to pivot; creating a timeline and budgeting resources as well as putting it in writing.
- Planning can help drive organizational accountability while boosting team confidence and motivation by establishing trust through well-executed plans.

CHAPTER EXERCISES

1. Make a list of the people in your organization who should be involved in your planning process. Identify which of the four key roles they fill.
2. Take a look at your to-do list. How many things did you put on it? How many items are assignments you got from someone else? Time for an honest assessment – are you working on your plan or someone else's?
3. In your current role, how many hours a month do you think you should spend on planning? Even if you can't fit that many hours on your schedule, can you put a small recurring block of time (weekly, monthly or quarterly) to start moving towards that as a goal?

CHAPTER NOTES

CHAPTER 7: Telling Your Product's Story To People With Short Attention Spans – The Power Of An Elevator Pitch

Speaking on a panel at the Future of Work conference in 2020, Microsoft CEO Satya Nadella said, "People are saying, 'data is the new oil,' but I fully agree with you that attention is the new oil. Data is plentiful. Attention is scarce, and we'll never get more of it."

Nadella is absolutely right. In today's age of constant distraction, it's more important than ever to be able to grab someone's attention and hold onto it. The internet has made information — and thus data — plentiful. But attention is still scarce. And it's only getting harder to get people to pay attention to anything for more than a few seconds.

So, how do you make sure your message cuts through the noise and gets people to pay attention? After all, a key attribute of a product manager is the ability to communicate concepts clearly at all levels and to all audiences. Remember, you're the hub, the person in the middle, talking to a customer to understand their problem and then swiveling in your chair and translating that into specific concepts for your developers to build.

Because communication with different groups is an essential part of the product manager's job, it's critical for the product manager to master a variety of communication vehicles. One of the most critical is learning to write and give a pitch. There are tons of resources available in this space and we'd encourage you to seek them out, but we'll hit on the highlights here and add some tips we've found useful during our attempts to build them.

Writing the Perfect Elevator Pitch

One of the most common pitches is the elevator pitch. An elevator pitch is a short, persuasive speech that you can use to sell your product, services, or business idea. Typically, these are going to be thirty seconds or less – about the time it might take to ride up a few floors in an elevator, thus the name. This abbreviated length also makes them a great tool for dealing with short attention spans. The key to a great elevator pitch is to be clear, concise, and confident. You need to be able to explain your idea in a way that is easy for people to understand and remember.

The main purpose of an elevator pitch is to get people interested in your product or service so that they will want to learn more about it. It's not a brain dump. It should not be too long or too detailed. You're basically creating a short commercial for yourself or your project. Edit yourself ruthlessly and polish what's left so that there are no rough edges. An elevator pitch is also sometimes called a "value proposition" or a "unique selling proposition" (USP).

"If you can't explain it simply, you don't understand it well enough." This quote by Albert Einstein is a good reminder that when you are developing your pitch, you need to make sure that you understand your product or service well enough to be able to explain it simply and concisely. This means that you should avoid using technical jargon or industry-specific language that your audience might not be familiar with. Instead, you should focus on using plain language that anyone can understand. If someone who doesn't work in your industry can get it on a single listen, it's probably about right.

The power of an elevator pitch comes from its ability to tell a concise and compelling story about your product. But to tell a great story, you need to know your narrative. The best way to do this is to develop a clear and concise elevator pitch that covers the following four points:

- What problem are you solving?
- What solution do you offer?
- What is the market opportunity?
- What is your business model, or how do you make money?

If you can answer these questions confidently, then you will be well on your way to telling a great story about your product.

When you are trying to *define the problem* you are solving, it is important to be as specific as possible. This means that you should avoid using general statements like "Our product solves the problem of unemployment." Instead, you should focus on a specific pain point that your product or service can address. For example, "Our product solves the problem of connecting American college graduates to a good well-paying job through establishing a marketplace of high-quality employers."

Once you have defined the problem you are solving, you need to *articulate the solution* that your product or service offers. The best way to do this is to focus on the benefits that your product or service provides. For example, if you are a job search platform, you might say that your solution helps people find their dream job by providing them with access to a database of jobs, personalized recommendations, and tips from experts.

When you discuss the *market opportunity* for your product or service, specificity is key. Avoid vague statements such as "There's a big market for this" and instead focus on a specific market segment that your product or service can address. A good example of this could be "The job search market is a $2 billion industry, and our platform specifically meets the needs of recent college graduates. There are over 2 million new college grads every year."

Likewise, an example of a bad statement would be something like "Our product has mass appeal across all demographics." This statement is overly general, as it fails to provide any concrete information about which particular markets are being addressed.

When crafting an elevator pitch, it's important to understand the concept of Total Addressable Market (TAM). Put simply, TAM is the total amount of revenue that a company could generate by capturing all its potential customers within a given market segment. By defining TAM in your pitch, you can help investors and other stakeholders understand how much demand there is for your product or service, thereby making it easier to decide if it's worth investing in.

As you define the market opportunity, you'll also want to be familiar with *Serviceable Available Market* (SAM) and *Serviceable Obtainable Market*, or sometimes just *Share of Market* (SOM) as your investors may ask you to refine your market estimates from the TAM. The SAM is the total market that could be served by your products. If the worldwide market was $3 billion, but you were only able to serve the North American market, the SAM would be something less than $3 billion. For this example, we'll say $1 billion. Then the SOM takes into account that there might be competition or other limiting factors to estimate a percentage of the market that could be realistically obtained. Let's say you estimate you could get 20% market share or $200 million for your SOM. While TAM provides insight into the potential scale of the opportunity, SAM and SOM may ultimately be the more realistic numbers for an investment decision, especially in a highly-competitive market.

Your *business model* is how you plan on making money from your product or service. There are a variety of different business models that you can use, so it is important to choose the one that makes the most sense for your particular product or service. For example, if you are a job search platform, you might make money by charging employers for access to your database of candidates or by charging users for premium features.

Getting Ready For Opportunity

One of the most important things that you can do when you are pitching your product or service to a team is to group the content into themes. This will help you to communicate the benefits of your product or service and to align it with customer needs. For example, if you are a job search platform, you might want to group your content into themes such as "finding a job after graduation" or "tips for job seekers." This will help your audience to understand your product or service in a way that is easy to digest and that is relevant to their needs.

It's critical to think about the pitch before you need one. Build out the right thirty-second soundbites and have them in your hip pocket so that when an opportunity presents itself, you're ready to go. There's nothing worse than bumping into someone who could be a significant ally in your product efforts and you fumble it. Then you're left with nothing but replaying the exchange in your head and thinking about the things you wish you'd said. Don't let this happen to you!

Another important element is to develop an expanded version of the elevator pitch. Don't be left flatfooted if someone hears the thirty-second version and says "That's interesting. Tell me more." That's the exact reaction you're hoping to get, so be ready for it with a more detailed two to five-minute version that expands on the key elements in a crisp and focused way.

Building Your Elevator Pitch in Less Than An Hour

You'll probably come up with your own approach for writing your pitches and product talking points, but here's the process that works for me and it takes less than an hour.

First, take the first five minutes and figure out what your goal/objective is for the pitch. Are you looking to simply communicate? Trying to get a project funded?

Then, spend the next ten minutes brainstorming all the things you might want to say to someone during your pitch. Remember the four key points outlined above – problem, solution, market size and how you make money.

Spend another ten minutes prioritizing the list from most important thing to least important thing. If you only answer the four key points in order, that's ok. But if you still have a few moments to work on a thirty-second elevator pitch, pick the top two or three things. Write them down on a 3x5 index card, the kind with ten ruled lines on it, and use a regular Sharpie pen. I'm not talking about making the kind of cheat card with a microprint that you might have used to study for a high-school history test. Think bullet points and use the ten lines on the card and no more. That's it. There's your basic elevator pitch.

For a longer (two to five-minute) talk, you'll need to decide if you want to use the extra time to take a shallow approach or a deeper one. With the shallow approach, you'll cover more of the high-level points on your brainstormed list but not as much detail. In a deeper approach, you'll take the original two or three top points and go into more detail about those areas.

Finally, before you can consider this done, write it down exactly the way you think you want to say it, then say it out loud to yourself. You'll develop an ear for narrative and flow. If it sounds awkward to you it's going to sound awkward to others because at least YOU know what you're TRYING to say and your listener won't. The goal should be to make the pitch sound conversational. Cycle on this a couple of times to polish the pitch, then try it out on a friend or business associate and ask for feedback. Ask them if they can tell you what your key points were. If your friend gets them close, you're probably ready for that elevator ride.

Here are reminders for creating a great pitch:

- Keep it simple and to the point. Use clear, concise language that can be easily understood. Avoid using jargon or technical terms.
- Focus on the benefits of your product or service. What problem does it solve? How does it make people's lives better?
- Make it memorable. Use stories, analogies, or examples to help people remember your pitch.
- Practice, practice, practice. The more you practice, the more confident you will be when delivering your pitch.

A pitch is a great way to quickly communicate the value of your product or service. By focusing on the benefits of your product and the solution it offers, you can create a memorable pitch that will resonate with your audience. With practice, you will be able to deliver your pitch with confidence and ease.

TL;DR

• Microsoft CEO Satya Nadella observed that attention is "the new oil" in the age of constant distraction, making it more important than ever to grab and hold someone's attention.

• Product managers must be able to communicate concepts clearly at all levels and to all audiences, including mastering a variety of communication vehicles such as elevator pitches.

• An elevator pitch should cover four key points: what problem are you solving; what solution do you offer; what market opportunity exists; and how does your business model make money?

• To craft a great story about your product or service, use clear language that anyone can understand while avoiding jargon or technical terms. Also, focus on benefits rather than features when explaining solutions.

• Finally, practice makes perfect - work on developing soundbites for short conversations as well as longer versions of the same message in order to deliver with confidence when opportunities arise.

CHAPTER EXERCISES

1. Identify a subject that you'd like to pitch. Answer the four key questions:
   a. What problem are you solving?
   b. What solution do you offer?
   c. What is the market opportunity?
   d. What is your business model, or how do you make money?
2. Go through the one-hour pitch process outlined in this chapter:
   a. Identify your goal
   b. Brainstorm possible content

c. Prioritize the content down to a top 2 or 3 things that'll fit on an index card
   d. Practice it out loud

CHAPTER NOTES

CHAPTER 8: The Four Whys – If Your Competition Reads This First, They'll Probably Take Your Customers Too

"There is no sport as competitive as business. It's 24 by 7 by 365 by forever, and there's all these young kids out here trying to kick your ass." - Mark Cuban

I've been tracking Mark Cuban for a long time. Back before he was one of the sharks on *Shark Tank* or dancing on *Dancing With The Stars*. Back before he was a billionaire. Way before all that, in the 1980s, Cuban had a company called MicroSolutions. This was back when PCs were desktop machines just starting to take the place of dumb terminals hooked up to mainframe computers. The devices had 16 KB (yeah, KB) of memory, which is roughly the same processing power and storage as one of your chip credit cards today. Your files were stored on 5.25-inch floppy disks that held 360 KB.

Cuban also had a regular column in one of the industry trade publications, *Computer Reseller News*. His stuff was the first thing I turned to each week. It was pretty clear that he had "it" even then. I remember his last *CRN* column where he told his readers that he was going off to work on a project that he couldn't talk about. That project turned out to be Broadcast.com, one of the first streaming services on the Internet. During the dot-com boom, Cuban sold the company to Yahoo for $5.7 billion.

Mark Cuban is a competitor. Nominated for an Emmy for *Shark Tank*. Owner of the 2011 NBA champion Dallas Mavericks. Cuban understands competition better than most of us. He says, "If you walk into a competitive environment and they still know more about the business than you do and more about your customers, you're going to lose."

In this next section, let's take a look at our competition. We'll learn about Jobs To Be Done and understand how we fit into our customers' lives. We'll also introduce something I call "The Four Whys" to get a handle on the psychology behind why people might buy from us.

It's always important to know more about your business than anyone else, but it's especially important in a competitive environment. If you walk into a meeting with potential customers and your competition knows more about the customer's business and needs than you do, you're not going to win. You have to be an expert. Ask the questions and get the understanding. You have to know more about your customers and their needs than anyone else in the room. Otherwise, you're not going to be able to sell them on what you're offering because you're not speaking THEIR language, you're speaking YOURS. Keep this in mind the next time you're preparing for a meeting or presentation. The more you know, the better chance you have of success.

Hard Work, Passion and Kicking Ass

"Work like there is someone working twenty-four hours a day to take it all away from you." - MC

More tough talk from Cuban. Not a surprise that hard work is a path to success. If you want something badly enough, you have to be willing to put in the hours to make it happen. We're a twenty-four-hour society now with a global labor market. If you're not constantly pushing yourself, someone else will be happy to take your place. Balancing this with the self-care that you'll need to survive long-term can be tricky. Job burnout is a real thing. But it's a tough world out there and if you're not prepared to work hard, you'll quickly get left behind. So remember, always work like someone else is working around the clock to take what you've achieved away from you. It's not just about the hours, but the effort in those hours, with a particular focus on always doing the most important work. Only by putting in the effort on the right things will you be able to stay ahead of the competition. It's ok to dream big and you should, but execution and hard work is what gets you across the finish line.

"Sweat equity is the most valuable equity there is. Know your business and industry better than anyone else in the world. Love what you do or don't do it." - MC

Have you ever known anyone who had an "Isn't there someone else that can do this?" attitude when faced with doing anything difficult? When you're building a product, you have to be willing to do the hard things required to make it successful. When no one else is there to do it, are you going to step up or step back? If you're passionate about what you're doing, it'll be easier to put in the long hours needed. Knowing your business inside-out is critical. You have to be the expert in your field, and you have to be able to make the tough decisions that will grow your company. If you're not willing to do all of those things, then it might be hard to hear this, but maybe you shouldn't start a business or launch a product - plain and simple. But if you are willing to put in the hard work and do the difficult thing, then you might stand a chance of winning.

"Figure out how to kick your own ass before someone else does it for you." - MC

It's not about finding the easy way out. It's about taking the hard things and making them look easy. Or at least easier. The same can be said of kicking your own ass. Before you can do great things, you have to be willing to put in the hard work. And that means figuring out how to kick your own ass. Maybe that means getting up early for a workout or pushing yourself to finish a project even when you're tired. Whatever it is, you need to find a way to push yourself to do better. Otherwise, someone else will end up doing it for you. And you don't want that. So, figure out how to kick your own ass, and make it look easy. Do it for yourself, and nobody else.

But kicking your own ass is not just about working hard. It's also about being self-aware enough to know your weaknesses. Ask yourself "If I were going to fail trying to do this, what would the reasons be?" And then spend time leveling up your weaknesses, turning your average skills into strengths, and upskilling your strengths into superpowers.

The Why Guy and The Infinite Game

Another person who has a strong take on the competition in the business world is author Simon Sinek. Sinek's TED Talks and his videos on YouTube have been viewed more than 100 million times. He's the author of several books including the best-selling *Start With Why: How Great Leaders Inspire Everyone to Take Action*. In it, Sinek argues that the key to success is not what you do (the "what"), but why you do it (the "why"). This simple yet powerful idea has resonated with people around the world, and Sinek has become a sought-after speaker on the topic of leadership. Outside of his work as an author and speaker, Sinek is also the founder of the nonprofit organization Start With Why, which is dedicated to helping leaders inspire others.

In his 2019 book *The Infinite Game*, Sinek suggests that there are two kinds of games in the world – finite and infinite. Finite games are games with a clock and established rules. Think basketball or soccer. If you're playing a finite game, you know who you're playing against. Someone keeps score and at the end of the game, you know if there's a win, a loss, or a tie.

Contrast that to what Sinek calls an infinite game. This is more like business or politics. In an infinite game, there are known and unknown competitors. The rules are much less clear, especially when determining whether something's legal or adheres to social norms (see certain rule-bending politicians). Scorekeeping is harder, although you can look at things like business revenues or election results to get a general feel for the current status. But there's no clock and the game keeps going into infinity with players joining and leaving the game over time.

In *Start With Why*, Sinek posits that the most successful businesses are those that start with a clear understanding of their purpose. Instead of fixating on beating the competition, these companies focus on fulfilling their own mission. As a result, they are able to attract loyal customers and employees who are passionate about their work and whose personal mission aligns with the company's why. This model can be applied to any organization, regardless of its size or industry. By focusing on your own mission, you can achieve long-term success, regardless of what the competition is doing.

The Two Most Important Things To Know

I wish I could sugar coat this. Your competition is out to crush you. Most of your customers are probably indifferent to you and you can't just run out the clock. If you're going to survive, it's essential to know two things whenever you're dealing with a competitive situation. First, you've gotta know why your potential customers are buying from someone else. Second, you've gotta know what you can do differently and better, so they should buy from you instead, and then execute on those things.

As a business owner or entrepreneur, it's essential to understand your customer's needs. The best way to do this is to ask questions and listen to the answers. What is your customer's problem? How are they solving it today? What are their pain points? How can you improve on the current solution? When you understand your customer's needs, you can develop a solution that meets their requirements and differentiates you from the competition. Asking questions is the key to understanding your customer's needs and developing a winning solution.

When you close your eyes and picture the best cheeseburger you've ever tasted, it's probably not a McDonald's cheeseburger. But it's hard to argue with the "billions and billions" of cheeseburgers McDonald's has sold. Different people have different reasons for buying one of those burgers. Being fast. Being "on-the-way." Being able to eat it in your car. There are a ton of reasons that McD's burgers can be the best choice even if it's not the best burger.

In my first job after college, I managed a McDonald's in Dayton, Ohio. It was a real-world business boot camp and an unofficial MBA in customer experience. Working there, you had a deadline every ten seconds as the food was prepared and customers were served. But flipping those burgers, even as I developed an appetite for Big Macs, one of the things that I learned was the importance of understanding the Four Whys.

So, what are the Four Whys?

The Four Whys are:

1. The Functional Why = I have a problem and I need a solution.
2. The Social Why = I want to be part of a community/tribe.
3. The Emotional Why = I want to feel a certain way.
4. The Logical Why - I choose this solution because it's the best, cheapest, fastest...

Let's look at each of these in a bit more detail.

The Functional Why: What's the Job To Be Done?

The Functional Why is usually the most important of the four because it's the core reason the customer buys your product in the first place. The Functional Why is table stakes. If you can't solve the customer's most basic problem, they're not going to buy from you.

Exercising the Functional Why, someone buys a McDonald's cheeseburger because they're hungry and want something to eat. But assuming there are other options available, you could also just as easily choose a hot dog off of the rollers at a gas station. But I'd probably stay away from the sushi.

Another perspective on this Why comes from Clayton Christensen. He was a renowned management thinker and author best known for his work on innovation and growth. Throughout his career, Christensen helped companies to better understand customer needs and develop new products and services that address those needs. He was also the author of *The Innovator's Dilemma*, a book that explores the challenges faced by disruptive companies. In another book, *Competing Against Luck*, Christensen focuses on the concept of "jobs to be done," which states that businesses should focus on creating solutions that help customers to get a specific job done. This approach has been hugely influential in the world of business, and it continues to shape the way that companies innovate and grow.

Christensen's "jobs to be done" theory is built on the idea that people buy products and services to fulfill a specific need or "job." They don't purchase products just for the sake of it, but rather because they have a need that they want to be fulfilled. For example, people don't need a drill as much as they need a hole-delivery system. In this view, drills are a way to deliver holes on demand.

The Functional Why, like all of the Four Whys, is a blend of Sinek's *Start With Why* and Christensen's JTBD theory. By understanding the customer's functional needs, businesses can better target their marketing efforts and create products that address those needs. Additionally, this theory can help businesses to understand why customers may switch to a competitor's product or service. If a customer feels that their current product isn't adequately fulfilling their needs, they'll be more likely to switch to a competitor who can better address those needs. Ultimately, by understanding and catering to customer needs, businesses can create products that are more likely to be successful in the marketplace.

The Social Why: Know Your Tribe

Have you ever bought something because you wanted to be a part of a group? Do you have a sports jersey or a band t-shirt in your closet? That's the Social Why at work. The Social Why is important because it's the reason the customer buys into your brand. It's how you connect with your customers on a deeper level and create a sense of community.

People who are exercising the Social Why to buy a McDonald's cheeseburger are doing it because it makes the customer feel like they're part of a larger community. According to the book *Fast Food Nation*, one in eight Americans have worked at a McDonald's at some point in their lives. When you bite into that juicy burger, you're a part of something bigger than yourself. You're a part of the McDonald's family. You eat at McDonald's because you see yourself as the kind of person that eats at McDonald's. Or Starbucks. Or roots for a particular sports team. Or votes for a certain candidate for president.

The Emotional Why: It's Called a Happy Meal for a Reason

Disneyland calls itself "the happiest place on Earth." A quote from their website:

"Discover a place that has all the happy you never knew could exist—so you're a new kind of happy every time you visit."

Disney is trying to tap into people's Emotional Why here. If you go to Disneyland, they suggest that you're going to feel a level of happiness beyond your imagination. They're trying to differentiate themselves from all the other happiness you could feel to create an emotional connection with their customers that keeps them coming back for more of that special Disney-branded happy.

If you're a loyal McDonald's customer, maybe when you eat a cheeseburger there, you're not just satisfying your hunger, you're also satisfying your emotions. There's something about that first bite of a Big Mac that just makes you feel good. It's the perfect comfort food when you're feeling down or needing a pick-me-up. Maybe it reminds you of being a kid again when you got that cheeseburger in the now-obviously named Happy Meal and it makes you happy all over again. There's a reason why McDonald's decided to launch adult Happy Meals in 2022. Could they be trying to connect with those childhood emotions all over again?

The Logical Why: A Path to Online Success

The Logical Why is important because it tries to quantify a reason for making a purchase decision by figuring out what your purchase criteria should be – let's say quality, speed, or price – and then using the available data to make the purchase.

In a world of online searches, we often make a purchase decision because something has more five-star reviews or because it was the cheapest option when we sorted by price. The Logical Why becomes increasingly important as we try to make data-driven decisions. We pick the item we buy on Amazon because it's got the lowest price or the best reviews. That's our Logical Why.

The key to winning when your customers are using the Logical Why is understanding their goals and strategies – their why – and then aligning your product with it. If your customers are trying to save money, be the low-cost solution or best value. If your customers are wanting a high-quality piece of equipment, be best-in-class and focus on positive online reviews.

A Cheeseburger Is Not Just A Cheeseburger

As mentioned before, a McDonald's cheeseburger is not necessarily the best-tasting solution. But it is the most sold cheeseburger in the world – over 300 billion of them. Being better isn't always enough and in other cases, it isn't even required. There are better cheeseburgers than McDonald's, but are McDonald's customers even buying them because they're the best?

In many cases, the answer is no. They're connecting the sandwich to one of the Four Whys. Functionally, it meets the basic criteria when they're hungry. But McDonald's customers are often buying because of convenience, price, and habit. McDonald's has become part of our culture and their cheeseburgers have become a symbol of that, giving it a strong emotional connection. When my mom took us there when I was a kid, it had nothing to do with the food – rather, it was because the restrooms were clean. While there may be better-tasting options out there, McDonald's is still the go-to choice for many people.

To wrap up this chapter, here are some final thoughts on competition from Mark Cuban...

"How am I going to crush them if I don't know what they're doing? How am I going to crush them if I can't stay ahead of them? And in order to stay ahead, I've got to keep on grinding to figure out not only how I can do what I'm doing better, not only how I can make my customers happier, but also how to anticipate what the competitors are going to do." - MC

By understanding the competition and what motivates customers to buy, businesses can create products that are more likely to be successful in the marketplace. To better understand your competition, ask yourself: Why do they exist? What needs do they fulfill for their customers? What are their goals and strategies? Once you have a clear understanding of these things, you can begin to develop a plan for how to best compete in the market.

To win against your competition, focus on customer needs and align your product with their goals and strategies, not just yours. By doing so, you'll be able to better meet their needs and exceed their expectations. Then, keep grinding. With a lot of hard work and dedication, you can carve out a spot and hold your own against even the toughest competition.

TL;DR

- Mark Cuban's advice on competition is to work hard and to know more about your business, customers and industry than anyone else.
- Simon Sinek suggests there are two kinds of games: finite (with set rules) and infinite (unclear rules). He argues that businesses should focus on their mission rather than beating the competition for long-term success.
- In Clayton Christensen's *Competing Against Luck*, he explores the idea of "Jobs To Be Done." His theory is based on people buying products or services to fulfill a need – they don't buy items just for the sake of it but because there is an underlying job they want accomplished (e.g., drills are used as hole-delivery systems).
- The two most important things for entrepreneurs to understand when facing competition is why customers buy from someone else and what can be done differently or better so they should buy from you instead.
- The Four Whys are a blend of Sinek's *Start With Why* and Christensen's JTBD theory, which helps businesses to understand customer needs and develop products that address them.

- The Functional Why is usually the most important of the four because it's why customers buy your product in the first place: they have a problem and need a solution.
- The Social Why helps to create an emotional connection with customers and build a sense of community around your brand.
- The Emotional Why taps into people's emotions by creating experiences that evoke certain feelings in them when they buy products or services from you.
- Lastly, the Logical Why quantifies reasons for making purchase decisions based on available data – such as quality, speed or price – allowing customers to make data-driven decisions (e.g., Amazon reviews).

CHAPTER EXERCISES

1. Think about a potential customer for your company or product. What problem are they trying to solve? How are they solving it today? What are their pain points? Why would they buy from one of your competitors? How can you improve on their current solution with a better and more differentiated alternative?
2. Name 2 or 3 things that you've purchased recently. Which of the Four Whys was the primary reason for the purchase? Can you think of any purchases you've made that fall into each of the Four Whys or do all your purchases fall into just one or two of them?

CHAPTER NOTES

CHAPTER 9: There's A Story In Your Product's Data — Do You Know What It Is?

"The most powerful person in the world is the storyteller. The storyteller sets the vision, values and agenda of an entire generation that is to come." - Steve Jobs

Storytelling is one of the most powerful tools we have for connecting with others. When done well, narrative can help us build rapport, empathize with our audience, and make complex concepts more relatable and understandable. Additionally, narrative can be a catalyst for change, inspiring people to act based on the insights we share.

Your product's data is more than a list of features and benefits. It's a story waiting to be told. And as the product manager, it's your job to tell that story. It's also often your job to decide what data you'll collect from your customers and how you'll collect, store and protect it. But where do you start? How do you use data to build a narrative that will engage and motivate your team, your customers, and your prospects? In this chapter, we'll look at a wide range of data-related issues ranging from data storytelling to common errors and biases along with ways to think more strategically about your product's data.

The most successful people I know are masters of narrative. They understand that the ability to communicate a compelling story is the key to influence and persuasion. And they use this power to their advantage, whether they're selling a product, pitching an idea, or simply trying to get their point across.

For all these reasons, we must learn to use narrative effectively when communicating about our product's data. By harnessing the power of story, we can make our data more impactful and meaningful, ultimately driving better decision-making and results.

But telling stories with our data doesn't always seem to get the emphasis it deserves. In a 2016 *Forbes* article called "Data Storytelling: The Essential Data Science Skill Everyone Needs," author Brent Dykes said the following:

"Much of the current hiring emphasis has centered on the data preparation and analysis skills—not the "last mile" skills that help convert insights into actions. Many of the heavily-recruited individuals with advanced degrees in economics, mathematics, or statistics struggle with communicating their insights to others effectively—essentially, telling the story of their numbers."

This is a problem. Are we relying too heavily on data scientists who can't effectively communicate their findings to non-technical people? The whole point of having data is to use it to make better decisions, and we can't do that if the data's relevance stays locked up in the heads of a few analysts. And that's why the person who can find the narrative in data science output is worth their weight in gold. They have the rare but essential skill of being able to take complex information and turn it into a story that people can understand.

That's why internal subject matter experts (SMEs) are often so valuable if they have strong communications skills. They also have the business or operational knowledge that adds context to the analytics. Using their business expertise, they can take complicated data and turn it into something that decision-makers and stakeholders can use to make informed choices.

Storytelling is the key to communicating your data. Data can be complex, and people can be confused by numbers. But people understand stories. Stories can inspire. Stories can provide context that connects the data to the business and drives action.

It's this simple. Not having a story to tell means you don't know your "why." Not understanding your "why" means you don't know what action to take. Not taking action means nothing changes.

In a world filled with numbers, data, and spreadsheets, it's easy to get lost in the details and forget the human element. This is where storytelling comes in. Stories connect us and help us make sense of the world. They provide context and meaning, and they inspire us to act. When used effectively, stories can help businesses understand their customers, connect data to real-world results, and drive change. In a fast-paced, competitive world, those who can tell stories will be the ones who succeed.

An Important First Question - Can You Trust Your Data?

"It's not what you look at that matters, it's what you see." – Henry David Thoreau

If you look at my Facebook page as of the writing of this book, I have just over 3000 "friends." (Yeah, I know.) Assuming that birthdays were evenly spread throughout the 365 days of the year, I would expect about eight birthdays on any given day of the year. But on January 1st, I have over thirty friends with birthdays. What gives? Is there something special about April Fools' Day that enhances the baby-delivery process nine months later? Probably not.

This is an example of Twyman's Law. In their book *Exploring Data: An Introduction to Data Analysis for Social Scientists*, authors Catherine Marsh and Jane Elliott call Twyman's Law "perhaps the single most important law in the whole of data analysis." Yet when

Tony Twyman died in 2014, this law named for him didn't even garner a mention in his obituary. Seriously. What gives? (https://www.mrweb.com/drno/news20011.htm).

Tony Twyman was instrumental in building out the now-standard methods and procedures used for measuring the size of radio and TV audiences in the UK starting in the 1950s up through his retirement in the early 2000s. His law was a simple one:

"Any piece of data or evidence that looks interesting or unusual is probably wrong."

Or, as Marsh and Elliott wrote in their book, "The more unusual or interesting the data, the more likely they are to have been the result of an error of one kind or another."

In the case of Facebook birthdays, I have almost four times the number of expected birthdays on January 1st. That's pretty interesting and unusual, right? But the explanation's straightforward. When people set up their FB profiles, especially if they're making a fake one, the easiest way to answer the question of when their birthday is if they don't want to use an actual one is to just type in 1's. And that's how you end up with a bunch of January 1st birthdays among your Facebook friends. You'll probably also find a lot of birthdays on November 11th for the same reason. Facebook's method of collecting birthdays has introduced an error or bias into their data that makes it less trustable.

Types of Data Bias

"The signal is the truth. The noise is what distracts us from the truth." – Nate Silver

There's a ton of data out there that we could collect. But there's a lot more noise than signal in that data. We often make choices in our collection techniques which effectively filter out some of that noise. But how do we know we're not also losing important parts of the signal that we really want?

We should always check our data collection method to make sure that we're not causing an issue at the source of the data. Collecting data is an essential step in any product or service development process. However, it's important to be aware of the different types of bias that can be introduced when collecting data. Here are a few:

- *Confirmation bias* can lead to overlooking important data that contradicts our hypotheses by only looking at the data that confirms our hypothesis.
- *Selection bias* can occur when we only collect data from a narrow subset of users that aren't representative of the entire user base.
- *Historical bias* can distort our understanding of trends if we don't take into account changes in the user base over time. For example, you might have some issues using a data set from the 1990s to make decisions today.
- *Outlier bias* can skew our results if we place too much importance on extreme data points, weighing them too heavily relative to their occurrence.
- *Systemic bias* can occur when our data collection methods favor certain groups of users over others.
- *Automation bias* can lead us to blindly trust automated data collection processes without verifying the results.
- *Location bias* can cause us to focus on users in a particular geographic area to the exclusion of others or to assume that

if we've sampled users in one region that we can use that data to make assumptions about users in all other regions.

Each of these biases can have a significant impact on our analysis and understanding of the product or service. Therefore, it's important to be aware of them and take steps to avoid them.

Improving Your Data: The Deming Wheel

"Without data, you're just another person with an opinion." - W. Edwards Deming

W. Edwards Deming is a name that product management leaders should know. Deming was an American statistician, professor, author, lecturer, and management consultant. He was a pioneer in the area of data and analytics. He is best known for his work in the field of quality control and for his advocacy of the use of statistical methods in industrial settings to make data-driven decisions. The renowned management consultant was one of the most significant figures in the total quality management (TQM) movement, where he developed the well-known Deming Wheel, also known as the PDSA cycle (Plan-Do-Study-Act cycle).

However, Deming's work goes beyond TQM. He emphasized the importance of data and how it can contribute to effective decision-making. In today's data-driven world, Deming's philosophy is still significant to organizations of all sizes and industries, especially when it comes to managing data.

The Deming Wheel is an iterative cycle that enables organizations and teams to continuously measure, analyze, and improve their business processes. The PDSA cycle is also at the foundation of Agile development. The purpose of the Deming

Wheel is to allow companies to find areas of improvement so they can increase efficiency while maintaining quality standards. As mentioned, the cycle includes four steps: Plan, Do, Study, and Act. Here's what each step means:

- *Plan*: In this step, you identify the problem, set a goal, and decide how to achieve the preferred outcome. This often involves studying data and analyzing trends to create an informed plan to improve a specific process or project.
- *Do:* After planning, you proceed to implement the plan. This step involves executing the chosen strategies while keeping track of the process's performance.
- *Study:* In this step, you evaluate the process's performance and measure its success. This stage assesses the data generated during the earlier stages and how it informs the organization's decisions.
- *Act:* If the results are favorable, you can adopt the changes to the process to promote continuous improvement. If not, you return to the planning phase to adjust the plan and try again.

The Deming Wheel can be an effective tool for organizations that want to optimize their data analytics strategies. By following these four steps, your organization not only improves its data management process but also enhances the overall efficiency of the organization.

For instance, if an organization wants to improve customer retention, it can use the PDSA cycle as a guide. In the Plan stage, the organization can study customer data and find why customers leave, set retention targets and develop a strategy to reach them. In the Do stage, the organization can execute the strategy and check its effectiveness. In the Study phase, the organization can decide if its initiatives are making a difference and in the Act stage, it can implement the most effective steps or iterate the process again to achieve better results.

With the increasing importance of data in running organizations, incorporating the Deming Wheel can help companies stay ahead of the curve in terms of business strategy, innovation, and growth. And while it may seem simple, it supplies a framework for collecting, analyzing, and implementing data-driven decisions. Deming's philosophy of using data to support informed decision-making is central to the wheel's impact.

Adding Value: Refining Your Data With The Callan Data Cycle

"Data! Data! Data! I can't make bricks without clay." – Sherlock Holmes (as written by Arthur Conan Doyle)

Looks like Mr. Holmes understood the importance of data insights way back in the late 1800's – over one-hundred and thirty years ago in 1892 to be exact. But beyond iteratively optimizing your data-centered decision-making, it's also important to understand how data flows in an organization. You've probably heard the phrase "Data is the new oil." But you can't use raw crude oil to power a car. And you shouldn't use raw data signals to make business decisions. In both cases, there's a process that refines the raw materials into something useful and more valuable. Since Deming's already got the Wheel staked out and, well, since I'm lacking a better naming idea as I'm writing this section, let's call this process the Callan Data Cycle.

The Cycle is a five-step framework that describes the process of how data is created and refined as it moves from the point of origin through a series of stages. This refinement takes the data from raw inputs to actionable tactics and it's how you'll extract the real value from your data assets.

The stages of the Cycle along with the corresponding result of each stage are as follows:

Stage	Result
Collect	Data
Order	Information
Interpret	Insights
Strategize	Tactics
Execute	Outcomes

Here's what happens in each stage:

1. *Collect:* The first stage of the Cycle is crucial for laying a solid foundation to ensure the business activities are working optimally. The aim is to establish accurate measurements for the outcomes of key business activities and avoid any bias or common errors. The significance of accurate data is pivotal since any further analysis would be

Callan Data Cycle

- Collect → Data → Order
- Order → Information → Interpret
- Interpret → Insights → Strategize
- Strategize → Tactics → Execute
- Execute → Outcomes → Collect

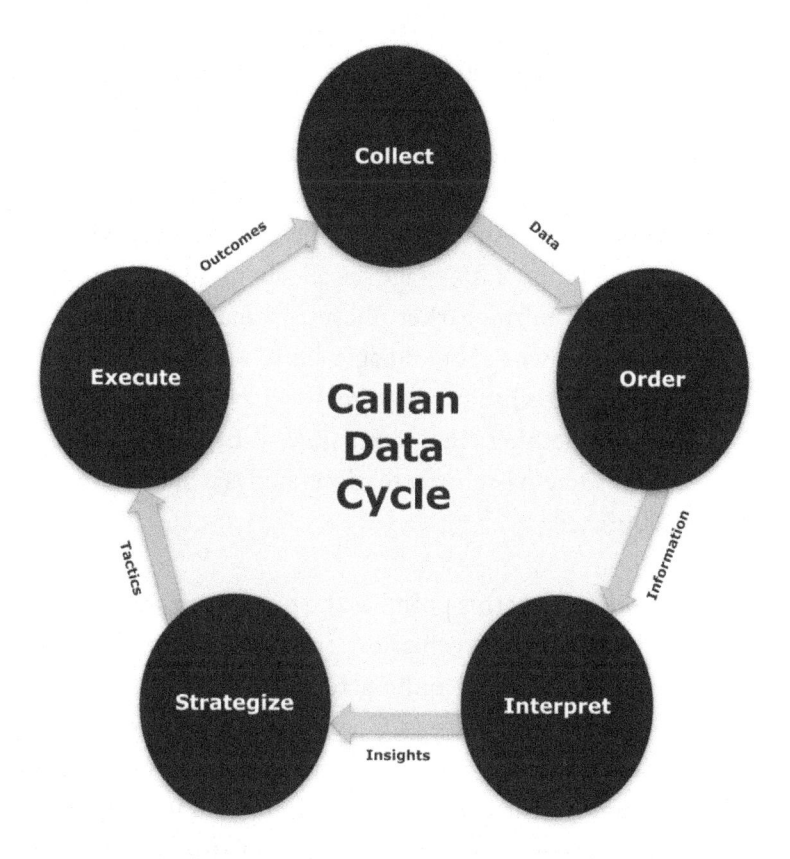

flawed without precision. To do this, the process of data collection begins with setting up systems to track and measure relevant events – for instance, Customer Relationship Management (CRM) tools, analytics tools, or surveys to gain direct feedback from clients. By choosing the right data collection method, the outcomes from the data collected can be translated into refined objectives and goals, unlocking insights that can result in better business decisions.

2. ***Order:*** Once you have collected your data, you move on to the Order stage. Now, data scientists and analysts come in to help transform raw data into something meaningful. They'll clean up data and start building data structures to organize data better, establish relationships, and identify possible correlations. This stage is all about taking the raw data collected in the earlier phase and making sense of it. Data scientists work their magic here, using mathematical and statistical techniques to transform rows and columns of data into something comprehensible. When they're done, you'll have some basic information, analysis and business trends identified.

3. ***Interpret:*** At this point, as the product manager, you'll start to put your information into context, interpreting the ordered data and pulling together insights to explain the trends in your datasets. Context is essential because it allows you to build a narrative around the data, which helps you understand it better and communicate it to others. While you can see the trends and analytics in the last stage, you need to answer the question "Why?" You're moving beyond looking at information and starting to come up with explanations. You're also tying the data back to events. For example, if sales have increased in the past month, you might note that there was a marketing campaign that drove the increase. By layering different types of data and analyzing them together, you can uncover hidden insights that can help you make informed decisions going forward.

4. ***Strategize***: In this stage, the insights obtained from the previous phase are transformed into strategic initiatives to propel fresh business activity. Should you rerun a specific marketing campaign? It may have succeeded in boosting sales last month but what if it underperformed in comparison to one launched six months ago? To craft a successful strategy, examine business goals and gather insights from past campaigns. Create tactics and actions that align with these goals. Upon completion of this stage, you should have a clear direction for the upcoming actions.

5. ***Execute:*** Finally, it's time to put the strategy into action. This stage focuses on implementing the strategic plan and generating new outcomes from those tactics. These results feed back into the front end of the Collection process and the Cycle spins around again.

Remember, the underlying data is only part of the puzzle – the rest of the process of refining the data into insights and strategies that can drive action is just as important for extracting the full value of your organization's data assets. By following the Callan Data Cycle framework, businesses can better understand their data and refine the signals into strategies based on actionable insights. For the rest of this chapter, let's take a more detailed look at each stage.

Cycle Stage One and Two: Collect and Order Your Data

Understanding what data your business needs to make decisions is your first step as a data-centric product manager. (What question or problem are you trying to solve? What data do we need to solve the problem?) This means that the business's data needs should be a part of the product design from the ground up. After all, products are often a primary source for a business's data and if you don't collect it, you can't measure it or manage it. Obviously, this is easier to do if your product is an app, website or some kind of software. But the point is still relevant even if we're talking about a physical good or service.

This data can come from a variety of sources, but it is typically collected through user interaction with the product. Once the business's data needs are understood, the next step is designing the product in such a way that this data can be easily observed, collected and stored. This often involves creating tracking mechanisms for user behavior and designing user interfaces that are intuitive and easy to use. By taking these steps, data-centric products can be designed that deliver invaluable customer insights for businesses and help them to make better-informed decisions.

Along the way, keep checking to make sure that you're asking the right questions and collecting the right data in your product. Data needs can change over time. So can the opportunity to collect new data.

Frequently, businesses will want to collect data to create forecasts for future performance. The most important thing you can do when it comes to making predictions is to focus on leading indicators, rather than lagging indicators. Lagging indicators are those that confirm what has already happened while leading indicators are those that signal what is about to happen. For example, consider your sales funnel. A lagging indicator would be to measure sales revenue which tells you how the sales team's performing after the money's in the door. But a leading indicator might be the number of sales calls that the team has made because if the volume of conversations increases, you could reasonably expect that revenue might also increase. The bottom line is that leading indicators are much more predictive than lagging indicators, so you should always focus on them when making predictions whenever possible.

When it comes to data collection, it's important to think beyond your team's needs and consider the value that other parts of the business might find in the data you're collecting. By aligning your data collection efforts with the needs of other stakeholders, you can bring added value to the organization as a whole. So, how can you discover what data other stakeholders might find valuable? One approach is to simply ask them! Talk to members of other teams and departments and find out what kind of data they would find helpful in their work. Ask them what problems they're trying to solve, what questions they need to have answered. By taking this proactive approach, you can ensure that your data collection efforts are aligned with the needs of the entire organization.

Once you have a good understanding of what data you need to collect, the next step is to put together a plan for how you will collect it. This plan should be based on the business's overall objectives and should consider the specific needs of each stakeholder. The plan should also be flexible enough to accommodate changes in the business's data needs over time. After all, as the saying goes, "the only constant is change."

Once you have a plan in place, it's time to start collecting data. There are a variety of ways to do this, but one of the most important things to keep in mind is that you need to collect accurate data. This means taking steps to ensure that your data is complete and free from errors. Frequently, someone will need to perform some data cleaning exercises. That's probably a data scientist or analyst, but you might be involved from an oversight or validation standpoint.

Data cleaning is the process of identifying and cleaning up inaccuracies and inconsistencies in data. It can also include the process of standardizing data in a particular format if it's collected in a variety of inputs. It is a crucial step in any data analysis, as it can help to improve the quality of the results. As an example, you might have been asked to confirm your street address or zip code when entering it during an online purchase. That's an effort to clean and standardize the data so that it's consistent since it could be entered slightly differently from each customer.

There are many different ways to clean data, but some common methods include:

- Remove invalid or inaccurate data: this includes removing data that is outliers or does not match the rest of the data set.
- Fix inaccuracies: this includes fixing errors in spelling, grammar, and formatting.
- Normalize data: this includes standardizing formats and units of measure.

Data cleaning is important because it helps to ensure that the data used for analysis is of high quality. This can make a big difference in the accuracy of the results. In addition, data cleaning can help to improve the efficiency of data analysis by reducing the amount of time spent on manual data entry or dealing with errors. As a result, it is worth taking the time to clean data before beginning any type of analysis.

But you should also ask yourself, "How clean does the data need to be to answer the question?" Don't over clean if the questions you're trying to answer don't need to have perfect data. One way to do this is to set up clear guidelines for how data should be entered into the system. This can help to minimize errors and ensure that the data is consistent across different departments and teams.

It's also important to make sure that your data is well organized. (Again, only as organized as it needs to be.) This will make it easier to find and use when you need it. One way to do this is to create a system for naming and tagging data so that it can be easily searched and retrieved. Another good idea is to create a central repository for all of your company's data. This repository should be accessible to all stakeholders and should be regularly backed up so that you don't lose any important information. Depending on your organization, you might not own the actual landing place for your product's data, but in most cases, you'll provide some business requirements for it at a minimum.

Cycle Stage Three: Interpret = Finding The Insights In Your Data

"If we have data, let's look at data. If all we have are opinions, let's go with mine." - Jim Barksdale, former Netscape CEO

Once you've got data you can trust, the next step is to turn that into something useful. In his book *The Black Swan*, Nassim Taleb talks about the difference between data and information. Data is just a collection of facts and figures. Information is data that has been processed in some way that makes it meaningful and useful.

As we discussed at the beginning of the chapter, data scientists are trained to bring order to data. They know how to clean it, how to manipulate it, and how to find patterns in it. But they don't necessarily know how to tell the story that the data is trying to tell. That's where you come in.

As the product manager, it's your job to take the data and turn it into a story that will engage and motivate your team, your customers, and your prospects. Start by analyzing the data your organization currently collects and determining how to optimize its use. Work with your team to develop a plan for collecting the data you need to tell the story of your product. And don't be afraid to get creative.

But not too creative.

Apophenia is the tendency to see patterns where none exist. It's a common error that people make when they're looking at data. They see a pattern and they assume that it means something. But often, the pattern is just noise. An example of apophenia is the gambler's fallacy.

The gambler's fallacy is a belief that past outcomes will have an effect on future results in a random situation. This phenomenon often leads to people making bad decisions when it comes to gambling, but it can also be seen in a variety of other contexts.

In gambling, the gambler's fallacy often takes the form of believing that if heads have come up five times in a row while tossing a coin, then there's a higher likelihood that tails must come up next. This misconception arises from attaching too much meaning to previous outcomes when they are all essentially unrelated - each toss of the coin has no effect on the results of any other toss, yet many gamblers will make bets based on their expectation that this one should be different due to what has happened before. In truth, this type of pattern recognition is simply apophenia at work — looking for meaningful connections where none actually exist.

Outside of gambling situations, apophenia plays an important role in many forms of decision-making processes. For instance, when analyzing complex datasets such as market trends or customer analytics, product managers may find themselves connecting variables that are actually unrelated — resulting in incorrect conclusions being drawn from incorrect interpretations of data. In order to combat this tendency towards apophenia, it is important for decision-makers across all disciplines to remain aware of potential pitfalls such as false correlations and not solely rely on logical analysis alone when attempting to make sense out of large amounts of data.

One way to avoid this error is to always question your data. Are there other explanations for what you're seeing? Could this be just a coincidence? Is there another way to look at the data that would show a different story? Don't let apophenia lead you down the wrong path. Be skeptical of your data and always question what it's telling you.

It's also important to remember that correlation is not causation. Just because two things are related doesn't mean that one caused the other. This is another common mistake. Just because X and Y are correlated, doesn't mean that X caused Y. There could be another factor, Z, which is causing both X and Y. Or it could be just a coincidence.

Let's take a look at an example: ice cream sales and shark attacks. On the surface it might appear that there is a connection between these two occurrences — more people buy ice cream when the weather gets hotter and more people go to the beach, resulting in more shark attacks — but it does not mean that buying ice cream causes sharks to attack!

At its heart, this example highlights the difference between correlation and causation - two concepts that are often confused due to apophenia. Correlation simply says that two things have a relationship while causation states that one thing directly causes another. In this case, while there is indeed an observable link between ice cream consumption and shark attacks (correlation), we cannot jump to conclusions and say that eating ice cream will bring about shark attacks (causation).

Therefore, understanding how apophenia can lead us astray when it comes to connecting disparate events is important - especially when attempting to discern false correlations from true causal relationships. It's easy for our minds to make assumptions about why something may be happening based on what we observe, but unless we have evidence of actual causation, no meaningful conclusion can be drawn from mere correlations.

In his book *Outliers*, Malcolm Gladwell tells a similar story of how a disproportionate group of Canadian hockey players are born in the early months of the year. Gladwell states that as much as forty percent of the players are born in the first three months of the year, while about ten percent are born in October through December. Is there something about being born in January that made them better hockey players?

The answer? Yes... and no. The cutoff for junior hockey eligibility in Canada is December 31st each year. The players born just after that date are essentially held back until the next season. This gives them extra time to develop physically, and when you're just eight years old, a few months of extra development can be a small but noticeable advantage on the ice. But it isn't just the physical size that gives them the edge over time.

Because they have that slight physical edge early, these kids are selected for opportunities to play against other early all-stars. They get more coaching and more ice time against higher-caliber competition. This early physical advantage means that they play against bigger, faster, better competition and for that reason, they become better hockey players themselves, going on to play in the National Hockey League.

But while there may be a correlation between being born early in the year and playing in the NHL, there is no causation. The players in the example weren't better because they had more natural talent. There was just a systemic bias introduced by the selection process in youth hockey that led to the results Gladwell found.

It's important to remember this when you're looking at data. Just because two things are correlated doesn't mean that one caused the other. Always look for other explanations and don't assume causation just because there's a correlation.

Cycle Stage Four: Strategy = Turning Your Insights Into Tactics

"The goal is to provide inspiring information that moves people to action." – Guy Kawasaki

Once you have analyzed and interpreted the data you've collected, it is time for product managers to develop a tactical plan in order to execute their strategy. We'll talk more about creating plans in much greater detail in Chapter 14. But at a high level here are some key steps for turning insights into tactical strategies:

1. *Know Your Goals*: Before you begin collecting and analyzing data, it is important that product managers first define their goals. Having this outline of objectives in mind prior will help focus their findings and keep them on track throughout the process.

2. *Create Statements of High-Level Strategy*: After defining your goals, come up with detailed statements of high-level

strategy which will provide more clarity around what needs to be done and why — further emphasizing these objectives while also making sure they are actionable, achievable and measurable.

3. *Identify Actions*: Once you have created your statements of high-level strategy, turn these into concrete actions that need to be taken for the set objectives to come into fruition. This could include tasks such as conducting user research or launch experiments depending on the context at hand.

4. *Determine Resources Needed*: Now that you know the tasks that must be completed, resource allocation should become an important step in the process as it will dictate what gets done and when as well as who handles each task. Make sure resources are distributed in such a way that critical tasks get priority over non-critical ones so that you can stay on budget without compromising quality results or sacrificing progress along the way.

5. *Create a Timeline*: Establishing a timeline with start dates, end dates and necessary deadlines is also beneficial for staying focused throughout the entire duration of planning - setting up checkpoints which can help hold stakeholders accountable while also allowing product managers themselves more clarity on how much time they have left before launch day arrives. This adds another layer structure around strategy development while also providing motivation during times when momentum may begin flagging due to unforeseen obstacles or bottlenecks that arise over time.

6. *Communicate Strategy with Organization*: Finally, make sure everyone involved understands your plan by clearly communicating your strategy with all relevant stakeholders across the organization. Having everyone on board from start to finish makes sure everyone stays informed about progress and any potential delays during testing phases or after launch periods have concluded. It also helps foster transparency between departments — leading to increased collaboration and engagement throughout strategy development while helping products avoid costly mistakes down the road.

By following these steps, product managers can set themselves up for success by developing more effective strategies based on accurate insights drawn from high quality data — ultimately leading to better products and customer experiences overall.

A Data-Driven Strategy is Not The Same as A Data Strategy

While we're talking about strategy and data, let's take a quick sidebar here to clarify a key point. A data-driven strategy focuses on making decisions based on data, while a data strategy considers how to protect and use data more effectively in an organization. The two strategies are closely related but have different aims and approaches. As an organization, you're probably going to want both. For the scope of this book, we're really focused on creating a data-driven product strategy here. That said, your product may become a major source for your organization's data and you may need to interact with the teams that manage and secure the data assets, so let's talk a little bit in this sidebar about data strategy.

A data strategy considers issues such as data security, privacy, and compliance. It should also consider how best to store and manage data so that it is secure yet accessible. The data strategy should also consider how best to present data in a way that is useful and informative. Visualization tools can help organizations make sense of complex data sets, while dashboards and reports can be used to keep stakeholders informed about progress. Finally, the data strategy should include a plan for how to use analytics results to improve the organization's performance. Real-time analytics can help organizations make better decisions quickly, while predictive analytics can deliver insight into future trends. With the right data strategy in place, organizations can make the most of their data and drive business growth.

A company's data strategy is an approach to managing data that has become an essential part of the modern world. There are several reasons for this. First, the volume of data that organizations have to deal with is growing exponentially. Second, the variety of data sources is also increasing, making it more difficult to manage and integrate data. Third, the need for timely and accurate reporting is higher than ever before. Fourth, the competitive landscape is becoming more challenging and organizations need to be able to use data more effectively to stay ahead of the competition. Finally, customers are becoming more demanding and expect organizations to be able to provide them with personalized experiences. A data strategy can help organizations deal with all of these challenges and create a competitive advantage.

A data strategy is an important tool for any organization that relies on data to drive decision-making. By clearly articulating the organization's goals and objectives for data, a data strategy provides a roadmap for how to collect, use, store, secure, and build value with company/product data. By aligning your product's data collection and use with organizational goals, a data strategy can help to ensure that data is used effectively and efficiently to drive business value. Additionally, a data strategy can help to identify and mitigate risks associated with customer data, such as privacy and security risks. By considering the ever-changing landscape of data, a data strategy can help organizations keep pace with the latest trends and technologies.

If your company has an overall approach to data, you'll want to make sure that your product's data strategy lines up with it. For example, if your company's approach to handling customer data privacy is to require customers to opt-in to allowing the company to use their data, you're probably not going to be able to use an opt-out process as a part of your product's onboarding.

Leveraging product data is a key part of improving your product. For example, collecting usage data can identify key features that you might want to enhance. Or looking at the support data from your help desk might tell you the most critical defects that you need to fix first. Having a product-level data strategy can help you make better-informed decisions, understand your customers at an individual and aggregate level, improve operations efficiency, optimize products and services, and measure and improve performance. Tying your product's data strategy back to your overall company data strategy is a critical way to ensure alignment across your organization.

As part of your assessment process, you'll need to understand the current data available in the organization. What's going on out there? Talk to stakeholders and identify any pockets of your product's data that are being collected by their teams as well as what their unmet data needs might be. Are there manual data collection efforts going on that roll up into spreadsheets or databases on someone's laptop or used by siloed teams that could benefit from a more systematic cross-company approach?

Usually, I'll recommend the following four steps to improve data availability in an organization:

1. Identify a single, high-value source of data and figure out what are the best ways to use that data.
2. Create data synergies by looking around the company for other high-value data that could be made more valuable by integrating it with your initial source. For example, do your support and sales databases share data?
3. Ask yourself, "what additional data could we collect that we don't have today that would drive new value from our data?" Maybe it requires a process change. Sometimes it's just adding another question to your collection process.
4. Finally, consider looking at third-party data that you could bring in from outside the organization and connect to your existing data. For example, maybe if you could get external purchase data about your customers, you could significantly improve your current targeting and sales conversions.

You might also find out that you need to improve the overall quality of your data. There's nothing worse than thinking you have great data only to find out upon closer inspection that it looks like Swiss cheese because you haven't been consistent in your collection efforts.

If you're not sure whether your data quality is up to par, you'll need to do a data audit. This could be as simple as looking at your database to see what you've got at an individual record level. If you've got massive amounts of data, you'll still want to take a closer look, but you'll be doing it from a random sample of the dataset to make the task manageable.

There are a few things you can look for. First, check to see if your data is complete. Are there any gaps or missing values? Second, take a look at the accuracy of your data. Are the values accurate, or are they off by a lot? Finally, look at the timeliness of your data. Is it up-to-date, or are you working with old information?

If you find that your data quality could use some improvement, don't despair. There are several things you can do to clean up your data and get it into shape. First, establish a set of standards for data collection and make sure everyone on your team is following them. Second, plan to regularly perform audits of your data to check for errors and inconsistencies. Third, establish some data-related KPIs so that you can set goals for improvement and measure progress. And finally, invest in some quality control measures, such as automated checks and manual data reviews to catch the things that your automation might miss. By taking these steps, you can ensure that your data is of the highest quality.

Companies are constantly collecting information about our online behavior to sell ads, improve their products, and generally make money. And while there's nothing inherently wrong with this, it does raise some important privacy and security concerns. For one thing, it's often unclear what data is being collected and how it's being used. This can lead to people feeling like they're being watched or that their personal information is being mishandled.

Additionally, there have been several high-profile data breaches in recent years, which has left many people feeling insecure about entrusting their data to companies. It might seem like common sense to keep data secure, but data breaches keep happening, so we'll touch on the issue here. The key thing to remember is that, even if a company is collecting data legally, there can be major consequences if that data ends up in the wrong hands. Before you share your product's information with anyone, make sure you understand how it will be used and what safeguards are in place to protect it. Also, consider the potential impact of your data decisions on your brand if the things you're doing with your data were to become public. You don't want to become a news story.

It's important to realize that if people inside your organization can get their hands on your data, they may assume they can do whatever they want with it – regardless of any legal or privacy issues. They may not even be trained on those topics. They don't have bad intentions. All they know is that they've been looking for exactly this kind of data and finally found it in an unprotected folder on a shared drive.

For example, someone might assume that everything collected in customer support is fair game for use by the marketing department. Could be ok, but it's probably more nuanced than that if you're in a regulated industry like telecommunications services. That's why it's important to keep your data secure and control access to it. Only give people the information they need to know and make sure they understand the consequences of misusing it. If you don't, you could end up in some hot water - or worse. So have a strategy to protect your product's data, and yourselves, by keeping a tight leash on who can see it and what they can do with it.

End of sidebar. Back to the last stage of the Cycle.

Cycle Stage Five: Execution = Turning Actions Into Data

"If you cannot measure it, you cannot improve it." - Lord Kelvin

Lord Kelvin may have lived in the 1800s, but he could have said that yesterday. In today's fast-paced world, it's easy to forget the importance of taking time to measure our progress. We're shifting from user data to performance data. You've set a strategy and recommended actions. Whether we're trying to lose weight, get fit, or achieve any other goal, if we don't take regular measurements, it's impossible to tell whether we're making progress. By taking the time to measure our progress, we can see exactly what works and what doesn't, and adjust our strategy accordingly. Consistent improvement is unlikely without taking effective action. How will you know if an action's been effective without measuring the results that come from it? In short, measurement is essential for improvement.

So next time you're working towards a goal, don't forget to measure your progress along the way. After all, if you don't know what you're starting with, how can you hope to improve upon it? The key is to find the right metric or combination of metrics that will give you the most insight into how you're performing along the path to improvement. We'll talk a lot more about KPIs in Chapter 20. Once you have a good understanding of what needs to be improved and how you're going to measure progress, you can set specific goals and start working towards them.

In the words of the late management guru Peter Drucker, "What gets measured gets managed." The idea is simple but profound: if you want to improve something, you need to track it and set goals. When you set goals and track your progress towards them, you are much more likely to achieve those goals. The key is to be specific and realistic. By setting clear targets, you can stay motivated and on track. And by measuring your progress, you can ensure that you are making progress.

Turning Product Data into a Compelling Narrative

"I think the best stories always end up being about the people rather than the event, which is to say character-driven." — Stephen King

So, we've walked through the Cycle, we've got data we trust, we've interpreted the data and we know what our strategy and tactics look like. We've started talking about execution. A critical part of execution and how we'll wrap up this chapter takes us back to the beginning – how do we communicate this as a narrative that will inspire teams and customers alike? In this section, we'll walk through five steps for turning data into an engaging story that will drive engagement and understanding.

Step 1: Identify the key questions
Before turning the data into a story, it's important to understand the key questions that the data seeks to answer. The purpose of the data should be clear and concise, and a roadmap to answer the key questions should be established. By doing so, teams will have a better understanding of what data to collect and how to present it in a way that is impactful and actionable. This step will also serve to identify any gaps in the data, which need to be filled before the data can be turned into a compelling narrative.

Step 2: Find a story worth telling in the numbers
Once the key questions have been identified, it's time to start making sense of the numbers. You're going to have people's attention, so don't waste it. Find a powerful story in the data and share it. While data visualization tools can make it easier to understand the numbers, it's important to dig deeper and find the

underlying story. This means analyzing the data, looking for patterns and trends, and thinking about the correlations between different data sets. Finding a story worth telling in the data is what makes data truly come alive and inspires teams to act.

Step 3: Create a clear and concise message

At the heart of every compelling narrative lies a clear and concise message. Once the story has been identified, it's important to create a message that is easily understood by those who hear it. This can be done by boiling the key takeaways down to a few bullet points, or by creating a visual representation that communicates the message visually. The message should be easy to internalize, easy to repeat, and relevant to the audience.

Step 4: Choose the right medium

Storytelling can be done in many forms, but not all mediums are created equally. Choosing the right medium depends on the audience and the message that is being communicated. For example, creating a video presentation might be the best way to engage a team when communicating a new product launch, while a blog post could be more effective in communicating the quarterly earnings report to shareholders. Regardless of the medium, it's important that it is used to its full potential to truly bring the story to life.

Step 5: Iterate and refine

Compelling narratives are not created overnight. They require iterations and refinements to create a story that is impactful and resonates with its audience. After presenting the data, collect feedback from the team and potential customers to see what resonates and what needs to be improved. It's important to continually refine the narrative until it clearly communicates the message and inspires action.

Turning product data into a compelling narrative is an essential part of product management. By following the key steps outlined in this chapter and using the Callan Data Cycle, teams can take the data they are collecting, improve it and turn it into a story that is not only inspiring but actionable. Teams need to remember to identify the key questions, find the story in the numbers, create a clear and concise message, choose the right medium, and iterate and refine. With these steps, teams can harness the power of data storytelling and turn data into a tool for driving growth and inspiring change.

TL;DR

- Steve Jobs famously said that the most powerful person in the world is the storyteller, and masterful storytelling can be a key part in connecting with others, influencing decisions, and inspiring change.
- Tony Twyman's law emphasizes the importance of verifying data—any interesting or unusual data should be suspected, as it is potentially incorrect.
- Data bias can distort data, such as selection bias (choosing a narrow subset of users), historical bias (not accounting for user base changes over time), and automation bias (blindly trusting automation).
- The Callan Data Cycle is a five-stage framework that explains how to refine data from raw inputs to actionable tactics to extract the value from an organization's data assets.
- Focus on leading indicators when making predictions for future performance instead of lagging indicators.

- When looking at data, it's important to remain wary of apophenia, the tendency to see patterns where none exist.
- Correlation is not causation - just because two things are related doesn't mean that one caused the other.
- To turn insights into tactical strategies, product managers must define goals, create statements of high-level strategy, identify actions, determine resources needed, establish a timeline, and communicate the strategy with the organization.
- A data-driven strategy focuses on making the best strategic decisions based on data, while a data strategy considers how to use data safely, securely and effectively in an organization.
- People should be aware of the legal, privacy, and security implications of collecting and sharing personal information. Before sharing product data with anyone, understand how it will be used and what safeguards are in place.
- It's important to find the story worth telling in your data, create a clear message and select the right medium if you want to communicate your product's narrative to your team and potential customers.

CHAPTER EXERCISES

1. Think about the contacts stored in your phone as a potential customer database. If you were going to go through the process of cleaning your contact data up for that use case, what would be some of the likely errors and biases you might have to address? What data gaps might you need to fill?
2. If you were going to try to convince a friend or loved one to join you on a vacation trip, what kind of data might you find useful? Using that data, what narrative would you use to inspire them?

3. What's a current project or decision that you need to make? Identify the key data elements that would be helpful to make this decision. Are they currently available to you? If not, how might you go about collecting them?
4. What patterns have you noticed in your own life? How might data be used to explain or predict them? Are there external factors that influence these patterns and how could they be identified?
5. Try to think of a product or service you use often and examine it from the perspective of collecting and using data. What kinds of data could be used to improve the product or service? What potential issues might arise from this data collection and use?

CHAPTER NOTES

CHAPTER 10: The Tour De France And What You Need To Know About Business Processes

When it comes to business processes, there's a lot that product managers, executives, and startup founders need to know. Business processes are important for a variety of reasons, including communication, quality, resource management, scalability, efficiency, prioritization, and strategic alignment. Too much or too little process can be detrimental to a company, so it's important to find the right balance. In this chapter, we'll explore what a business process is and why it's so important. We'll also look at how to tell if you have too much process, not enough process, or bad process.

But let's start by taking a look at the world of professional cyclists. The best known bicycle race in the world is probably the Tour de France. The Tour is one of the most exciting and demanding events in all of sports. It pits some of the greatest cyclists from around the world against each other in a grueling three-week tour across France. The race is typically more than 2000 miles over that period. Each day is a different challenge from flat sprinting sections across farmland to difficult, treacherous mountain climbs and descents in the Alps and Pyrenees.

In the Tour, many of the mountain routes have hills that are more than ten kilometers long and have gradients over 10% - these slopes get graded from Category 4 to Category 1 with Cat 1 being the toughest.

But there are also some mountain routes, like the famed Alpe d'Huez, that are graded "HC" - Hors catégorie - or "Beyond categorization." The Tour de France is usually won or lost each year based on how the riders perform on these HC mountain stages. Climbing these mountains can require the cyclist to generate 450 watts of power for more than 60 minutes. An average cyclist like you and me typically rides at around 100 watts and could likely only maintain a 450-watt pace for a minute or two tops. The world's best challenge each other's pace up the mountain, hoping to crack the other riders and leave them behind.

The rider's power-to-weight output ratio becomes a key element of their success. Every extra ounce on the bike becomes an ounce that you have to pedal up and over those mountains. For that reason, there's a major focus on making the bikes, gear, and riders as light and efficient as possible. Carbon fiber has replaced metal as the material of choice to keep the bike light but strong. A typical TDF bike weighs just over 15 pounds and costs about $15K.

But this weight has to be balanced, because if you take away too much weight from the bike, it wouldn't hold up under the extreme amount of energy being exerted on it. There are examples of bikes snapping in half during a race under this intense effort. And if the riders themselves lose too much weight, they're at risk of losing the very muscle mass they need to pedal themselves up the peaks.

The key here is to have just enough bike and rider to efficiently and quickly get over those mountains and not one ounce more.

I'd argue that this is exactly like how much process is needed in an organization – enough process to efficiently and quickly get the job done but not one ounce more.

Why You Need Some Process

You might not think that you have or need a lot of processes, but it's almost impossible to make a business work without them. What if you had a completely different way of billing a customer each time? What if everything you did was just like the first time you ever did it? What if there were no clear roles and responsibilities?

If there's no process in place, we end up swarming the work like eight-year-olds chasing a soccer ball. This creates chaos. Eventually, the increasing levels of chaos from a lack of process causes enough pain, error, confusion and inefficiency to lead us to start writing things down and creating documentation. Eventually, those documents become the work flows that define a process. Business process actually emerges as a response to tame the business chaos.

A business process is a set of activities that are conducted to achieve a specific goal. It can be helpful to think of a business process as a recipe for success. Just as a recipe tells you what ingredients you need and what steps you need to follow to make a delicious meal, a business process tells you what tasks you need to complete and in what order you need to do them to achieve your desired outcome.

Processes are important because they supply structure and establish a workflow. Business processes can help define each person's roles and responsibilities and level-set expectations while delivering consistent and predictable results. Without a process, it would be very easy for things to get disorganized and for deadlines to be missed. By having a set way of doing things, businesses can ensure that everyone is on the same page and that tasks are completed efficiently and effectively.

But Process Is a Balancing Act

While having a bit of process is important, it's also possible to have too much of it. If a business has too many processes in place, this can lead to bureaucratic inefficiencies and bottlenecks. Employees struggle to make progress on projects because they're lost in overly complicated mazes of rules and procedures. As a general rule, you should only put in place the minimum amount of process necessary to get the job done efficiently and effectively. If things intuitively feel like they're moving too slowly, you may have too much process in the way. Take a look at your workflows and make sure that each step adds enough value to justify its existence.

Often, a company will over-correct back to a place with too little process. It can happen often during a transition where the new process owner is trying to streamline and doesn't fully understand the why behind a specific activity. This can lead to a lack of protocol and structure, which can in turn lead to missed deadlines and goals not being met. While it's important to keep your processes simple, you also need to make sure that there are enough of them in place to provide the guidance and structure that your business needs. If your workplace still feels like barely managed chaos, you probably don't have enough process in place yet. Essentially, when it comes to a business process, you're trying to strike a balance between chaos and speed.

Finally, it's also possible to have processes that are not really too much or too little but just poorly designed. This can happen when processes are put in place for the wrong reasons, the goal of the process is unclear or when they are overly focused on one aspect of the situation instead of taking a more holistic approach. You might have a recurring situation and know you need to do something to provide structure, but what you've got in place just isn't optimized or maybe it fixes one thing and makes another harder. Or maybe a procedure worked well at one point but over time things have evolved and it's no longer in sync with business needs. Bad processes can be especially frustrating for employees and can once again lead to inefficiencies, errors and even employee turnover. If you think that your business might have some bad processes, it's important to look at your processes as part of a regular review and make sure that they are still fit for their purpose. Don't get pulled into the "we do it this way because this is the way we've always done it" trap we mentioned in an earlier chapter. (See Chapter 4.)

Key Principles of Process

There is no one-size-fits-all approach to business processes – the best way to create them will vary depending on the specific goals and needs of your organization. To ensure your processes are effective however, some key principles should always be followed:

1. First of all, it's important to make sure that each process is well-defined and documented so that every employee knows what they need to do and how and when to do it. This can be especially important when people change roles.

2. Strive for simplicity in process design – excess complexity can make it hard to keep track of your operations, leading to potential errors. Simpler methods are easier to execute and tend to more consistently deliver higher-quality results.

3. Remember to review and update your processes regularly as the demands of your business change over time. This will help you stay ahead of the curve so that you can continue running efficiently regardless of the challenges you face. Establishing a scheduled quarterly review is a good idea.

4. Having a clearly written sharable process in place can help you to explain your thoughts and ideas more clearly, and it can also make it easier for others to understand what you're trying to say. In addition, the process can improve efficiency by helping you to organize and prioritize your tasks. It'll help you to manage resources more effectively, making sure that you're using your time and energy in the most productive way possible.

5. Finally, establishing a process can help to ensure that your actions are aligned with your overall strategy. We'll talk more about strategy alignment later. By taking the time to plan out your steps, you can make sure that everything you do is working towards your larger goals. Having a process in place can make it easier to scale up as your business grows. As you add new team members or take on new projects, you'll already have a system in place that everyone can follow.

How To Assess Your Current Processes

If you're not sure whether or not you have the right balance of process in place, there are a few signs to look out for. First, take a look at your results. Are they consistent? If the same task is being completed differently each time it's undertaken, there's likely a problem with the process. There may be confusion around roles and responsibilities. If people are unsure of what they should be working on, it can lead to inefficient use of time and resources as well as delivering unpredictable outcomes.

Next, look at the quality of your products. If you're receiving a lot of customer complaints or support tickets around the same set of issues, it could be an indication that your quality assurance and testing processes are insufficient. Customers really shouldn't be finding product defects if you're supposed to be caring about the customer experience.

Business profitability can be another key indicator that you've got too much process. Remember that your workflows drive organizational resource usage. If the business isn't making money, especially if it used to, there's a good chance that some of what you're doing needs to be simplified, streamlined or eliminated completely.

Ask yourself if everything is being documented. If nothing is ever written down, there are likely some areas where people aren't being properly trained and the process is lacking. Beyond that, a bad process can cause frustration for employees. If people feel like they're constantly fighting against the system, it's likely that the process is not serving them well. For the record, I'd say that you can get a long way just with clear roles, a documented workflow and a prioritized kanban work queue. A kanban board is a visualization of your work queue. While they can get more complex, the simplest version breaks work into three columns: "To-Do," "Doing" and "Done."

Are you spending more time in meetings than actually getting work done? Could be a sign that you have too much process. For sure, meetings are usually a part of the process, but if they're filling up your day and you're still on the hook for deliverables, then your work-to-process ratio is out of whack. If you're spending more time on process than on actual work, it's a sure sign that something is out of balance.

When your process becomes more important than the output it generates, that could also be an indicator that you've become process-heavy. The process should be about generating the output, not the other way around. Additionally, if you find that you're spending more time on process-related activities than on activities that directly serve the customer, it's another sign that you have too much process. The customer should always be the focus of your business, and if the process is getting in the way of that, it needs to be simplified.

If people need excessive permissions to complete tasks, it's another sign that there is too much process in place. People should be allowed the freedom and autonomy to do their jobs without needing approval at every step of the way. If this is not the case, the process is preventing them from getting things done efficiently. Additionally, if you're having to ask for someone's approval constantly throughout a routine task, it suggests that your process is overly restrictive. Permissions should only be needed in rare cases and usually at the very beginning of a workflow - if they are required more often than not, it's a clear indication that your current process needs to be reevaluated.

Sometimes, you might find that you're constantly having to force a process to fit your needs. Or maybe people are working around an existing process. This might be the result of a process that's too complicated or time-consuming and not flexible enough to meet the real-world needs of the organization. Flexibility is important in business and if people perceive the process as not adding value, it's a sign that it's not serving its purpose. In either of these situations, what you're doing today likely needs to be modified.

In the end, simplifying your business process can be difficult, but it's important to do if you want to be successful. Don't let your business be controlled by a complicated process; keep it simple and focused on what's important.

What Does A Typical Product Development Process Look Like?

The typical workflow of a product development process generally includes the following steps: ideation, research and prioritization, requirements and design, iterative prototype/development/test loop, product launch, improvements/enhancements, break/fix, and scaling/life-cycle management. This workflow can vary depending on the specific industry or product, but these are generally the most common steps involved in developing a new product. We'll go over these steps in much more detail throughout this book, but here's a quick overview of each step.

Ideation typically kicks off the process. This is when you come up with an idea for the product, feature or project. You can do this by yourself or with a team. It is important to come up with as many ideas as you can at this stage. Once you have an initial idea, you can move on to research and prioritization.

The *research and prioritization* steps entail investigating the feasibility of the product idea and determining whether or not it's something that can and should be pursued. This stage often includes creating a business plan (or at least some high-level resource estimates) and setting priorities for the development process. After research and prioritization have been completed, it's then time to move on to requirements and design.

The *requirements and design* phase is like a map that shows us what we need to do to make the product. This stage is often very complex because we have to start figuring out the product and user experience and how everything will work together. This can be tricky, but it's critical to get a handle on what we're going to do before we start doing it. Once the initial requirements and design are done, then we can begin creating a prototype.

The *prototype development* stage is where the product begins to take shape. During the prototype building phase of product development, teams take their ideas and begin to design a model that can be tested and refined. Depending on the concept, this can take a variety of forms such as a physical model, a series of screenshots or some kind of limited working version of the product. No matter the form of the prototype, it's important to form an iterative development loop with the testing phase to gain valuable feedback and insight from customers or stakeholders to refine and improve the prototype.

Testing is an important step in the product development process. As a part of the prototype work, beta testing is conducted with a small group of users to get feedback on the product before it's launched. This info helps to shape the prototype into a real product that's ready to go to market.

After testing has been completed, you should be ready to *launch* the product. This is usually done through a sales and marketing campaign and/or by making the product available for purchase through a variety of sales channels. You'll find a detailed go-to market checklist in Chapter 23. Once the product has been launched, it's important to monitor how it's being used and to make improvements and enhancements as necessary. You'll also be fixing any broken elements that don't seem to be working as expected. You can also start doing some user testing, since you have real users, to better understand how your product works in the real world.

The final stage of the product development process is *scaling and life-cycle management*. This involves ensuring that the product can meet the demands of a growing user base and that it continues to function properly over time. It's also important to put a plan in place for how the product will be supported and maintained over its lifetime. We'll talk more about the product life-cycle in the next chapter.

How To Measure Progress In A Process

Measurement and feedback are an essential part of having a good process in place. Make sure that you're measuring the right stuff. We'll talk about setting goals and managing OKRs (Objectives/Key Results) elsewhere. (See Chapter 20.) But there are a few types of measurements that are more specific to process management. One of the most basic ways to measure progress is by looking at *the time it takes* to complete each stage of the process. This can be done pretty simply by tracking the start and end dates for each stage and then calculating the average duration.

Another way to measure progress is by *milestone completion*. This involves breaking out the process into smaller steps or milestones and then tracking the completion of each one. You can also combine milestone tracking with the time for completion to establish benchmarks for each procedure. This can be a useful way to identify bottlenecks in the process or to see where things are falling behind. Once you have some historical data gathered from previous projects, you can also use that information to make more accurate estimates for business cases and project timelines.

Throughput is another way to measure progress. This is a measure of the work volume that's being done compared to the estimated capacity. If you find that certain aspects of the workflow require significantly more time than others, this can indicate areas where maybe you have an oversubscribed resource or an overly complex process in need of simplification.

Performance is yet another way to measure progress. Tracking the accuracy, quality, and defects of our outputs can be a good indicator of how effectively we are executing tasks and how well our processes are working. High defect rates can suggest that a process is poorly defined or inconsistently executed. This type of measurement allows us to find areas that need improvement so that we can make informed decisions about where to allocate resources.

Finally, *resources and budget* can also be used as measures of progress. Compare actual resources and money spent against your plan to see where you're using more resources than planned or where it's going over budget. This is especially important with new activities since your planning estimates are likely to be based more on assumptions if you don't have data.

Choose whatever measurements make sense and fit the needs of your project and team. Make sure that you're constantly measuring and reviewing your metrics to ensure that the process is running smoothly.

Whether you're riding in the Tour de France or building mobile apps, it's clear that processes are a crucial tool for every business and it's essential to find the right balance. Processes help provide structure, roles, and expectations making businesses more efficient and organized. They should be well-defined, documented, reviewed regularly and aligned with the overall strategy of the business.

Too much process can lead to stagnation, and not enough process can lead to chaos. The key is to find a happy medium. By following these steps, you can simplify the product development process and focus on what's important: creating a great product that meets the needs of your users.

TL;DR

- Riders in the Tour de France have to get up steep mountains efficiently and quickly without carrying any extra weight on their bike or body; this can be compared with how much process should be present in an organization - enough to get the job done but not one ounce more.
- Processes are necessary to tame business chaos and provide structure, workflows, roles, responsibilities and level-set expectations.
- It's important that processes are well-defined, documented, reviewed regularly and aligned with the overall strategy of the business.

- Too much process can lead to bureaucratic inefficiencies while too little leads to missed deadlines or goals not being met.
- Processes should be kept simple, but also provide enough guidance and structure to complete tasks efficiently.
- If people are spending more time on process-related activities than those directly serving the customer or if excessive permissions are needed to complete tasks, it is a sign that there is too much process in place.
- The typical product development workflow includes ideation, research and prioritization; requirements and design; iterative prototype development: testing; launch; and scaling/life-cycle management.
- Measuring progress in a process involves looking at the duration it takes to complete each stage; tracking milestone completion; measuring throughput (work volume vs estimated capacity); performance quality; and resources used compared with budget allocated for projects.

CHAPTER EXERCISES

1. Think about a process that you currently use. Write down the key steps in the process and identify the owner of each step if it's not you.
2. How are you measuring the progress through the process today? After reading this chapter do you have any new ideas about how you'd like to track it going forward?
3. Estimate the amount of time it takes for each step of the process. Are there any bottlenecks? Does each step add value? Take a look at the longest step. Could you shorten the time it takes by using resources differently?

CHAPTER NOTES

CHAPTER 11: What Is The Product Life-Cycle? Or, How To Kill Your Product (Or Maybe Not)

In 1947, John Bardeen and Walter Brattain invented the first transistor at Bell Labs. By 1959, the MOS transistor was invented. MOS stands for Metal-Oxide-Silicon, officially putting the Silicon into Silicon Valley. The transistor became the foundation of modern electronics. The MOS transistor would go on to become the most manufactured object ever, estimated at thirteen sextillion units in 2018. Ultimately those two scientists, plus William Shockley, would win the Nobel Prize in Physics in 1956 for their work. The transistor is still an essential part of electronic devices today and is used in everything from computers to cell phones.

In 1954, the transistor radio was invented, which put music on a path of evolution that it is still following today. Before the transistor radio, there were only vacuum tubes in radios, which made them larger, hotter, and not very pocket-sized. In 1957, Sony came out with their first generation product, the TR-63. The TR-63 was available in four colors and sold in the millions. For twenty years, not much changed; then, in 1979, the Sony Walkman was launched. With the Walkman, you could choose your own music on cassettes. Viva mix tapes! By 2010, Sony had sales of over 200 million Walkmen.

When the iPod was first introduced in 2001, it revolutionized the way we listen to music. With the iPod, per Steve Jobs, you could now hold "1000 songs in your pocket." For the first time, we could carry our entire music collection with us wherever we went. Viva playlists! The small, sleek design of the iPod made it perfect for listening to music on the go. In the 2010s, Apple's iPhone started out selling iPods. As cellular networks became more robust and streaming music services became more popular, people began to rely less on their iPods for music playback. By 2017, Apple had stopped making most standalone music devices, leaving only the iPhone and iPod Touch. In 2022, Apple dropped the iPod product line altogether. Although the iPod was a short-lived product, it had a huge impact on the way we listen to music today. Thanks to the iPod, we can now take our music with us wherever we go, either stored on our device or streamed over a network connection. Viva 5G!

Welcome to the product life-cycle.

The Phases of the Product Life-Cycle

The product life-cycle is the process that products go through, from when they are first thought of, to when they are eventually removed from the market. There are various stages to the product life-cycle and each stage has its objectives and strategies. As seen with music, the user's general need (for music, in this case) stays the same while the product that meets the need evolves and changes. This cycle of persistent need and constant change defines the life-cycle process.

Product Life-Cycle

A bar chart with Sales on the y-axis and Time on the x-axis, showing five phases: Build (smallest), Launch, Scale, Harvest (largest), Sunset.

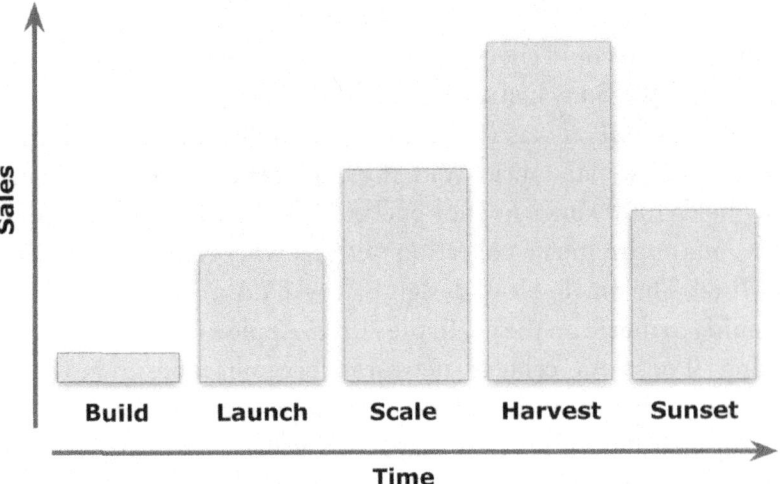

When you're managing a product, it's important to understand the different stages of the product life-cycle. This will help you make decisions about when to launch, how to scale, and when to remove the product from the market. In this chapter, we'll take a closer look at each stage.

> Build

The build stage is where we actually create the product. This is where you take your idea and make it a reality. It can be costly at this point and there are no offsetting sales revenues to support the product, so it's important to have a solid plan in place before moving forward.

Some of the key activities during the build stage include:
- market/customer research and validation
- identifying the feature set for a Minimum Viable Prototype, which we'll discuss in great detail later in the book (see Chapter 19)
- writing product spec/requirements/user stories
- development /test/adjust cycles
- filing for IP/patents, if any
- customer interaction = user trials, alpha/beta releases

It's important to note that the build phase is a heavy investment phase. This is because you are investing in the solution itself, one that doesn't yet exist or needs to be developed.

If you're building software or mobile apps, you'll also need to consider the following during the build stage:
- what platforms you will support (web, mobile, etc.)
- what devices you will support (phone, tablet, desktop, etc.)

- what operating systems you will support (iOS, Android, Windows, etc.)
- what browsers you will support (Chrome, Firefox, Safari, etc.)
- what languages you will support (English, Spanish, French, Mandarin, etc.)
- what countries you will support (US, UK, Australia, China, Japan, etc.)

But even if you're not building a technical product, there will still be considerations around the scope, scale, and audience for the product. The build stage is a critical part of the product life-cycle. It's important to make sure that you have a solid plan in place before moving forward.

> Launch

The launch stage gets the product out there and makes it available to customers. It's an oversimplification to say that this is only about marketing and advertising campaigns. You'll find a fifty-eight-point launch checklist elsewhere in this book (see Chapter 23). But in general, make sure that the product is ready for launch across all the essential work lanes such as sales, product fulfillment and customer support. This stage is less heavy on development than the build stage, but still a bit more dev-centered than future stages.

More focus during launch shifts towards marketing. Some of the key activities during the launch stage include:
- creating marketing and advertising materials (e.g. website, landing pages, social media posts, etc.)
- developing go-to-market strategy and plan

- setting up channels for distribution / sales / customer support
- onboarding initial customers

During the launch stage, you'll want to focus on creating awareness for the product and establishing initial demand. This is usually done through various marketing and advertising channels. You'll also want to focus on setting up distribution channels and getting the product into the hands of customers.

Gathering customer feedback is always important, but it's especially critical during launch. Understanding and fixing any product gaps can be essential to driving toward product-market fit, which we'll talk about at length later in the book (see Chapter 21). This is also likely the point where your product differentiation is greatest since your competition will have to react to you as a new entrant.

It's important to note that the launch stage is also a critical part of the product life-cycle. This is because it's during this stage that you'll be establishing initial demand for the product. Don't underestimate this stage. If there is no demand, then the odds of long-term product success are very slim.

> Scale

The scaling stage is about growing the product's user base and making it available to even more customers. This stage is focused on profitable growth. This can be done through various marketing and sales channel strategies. During this stage, you're likely also finding ways to build more products faster and more efficiently. Hopefully, the scale that comes with growth will improve your cost structure and the overall profitability of the product.

By the time you reach the scale stage, you've hopefully established a product that people want and need. You've also hopefully reached product-market fit. At this point, focus shifts from building the product to establishing the processes that enable you to repeatedly deliver a quality product in a reasonable timeframe.

Investment during the scale stage will shift towards systems and processes. This is because you need to be able to support a larger customer base and higher volume of sales. Other key activities during the scale stage include:
- creating and documenting repeatable processes
- establishing quality control and assurance procedures
- setting up automated build and release pipelines
- optimizing distribution channels
- scaling customer support

During the scale stage, you'll want to focus on setting up processes and procedures that can be repeated easily and with a high degree of accuracy. This is essential for maintaining quality control of your product and services as you expand your customer base. You'll also want to focus on optimizing your distribution channels so that you can get the product to market quickly and efficiently.

Gathering customer feedback is still important at this stage. However, the focus will be more on understanding how well the product is meeting customer needs and what areas need improvement. This feedback can help you fine-tune your processes and procedures so that you can continue to improve the quality of your product.

> Harvest

The harvest stage marks a shift from a focus on growth to a focus on profitability. You're gathering the fruits from the seeds you planted in the previous stages. Investment moves to continue improvements in efficiency and maintaining the marketability of your product. You're looking at ways to drive costs out of the business and maximize those profits. You may also be using the revenue from this product to fund a new and improved solution that will ultimately replace it.

By the time you reach the harvest stage, your product is likely well-established and generating significant revenue. Some of the key activities during the harvest stage include:
- reducing product costs
- improving production efficiency
- managing customer churn
- extending the profitable lifespan of the product

During the harvest stage, you'll want to focus on reducing costs so that you can maximize profits. This can be done by improving production efficiency or by finding ways to extend the profitable lifespan of the product.

It's also important to continue gathering customer feedback during the harvest stage. This feedback can help you understand what areas of the product are most important to customers and where there may be opportunities for cost savings. Customer feedback can also identify areas which might be causing your customers to churn off the product. Customer retention is an especially critical element in the harvest stage.

> Sunset

The sunset stage marks the end of the product's life-cycle. Eventually, the product may be removed from the market. This is usually done when the product is no longer profitable or when it is no longer needed. This can be due to a number of factors, such as changes in customer needs or the introduction of newer, better, cheaper, or more efficient products. These new products may be better positioned to grab market share away from your product. Hopefully, you've seen this coming and your next generation solution is already in the market and ramped up to replace the revenue of the sunsetting product.

As you enter the sunset stage, there are some key questions to ask yourself. They include:
- Can the product be extended with "new and improved" features?
- Can value blocks from the product be recycled as part of a new replacement product?
- Do existing customers find enough value in the product to be willing to pay a significant price increase in order to continue to have it at the current levels of development and support or can you continue to sell "as-is" with minimal development and support to a profitable niche?
- Can you cut some of the more costly features and still sell a more streamlined offering?
- Can you sell the product and user base to a company that's interested or better positioned to continue with it?

If you're coming up with "No" to these questions, as the cost and effort to extend the product's market starts to exceed the value it's bringing to your organization, you've got a decision to make. At some point, you're likely to stop selling to new customers and begin to transition existing customers to your newer solutions. Make sure that you have a place for those existing customers to go before you take the final steps.

How to Kill a Product or Feature

When you think it might be time to pull the plug, don't make it an emotional decision. Look at your usage data if available.

Try not to let loud or biased customers and stakeholders drive the decision, unless they're willing to step up and subsidize the financial gap in the product's revenue. But also keep in mind that it can be a very emotional or comfort-impacting decision for your customers. In the case of a business-to-business (B2B) product, this might include companies that have made a significant organizational investment in your product such as training, process, workflows, and any customizations that they've built around the product.

Maybe it's an option to keep some parts of the product to offer as a premium service for the remaining users. If they'll pay an increased price to keep key functionality available, does that change the economics of your "kill it" decision? On the other hand, maybe you're supporting custom or high-maintenance features that cost a lot to provide but no longer drive value. Can you shut down just those features and "save" the remaining product?

After asking these questions, if you still land on "kill," there are a number of ways to kill a product or feature. Here are some of the most common:

- Stopping investment: Once a decision has been made to kill a product, it's important to stop investing in it. This includes both financial and human resources. Continuing to invest in a product that's no longer profitable is a drain on company resources.
- Redirecting resources: Once investment has been stopped, any remaining resources should be redirected to more profitable products or areas of the business.
- Communicating the decision: Once you know for sure that you're doing it, communicate the decision to kill a product or feature to all relevant stakeholders. This includes employees, customers, partners, and investors. Failing to do

so can lead to confusion and frustration. Be prepared for (and open to) feedback on your decision as this is the moment it will become real for a lot of people.
- Implementing a plan: Once the decision has been made and communicated, it's important to implement a plan for killing the product or feature. This plan should include a timeline, budget, and resources.

A few more considerations and options for killing a product:

- Give lots of notice: If you're going to kill a product or feature, it's important to give customers and employees plenty of notice. This will allow them to make alternative arrangements.
- Offer alternatives: If possible, offer customers and employees alternative solutions. For example, if you're killing a product, you might offer a discount on a similar product.
- Run new and "classic" experiences side by side: This will give people time to transition to the new experience.
- Give incentives: To help people transition to the new experience, you might want to offer incentives, such as discounts or rewards.
- Remove "classic" when usage drops: Once usage of the "classic" experience has dropped to an acceptable level, you can remove it.

Killing a product or feature is not an easy decision. However, it's sometimes necessary in order to focus on more profitable areas of the business. If the product's sunset is not handled properly, then it could come back to haunt you later.

The product life-cycle is an important concept for all businesses to understand. There are different activities and strategies tied to each stage of the product life-cycle. It's important to understand each stage and what needs to be done in order to successfully move through each one. By understanding the product life-cycle, you'll be able to create a roadmap for your product and ensure its success.

TL;DR

- The product life-cycle is the process that products go through from when they are first thought of, to when they are eventually removed from the market.
- During the build stage, there is a heavy investment phase in creating and validating a Minimum Viable Prototype. If building software or mobile apps, other considerations include platforms supported as well as languages and countries.
- The Launch stage gets the product out there by building demand across sales channels, creating marketing materials, developing a go-to-market strategy and onboarding initial customers while gathering feedback for improvement.
- In Scaling up, emphasis moves to setting up processes that enable repeatable delivery of quality products in reasonable timeframes as well as optimizing distribution channels for growth.
- Harvest marks the shift to managing the product's profitability where cost reduction strategies are employed along with production efficiency improvements and management of customer churn; feedback is still important here, but that feedback is more purposed toward understanding how well needs are met rather than generating new ideas.
- Sunset signals end of life-cycle when it's no longer needed or profitable - questions should be asked about extending features or recycling value blocks into new replacement products before transitioning existing customers away from current offering.

- It is important to make decisions about killing a product or feature based on data and not emotions. But it's also important to know that it can have an emotional impact on your customers.
- Give customers and employees notice of the change and offer alternatives where possible; run new and classic experiences side-by-side before removing classic when usage drops; give incentives to help transition people over.

CHAPTER EXERCISES

1. If you're currently managing a product, where would you say that it is in the product life-cycle?
2. Think about some of the products you use in your day-to-day life. Can you come up with examples of products in each of the different life-cycle stages?
3. Have you ever had a product you used get discontinued? What was the experience like? Is there anything you might have done differently from the perspective of a product manager?

CHAPTER NOTES

CHAPTER 12: Creating A Feedback-Rich Product Environment

At one point in my career, I managed a turn-by-turn driving navigation mobile app called Sprint Navigation. Think Waze or Google Maps.

Frequently, as we'd go through the detailed notes from customer support calls to find the issues we needed to resolve with the product, we'd find that the extent of the detail was "Customer had a problem with Sprint Nav." Unfortunately, there was nothing we could do with that information to resolve the issue. There wasn't enough information to even guess at what the customer had experienced. So, I met up with the Customer Support manager and the conversation went something like this...

"Hey, when a customer calls in with a Sprint Navigation issue, could you tell your team to just ask one more question? We'd like to know where they were located when they had the problem and what time of day. This will give us the information that will let us look into network conditions at the time that they had their issue."

"We can't do that."

"Uh... why not?"

"We get measured on how quickly we can resolve the customer's issue and adding questions will add to the time we spend on the phone."

"But we can't hope to actually fix the customer's problem without that information, which means that the same customers will call over and over with the same problem."

"We don't get measured on fewer calls. We get measured on shorter calls."

I never got the information we needed to fix those problems. While we were still able to do a few things to reduce our support calls, we could have done even better with that data.

As a product manager, one of your key jobs is to ensure that not only feedback, but useful feedback, about your product is constantly flowing in from all stakeholders. The right feedback is essential for identifying problems with your product and making improvements. In this section, we'll talk about how to establish feedback loops and discuss ways to manage the stakeholders that you'll work with as part of this process.

How To Create a Feedback-Rich Environment

There are several ways to create a feedback-rich environment for your product. One way is to set up feedback loops with stakeholders, care, sales, and customers. Another way is to conduct regular stakeholder and customer interviews. Finally, you can build out a product team from your stakeholder groups.

By taking these steps, you can ensure that you are constantly receiving feedback about your product. This feedback will be invaluable for making your product the best it can be.

A lot of people in the business world talk about feedback loops, but what are they? And how can they be used to improve your product and boost your bottom line? Feedback loops are simply a way of incorporating customer feedback into the product development process. By constantly gathering feedback and using it to inform your decisions, you can ensure that your product is always meeting customer needs. This can be done in several ways, from conducting surveys and focus groups to tracking customer satisfaction levels. In addition, it's important to create a system for quickly implementing changes based on feedback. By doing so, you'll be able to continually improve your product, making it more appealing to customers and more profitable for your business.

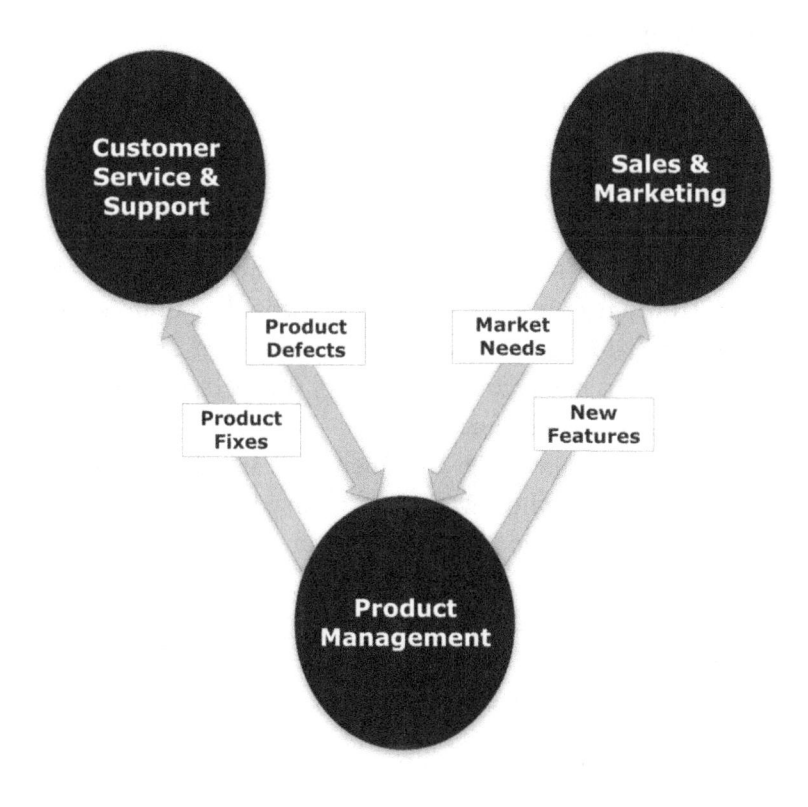

If you have a care or sales problem, it probably has at least part of its roots as a product problem. If you have a churn problem, you also probably have, in part, a product problem. Feedback loops are critical to product improvement and can directly impact product success and profitability.

For example, capturing information on what drives your customer complaints, like I was trying to do with Sprint Nav, can (a) reduce support costs by removing the cause for the calls and (b) reduce customer churn by removing points of dissatisfaction. Getting market feedback from your sales team can (a) provide competitive insights and (b) indicate features you might need to increase sales volume.

How To Conduct a Stakeholder Interview

The simplest feedback loop is to have a one-on-one conversation with one of your stakeholders. The goal is to gain insights that will help you make better product decisions. This type of interview is different from a user interview, which is focused on understanding the needs of your users. Stakeholder interviews are important because they can help you understand the perspectives of key decision-makers and influencers.

To conduct a stakeholder interview, you will need to identify individuals or groups who have an interest in your product's success, develop a list of questions, and schedule an initial session. During the interview, be sure to listen carefully and take notes. Some typical stakeholder groups for the product team include sales, marketing, developers/engineers, customer support, investors/ finance, users, your boss, and the executive team. By conducting stakeholder interviews, you will be able to gain valuable insights that will help you make better product decisions.

As you consider how to move forward with your stakeholders, you'll need to ask yourself "Do I have a potential HiPPO problem?"

That stands for "highest-paid person in the room's opinion." And it can be a big problem if you're trying to run a tight product ship. Group discussions with a loud and vocal HiPPO in the room are a bad idea if you want to maintain any control. You'll get more unfiltered feedback if you talk to people one-on-one. Yeah, it takes longer, but so does damage control if a group session spirals out of control. Plus, it helps to neutralize HiPPOs and get them on your side. So next time, skip the group discussion and go straight for the one-on-ones. You can always get the group together after you've got the most likely source of dissent on board with your vision. Having the HiPPO as an advocate is where you want to be.

As anyone who's ever been in a business meeting knows, stakeholder interviews are essential for getting buy-in and feedback on projects. But how do you make sure you're getting the most out of your stakeholder interviews? Here are six key steps:

1) *Know your goal(s).* What are you trying to accomplish with the interview? Is it to get feedback on a project proposal? To understand how a certain decision will be received? Knowing your goals up front will help you focus your questions and get the information you need.

2) *Identify stakeholders.* Who do you need to talk to in order to achieve your goal? In many cases, it will be obvious who the stakeholders are. But sometimes, especially in large organizations, it can be helpful to map out all the potential stakeholders and their interests before narrowing down your list.

3) *Develop a list of questions.* Once you know your goals and who you need to talk to, you can develop a list of focused questions that will help you get the information you need. Questions should be open-ended and aimed at understanding the stakeholder's point of view, rather than at getting yes or no answers.

4) *Schedule the initial session.* Once you have your list of questions, you can reach out to schedule an initial meeting with each

stakeholder. It's important to have a clear goal and agenda for the meeting, so the stakeholder knows what to expect.

5) *Listen carefully and take notes.* During the meeting, be sure to listen carefully to the stakeholder's answers and take detailed notes. This will help you remember key points and follow up on any action items after the meeting.

6) *Follow up and thank them.* After the meeting, be sure to follow up with the stakeholder to review any action items and thank them for their time.

Stakeholder interviews are a valuable tool for product managers, but it's important to use them correctly to get the most out of them. By following these six steps, you can ensure that your stakeholder interviews are productive and informative.

You'll want to come up with your list of questions, but here are ten stakeholder questions that we've used successfully.

1. Define success from your perspective — are there specific KPIs that you think we should be using?
2. How does this product align with your team's strategy?
3. How could we be better aligned?
4. What are your biggest concerns?
5. What are you most afraid of that you think we don't know?
6. If you were in charge of this project, what would be your top priorities?
7. If we needed to move faster or be more efficient, do you have any ideas on how we could?
8. How would you like to be engaged in this going forward?
9. Who else should we be talking to?
10. Are there any internal conflicts or blockers that we should be aware of?

STAKEHOLDER QUESTIONS CHECKLIST

- ❏ Define success from your perspective -- are there specific KPIs that you think we should be using?

- ❏ How does this product align with your team's strategy?

- ❏ How could we be better aligned?

- ❏ What are your biggest concerns?

- ❏ What are you most afraid of that you think we don't know?

- ❏ If you were in charge of this project, what would be your top priorities?

- ❏ If we needed to move faster or be more efficient, do you have any ideas on how we could?

- ❏ How would you like to be engaged in this going forward?

- ❏ Who else should we be talking to?

- ❏ Are there any internal conflicts or blockers that we should be aware of?

Asking these ten questions never fails to open up some interesting conversations and frequently uncovers not only product issues, but perhaps also stakeholder motivations that you didn't know. The latter can help you get a better understanding of the context that your stakeholder sees when they think of your product. For example, as in the story that opens this chapter, you might find out that they're getting their annual bonus based on reducing their average call time.

Turning Key Stakeholders Into a Product Team

As anyone who has ever tried to develop and launch a new product knows, it takes a team of dedicated individuals with a wide range of skills to make it happen. From the initial concept through to marketing and sales, every stage of the process requires input from different people with different areas of expertise.

Having a product team in place helps to ensure that all the necessary skills and knowledge are brought to bear on the project on a regular basis. It also helps to create an ongoing feedback loop between different stakeholders, so that everyone is kept up to date with progress and can offer their input at each stage. Furthermore, a product team can help with implementation and operational support once the product is launched, as well as with long-term stakeholder interaction.

In short, a product team can be a critical piece for successful product life-cycle management. As the product manager, one of your key roles is to establish and maintain communication between all the different stakeholders involved in a project. This includes not only the product development team, but also other departments such as marketing, sales, and customer support. Establishing regular communication channels and rhythms is essential for keeping everyone on the same page and ensuring that the project runs smoothly.

By bringing together the right mix of people and skills, a product team can help to make the process run more smoothly and improve the chances of success. It doesn't have to be **all** the stakeholders. You'll likely know who the essential players are. But if you're not sure, I'd err on the side of being more inclusive at the beginning. People can always opt out later if they're not getting or bringing value to the team.

There are a few different ways to do this, but one of the most effective ways to establish a product team is to simply set up a recurring product team meeting and invite the key players. These can be weekly, bi-weekly, or even monthly depending on the needs and pace of the project. During these meetings, you can provide updates on progress, get status on open action items, solicit feedback from team members, and discuss any issues that have arisen. Team meetings are a great way to keep everyone informed and ensure that everyone is on the same page.

In addition to team meetings, another effective way to communicate with stakeholders is through the publication of regular status updates. These can be in the form of emailed reports, newsletters, blog posts, or even video updates. Whatever form they take, regular updates help to keep everyone informed about what is going on with the project and allow them to offer their input. These notes can also be a great way to engage the rest of the stakeholders who don't sit in on your meetings.

As a product manager, it's important to always balance input from all your stakeholders (product team or otherwise) with your knowledge of the market and competition. It's your full-time job to have the broadest perspective of the issues and to synthesize strategy across all of them. Most of your teammates will be focused on their specific area and their required interactions. Even with a product team in place, you're likely to be the only person who talks individually on a regular basis to all stakeholders, especially those who aren't represented on the core product team. The key is to provide each stakeholder with the information they need, while also keeping an eye on the big picture. By doing so, you'll be able to make the best decisions for your product.

How To Conduct Customer Interviews

While the feedback you get from your product team and internal stakeholders is a critical starting point, it's not the only input you should be looking to collect. An important part of the product feedback you need to seek comes from customer interactions. Customer feedback is essential for any product team. Without it, it would be very difficult to improve the product and make sure that it meets the needs of customers. There are a few different ways to get feedback from customers, but one of the most effective is through customer interviews.

Customer interviews are a great way to get in-depth feedback about the product. They allow you to ask follow-up questions and drill down into the specifics of what customers like and don't like about the product. Furthermore, customer interviews can help to uncover unanticipated use cases and value blocks which can open up new market opportunities.

Picking the right customers to interview is also important. You want to make sure that you're talking to a mix of both prospects and customers, as well as to both management and end users. It's also important to include customers who have a strong relationship with the company, as they'll be more likely to give honest feedback.

Finally, you want to talk to both new users and experienced users, as they'll frequently have very different perspectives on the product.

Before you schedule any customer interviews, make sure that you have awareness and support within your organization — especially from sales or marketing or whoever owns the customer relationships internally. Don't just do it on your own. It's also not something that you can do one time and permanently check off your to-do list. You can't assume you know all your customers from talking to one. Commit and budget for a regular schedule of customer visits — monthly, quarterly or annually as your time and budget allow.

This is your chance to get feedback directly from the people who use your product and learn how they're using it. Customer interviews can also help you find unmet needs that your product could address. You might find that they're using the product in an unexpected way that opens up new value blocks and narratives you can use in your marketing. And finally, try to talk to customers in the environment where they use your product. By talking to customers in that space, you can get a better understanding of the context in which they use your product. By taking the time to talk to your customers, you will gain valuable insights that will help you improve your product.

Always remember that this is not the time for a sales pitch. You are not trying to close the deal. This is an information-gathering mission, pure and simple. The goal is to gather as much useful information as possible so that you can improve your product or service. Be humble and open-minded. The customer knows more about their own experience than you do, so resist the urge to argue or defend yourself. Just listen, take notes, ask more questions and try to see things from their perspective. You may not like what you hear, but it's better to have an honest picture of reality than make decisions based on a happy pile of BS. Remember, this feedback will help you make your product or service better, which will ultimately lead to more sales down the road. So even though it may be painful at the moment, customer feedback is essential for long-term success.

Getting Prepared for Your Customer Interviews

Don't think that you're going to walk into a customer meeting unprepared. Do your research ahead of time. First, look up the customer online and see if there is any information about them that you can find. Know what's going on with the company – news stories, merger talks, new product launches, etc. – all of this provides valuable context for the conversation you're going to have. Next, check to see if there are any current sales issues or support tickets that you should be aware of. There's nothing worse than being in front of a customer and hearing about their problems for the first time directly from them. You should be anticipating the kinds of things that could come up in conversation, so you better know if the customer has a "hot button" issue. They'll expect you to know what's going on with them so don't let yourself get blindsided by something you should have known.

This is critical so let me say it again. If you're talking with an existing customer, they're likely to have had several conversations with your sales teams. They might also have had support issues and opened support tickets recently. That's their reality as it relates to your product when you walk in the door. Even though you don't know everything they're going to say during your interview, understanding the customer's context before you walk in the door and maybe doing some research into any issues they've had can help with some very uncomfortable parts of the conversation. This is especially the case if you're supposed to be the product expert and you had no idea their sales or support issue existed. Ask me how I know...

Finally, make a written agenda for the meeting, even if you don't share it with the customer. This will help you keep track of the discussion and make sure that you cover all of the relevant topics. Once you've done your preparation, you'll be ready to have a productive and informative conversation with the customer.

The result of these customer interactions should be improvements in customer retention and churn. Why is retention and churn such a key issue? A Harvard Business Review article suggests that acquiring a new customer is anywhere from five to twenty-five times more expensive than retaining an existing one. That's a pretty big difference. And it makes sense when you think about it. It costs more to find new customers, get their attention, and then convince them to buy from you. In contrast, existing customers already know who you are and what you do. They're also more likely to buy from you again if they had a positive experience the first time around.

Handling Customer Feedback

How you handle customer feedback is also important. First of all, track the feedback so that you know where you got it from. This way, when you act on it, you can ensure that you're providing feedback to the customer to close the loop. Letting a customer know that you heard them, did something about it, and then followed up with them afterward is a good way to turn a regular customer into a fan for life.

Typically, there are three main categories for customer feedback: usability issues, bugs/defects, and feature requests. *Usability issues* involve anything that makes it difficult for customers to use your product. *Bugs/defects* are problems with the product itself, while *feature requests* are suggestions for new features or improvements based on new value blocks and use cases. Going back to the Sprint Navigation example we discussed earlier, proper categorization of support calls can help you stack rank problems to decide how you prioritize fixes. For example, knowing that a specific feature or bug is driving 43% of current customer calls gives you valuable prioritization information rather than just managing your bugs in a first-identified, first-fixed manner.

Where possible, standardize a handful of key questions for your customers so that you can measure changes over time. A well-known example of this technique is Net Promoter Score (NPS). The Net Promoter Score is a management tool that can be used to measure customer loyalty and satisfaction. Created by Fred Reichheld of Bain & Company, the NPS system is based on a simple question: "How likely are you to recommend our company/ product/service to a friend or family member?" Customers are asked to rate their answer on a scale of 0 to 10, with 0 being the least likely and 10 being the most likely. The NPS score is calculated by subtracting the percentage of customers who are "detractors" (those who rated their answer 0-6) from the percentage of customers who are "promoters" (those who rated their answer 9-10). The resulting number can range from -100 to 100, with a positive score indicating more customers are promoters than detractors, and vice versa.

So why should you care about your company's NPS score? For one thing, it's a uniquely powerful metric for gauging customer loyalty. Unlike other measures of customer satisfaction, the NPS score captures how likely customers are to recommend your company to others, which is a key driver of growth. Additionally, research has shown that companies with high NPS scores outperform their competitors financially. Several studies have shown a direct correlation between improvements in NPS scores and revenue growth.

Other Ways to Get Product Feedback

The best product managers know that feedback is essential to building a great product. But getting meaningful feedback can be difficult, especially if you don't have a system in place. Fortunately, there are a few simple steps you can take to set up feedback loops that will provide valuable insights into your product.

1. For apps or web-based experiences, set up Google Analytics. Google Analytics is a free tool that allows you to track user behavior on your website or app. By setting up Analytics, you can see how users are interacting with your product and find areas for improvement.

2. Use customer surveys and focus groups. Customer surveys are an easy way to gather feedback on your product. You can use surveys to ask for feedback on specific features, or you can use them to get general feedback on the user experience.

3. Conduct user tests. User testing is a more comprehensive way to gather feedback on your product. By conducting user tests, you can see how users interact with your product and identify areas for improvement.

4. Set up a system for tracking bugs. Bugs are inevitable, but they can be frustrating for users. By setting up a system for tracking and fixing bugs AND by reviewing and prioritizing

it often, you can ensure that users have a positive experience with your product.

5. Consider other passive methods of data mining to gather information. For example, chat transcripts and recorded calls can give valuable insights. These can be run through speech-to-text software to generate word clouds or be analyzed for user sentiment. Twitter can also be a goldmine of customer feedback, and there are various tools available that can help with analyzing sentiment.

Wrapping up, it's essential for product managers to create feedback loops with stakeholders, care and sales teams as well as customers in order to ensure that useful feedback about the product is constantly flowing in. Stakeholder and customer interviews are effective ways of gathering invaluable information. Leveraging your stakeholder groups to build a product team helps to keep the project on track and bring together the necessary skills and knowledge. Other methods such Google Analytics, surveys and focus groups plus user tests can also provide valuable insights into how users interact with a product and find areas needing improvement. Creating, tracking and analyzing these feedback loops will help make better decisions that will lead to a better product and increase your company's bottom line.

TL;DR
- As a product manager, it is important to create feedback loops with stakeholders, care and sales teams as well as customers in order to ensure that useful feedback about the product is constantly flowing in to help make better product decisions.

- Stakeholder interviews are a great way of gathering feedback from key decision-makers and influencers. Conducting one-on-one conversations is the best way to get unfiltered responses and neutralize HiPPOs (highest paid person's opinion).
- To get best results from stakeholder interviews, six key steps should be followed: know your goals; identify stakeholders; develop questions list; schedule initial sessions; listen carefully and take notes; follow up and thank them.
- A product team helps to ensure all necessary skills/knowledge are brought together on a regular basis to create an ongoing dialogue between the different stakeholders involved in the project. This team should include individuals from sales, marketing, developers/engineers etc., who will offer input throughout the process.
- Customer interviews are a great way to get in-depth feedback about the product and uncover unanticipated use cases and value blocks.
- Before conducting customer interviews ensure you have awareness and support within your organization - especially from sales or marketing or whomever owns the customer relationships internally.
- During customer interactions focus on gathering information - not making sales pitches - be humble and open-minded when listening to feedback.
- Prepare ahead of time by researching the company online; make sure you know any current issues they have with your product or service.
- Proper use of customer feedback can improve customer retention and reduce churn. Remember that it costs more to acquire new customers than retain existing ones; Net Promoter Score supplies valuable information on measuring customer loyalty and satisfaction.

• Other methods such as Google Analytics, surveys and focus groups plus user tests can provide valuable insights into how users interact with a product and identify areas needing improvement; setting up systems for tracking bugs and getting team member feedback are other ways of gathering information about your products.

CHAPTER EXERCISES

1. Think about the current feedback that you get about your product. After reading this chapter, are there any new information flows that you think would be valuable to add?
2. Make a list of your product's stakeholder groups. Include any specific individuals that you think could be influential in making it successful.
3. How many of the people and groups from your stakeholder list have you met for a recent conversation about your product? Pick at least one person and schedule some one-on-one time with them to collect some feedback.

CHAPTER NOTES

CHAPTER 13: What Is A North Star And Why Is It Important?

Imagine that I airdropped you somewhere in Europe with a simple instruction: "Go to Champ De Mars." To complicate matters, I told you no devices, no Google, and no outside help was allowed. To raise the stakes, let's say that there was $1 million on the line — like in *The Amazing Race*.

Could you do it?

Unless you were lucky and already knew where it was, it would be tough, right? A lot of trial and error and wasted efforts could be the result as you guessed over and over where you might need to be. You might figure out that the name Champ De Mars was French, which could narrow the playing field a bit. But even so, there are over 600,000 square kilometers in France and Champ De Mars is less than one of them.

But then imagine that I gave you a five-word clue. "Base of the Eiffel Tower." You wouldn't even need a map. Once you got to Paris, you'd still know exactly where you needed to go just by looking at the horizon and finding La Tour Eiffel. Once you got there, you'd easily figure out that Champ De Mars is a large public green space at the southern base of the Eiffel Tower.

This is the power of having a north star. In the next few pages, we're going to use a template to create one. We'll also learn a few key characteristics of a good one.

Baseball legend Yogi Berra once famously said "If you don't know where you're going, you'll end up somewhere else." A north star can be the framework to set priorities and drive action in your organization. Think of your product's north star as a product vision statement including a key metric. It should answer these questions:

- Where do you want to be in five years and why?
- How will you track your progress getting there?

A product's north star should be a point of alignment with the overall business strategy. It should deliver focus and help set priorities. Think about the Champ De Mars example — "Go to Champ De Mars" vs "Base of the Eiffel Tower." With the latter, you have focus as a team and know very quickly that any effort that takes you to London is probably taking the team in the wrong direction.

Product north stars lead to an overall improved product. They help to ensure that everyone is working towards the same goal. Product north stars provide a clear and concise way to communicate what the end goal is for a product. They can link to your overall business strategy and connect back to your company's "why" statement. They will help foster improved cross-team communication by setting a common goal. A good north star can build and drive your narrative and can even be a source of inspiration for your team.

The North Star/Product Vision Template

To help you get started on putting together a north star (or product vision), we've put together a template (see Product Vision Worksheet).

You'll need to answer the following questions:

Problem - What is the key problem you are trying to solve? How do people with that problem currently solve it?

Solution - What do you propose as a solution? How is it different from other current solutions?

Target customers – Who are the people that you think would be interested? Why do you think this? What are the benefits of your solution for them?

Business goals - What are the benefits to the business? What are the timelines for delivering these benefits?

North star metric – What could be the single leading metric that best measures progress towards your north star? This metric should be tied to your primary business goal. It can be a count, ratio, weighted score, or maybe a ranking. For example, if your goal is to become the market leader, then your north star metric might be market share. If your goal is to reach a certain level of profitability, then your north star metric might be profit margin.

Now that you have these five things defined, try this format for a first cut at creating a north star.

> For (target) who experience (problem), we propose (solution). Our primary goal is (business goal). We will know we're successful when (north star metric).

You can always shorten it up as you iterate but start here. The idea is that by focusing on this one statement, you will be able to make the necessary trade-offs and decisions to grow your business.

For example, if your north star metric is Daily Active Users, then you might sacrifice short-term revenue to get more users. Or if your north star metric is Profit Margin, then you might focus on selling higher-priced items even if it means fewer sales. But once you think you have your metric, it's critical to understand its drivers. For example, let's say that you decide to focus on sales revenue. Revenue drivers include the number of sales calls, close rate, revenue per sale, etc. This is going to help you effectively drive the actions which will insure you achieve your goals.

Product Vision Worksheet

PROBLEM:
What is the key problem you're trying to solve?

SOLUTION:
What is your proposed (differentiated) solution?

TARGET CUSTOMER:
Who do you think will be interested in this solution?

BUSINESS GOALS:
What are the benefits and timelines for the business?

NORTH STAR METRIC:
What is the single leading metric to measure progress towards your goal? What's a reasonable target that would define success?

NORTH STAR/VISION
For (target) who experience (problem), we propose (solution).
Our primary goal is (business goal).
We will know we're successful when (north star metric).

The important thing is that you have a clear north star that everyone in your organization is aware of and working towards. To make sure this happens, it's essential to gain organizational buy-in. One of the greatest complaints about a product north star is that the vision doesn't drive any action. Don't let this happen.

Getting Buy-in On Your Vision

The vision for your product should be something that everyone in your organization can get behind. The best way to do this is to collect input from all of the stakeholders and then collaborate on the vision via workshop. This will ensure that everyone has a say in the direction of the product and that the vision is something that can realistically be achieved. Additionally, talking to potential customers is essential to ensure that the product is something that people want. Getting buy-in during the creation stage is important. Without buy-in from all sides, it will be very difficult to launch and maintain a successful product.

Having your organization bought into the vision helps ensure that they're committed to its success. It gives everyone focus. Without a north star, it's easy to get caught up in short-term goals and objectives that might not be aligned with your long-term vision.

For example, you might be tempted to chase after vanity metrics such as page views or social media followers. But if those things don't help you grow your business, then they're ultimately a waste of time. Having a product north star helps you stay focused on what's important and makes it easier to say "No" to distractions.

It also helps you make better decisions. When you have a north star, you can use it as a litmus test for all of your decision-making. For example, if you're considering launching a new feature, you can ask yourself, "Will this help us achieve our north star?" If the answer is no, then it might not be worth doing.

Once you've identified your north star, it's important to communicate it to everyone in your organization. Everyone should be aware of what the north star is and why it's important.

You should also make sure that your north star is visible and accessible to everyone. It should be prominently displayed in your office or maybe even on your website if it's customer appropriate.

And finally, you need to make sure that you're tracking your progress towards your north star. You should have a clear understanding of where you currently stand and what needs to be done to reach your goal.

Five Key Characteristics of a Good North Star

Not all north stars are created equal. Certain characteristics make a good north star.

First, a good north star should be *aligned* with your company's long-term goals. If it's not, then it's not going to be very helpful. Ask yourself, "If we improve against this north star, does that mean that we are successful?" Your answer should be yes – otherwise, you should keep working on it.

Second, a good north star should be *actionable*. That is, you should be able to take specific actions that will impact the metric. For example, if your north star is market share, then you should be able to take actions that will increase your market share.

Third, a good north star should be *measurable*. You should be able to track it and measure your progress over time. Many companies will create a company dashboard which includes the north star metric so that everyone has visibility into how the organization is performing.

Fourth, a good north star should be *understandable*. Everyone in your organization should be able to understand it and know how it relates to your long-term goal.

And finally, a good north star should be *inspiring*. It should motivate people to act and do their best work. A product vision can do more than help you focus on what your team should be building—it can also be an inspirational rallying cry that gets everyone excited about their work. It should create a sense of shared purpose that gets everyone working towards a common goal.

In conclusion, a product north star (or vision) is an essential tool for any product leader. It sets the direction for the product, brings focus and provides clarity in decision-making. The act of creating a north star will bring clarity to your product's narrative as you answer the key questions included in this chapter. Ensure it is aligned with long-term goals, actionable, measurable, understandable and inspiring. Share this with stakeholders throughout your organization - getting buy-in from them will be instrumental in achieving success with your product. Crafting an engaging product vision is no easy task. But the effort is well worth it, as a strong vision can be the difference between a team that is just going through the motions and one that is truly enthusiastic about their work.

TL;DR

- A product north star is an important tool for any product leader as it provides focus, helps make better decisions and aligns with the overall business strategy.
- To create a north star/product vision, answer key questions such as what problem are you trying to solve, who are your target customers, and what business goals do you want to achieve?

Additionally find an appropriate metric for tracking progress towards the goal.
- A good north star should be aligned with long-term goals, actionable, measurable, understandable and inspiring.
- It's important that everyone in your organization is aware of and working towards this vision; gaining buy-in from all stakeholders helps ensure success.

CHAPTER EXERCISES

1. Ok, you probably expected this exercise. Let's take a moment and fill in the Product Vision template in this chapter. What are your answers for the first four sections?
    a. Problem
    b. Solution
    c. Target Market
    d. Business Goals
2. What are some possible north star metrics you could use to measure success? Make a list of 3 or 4 and think about the advantages for each one. Now pick one to use in your vision.
3. Put together all the answers into a single vision statement using the framework:
    > For (target) who experience (problem), we propose (solution). Our primary goal is (business goal). We will know we're successful when (north star metric).

CHAPTER NOTES

CHAPTER 14: Your Product Plan - The Bridge Between Vision And Execution

"A goal without a plan is just a wish."

That's a quote from Antoine de Saint-Exupéry. If that name sounds familiar, he's the author of one of the best-selling novels of all-time, *Le Petit Prince* (*The Little Prince*). Wikipedia suggests that the book has sold more than 200 million copies and sits atop the all-time best-selling novels list with Dickens, Tolkien and Rowling.

But de Saint-Exupery didn't make it into this chapter because he wrote *Le Petit Prince* or because I'm hoping some of his best-seller magic rubs off on this book. He's here today because he's right about goals. You can have big dreams, but if you can't execute then they'll just stay dreams. And in the world of product management, product plans are the product leader's primary tool for turning wishes into goals and goals into reality.

In this chapter, we'll take a closer look at the basics of product planning, including the key elements you need in your plan. We'll talk about the critical first step – research. And we'll walk you through a one-page product plan template that you can use to communicate your plan to the rest of your organization.

What is a Product Plan?

A product plan is a roadmap that details the steps that need to be taken to bring a product to market. The plan outlines the resources that will be required, the milestones that need to be achieved, and the risks that need to be managed. A product plan is important because it provides a clear and concise overview of the entire product development process. It helps to ensure that all stakeholders are aligned on the goals and objectives of the project, and it provides a framework for tracking progress and identifying areas of potential risk. Without a product plan, it would be very difficult to bring a new product to market successfully.

Many different elements go into a product plan, but the key components are research, situation assessment, vision, goals, strategies, and tactics. Let's take a closer look at each of these elements and how to do your research to develop a strong product plan.

Research is the first step in the product planning process. It is important to understand the needs of your target market and to assess the competitive landscape. This can be done through market research, surveys, interviews, and focus groups. It can also be done by doing a deep dive on your product and competition on the Internet. Once you have a good understanding of the market, you can begin to develop a vision for your product.

The next step is to *assess* your current situation and *identify* your product and company's strengths and weaknesses. A primary method for this is called a *SWOT analysis*. A SWOT analysis is a tool that helps you to identify the Strengths, Weaknesses, Opportunities, and Threats facing your business. Once you have your SWOT completed, you can begin to work on your *situation assessment*. We'll go over that in the next section.

After you have done your research and assessed your current situation, it is time to *develop a vision or north star* for your product. You may have already done this in the previous chapter. Your vision should be clear, concise, and achievable. It should be something that inspires you and motivates you to keep going when things get tough. Once you have developed a vision for your product, you can begin to set goals.

Goals are the next step in the product planning process. Goals should be SMART (specific, measurable, achievable, relevant, and time-bound). They should be aligned with your vision and your overall strategy. Once you have set goals, you can begin to develop strategies for achieving them.

There are many different types of strategic approaches you can take, but the most important thing is to choose strategies that are aligned with your goals and your vision. Keep them high-level for now, as you'll go into more detail with your tactics at a later stage in the planning process. Some common product development strategies include market/channel expansion, product differentiation, cost reduction and improved production efficiencies. Once you have identified a few strategies that are relevant to your goals, you can begin to develop tactics for implementing them.

Tactics are the final step in the product planning process. Tactics are specific actions that you will take to achieve your goals. They should be well-thought-out and aligned with your overall strategy. Tactics can include things like marketing campaigns, sales initiatives, and new product feature rollouts.

A Good Plan Starts with Research

"If I had an hour to solve a problem I'd spend 55 minutes thinking about the problem and 5 minutes thinking about solutions."
— Albert Einstein

When it comes to building a product plan, research is key. You need to take the time to understand the problem you're trying to solve, as well as the needs of your customers. What are they looking for? What are their pain points? What are your competitors doing? It's also important to understand the financial and legal environment in which you're operating, as well as any relevant tech trends. Only once you have a clear understanding of all of these factors can you start to put together a product plan that makes sense.

Take a look at the research template that we've provided. Key areas to focus on for your research are:

- Internal company environment - what's going on inside your organization? Are there things that might affect your initiative positively or negatively? Strengths? Weaknesses?
- External company assessment - how do people outside the company view it?
- Competition - What are they doing (features, business models, etc.)?
- Customer needs/problems
- Financial environment
- Legal and regulatory environment
- Technology trends
- Current macroeconomic trends

During the research phase, one of the most important things you can do is to set a timebox in advance for how much time you're willing to budget for this effort. It's very easy to end up down a long deep rabbit hole and never feel like you have enough information. You can get stuck in this phase forever if you're not careful.

Here's a chance to leverage the heck out of the 80/20 rule and spend just twenty percent of the time you'd otherwise like to spend on research. If you think you could spend an entire work week (five days) exhaustively researching a category, you can get 80% of the value just by spending a single high-quality focused day.

Follow your instincts when doing research. If your gut tells you it could be relevant, carve out some time in your timebox to review it. But stay out of the rabbit hole and don't give in to the temptation to expand your timebox.

Situation Assessment Research

Internal:
- What's going on inside your company?
- Key initiatives
- Company strengths and weaknesses
-

Customers:
- What's going on with your customers?
- Any issues with your most important customers?
- Shifts in customer demographics?
-

Financial:
- How do the numbers look?
- Impacts to the business case, business model, cost structure or profitability?
-

Legal/Regulatory:
- What's the current legal landscape?
- New laws or regulations that could be on the way?
- Privacy? Data security?
-

External:
- How do people outside the company view it?
- Threats?
- Opportunities?
-

Competition:
- What are they doing?
- New features or business models?
-

Technology:
- New tech on the horizon that could have an impact?
- Examples could be things like cloud, 5G, blockchain, etc.
- Faster, cheaper or better ways on the horizon?
-

Macro Trends:
- Any major economic trends like shifts in the market?
- Interest rates?
- Changes to overall usage patterns?
- Other longterm shifts that are out of your control?

If you have the time and/or budget during your research phase, it's a great idea to include customer research and stakeholder interviews – key customers, sales, customer support, and other internal stakeholders. Include your developers in your stakeholder survey as well. You'd be surprised by the deep insights that developers might have from working on the product all the time. Queue this up in advance of the actual product planning process so you don't get delayed, as good research can take some time.

Wherever possible, use real customers, not personas. Don't fall into the popular trap of creating personas — if possible, find actual customers with real problems and needs. Creating a fake customer that's a hybrid of attributes which doesn't exist in the real world won't help much if you want to actually talk with them, right? If you want to put an alias on the real customer to protect privacy, absolutely go ahead. But that's different than making up a blended persona that will never really use your product. If you're having problems with finding them, this could be a message for you about your market.

Next Step: The SWOT Analysis

Once you've done the baseline research, it's time to move over to the SWOT analysis we mentioned earlier in this chapter. Again, the acronym stands for Strengths, Weaknesses, Opportunities, and Threats.

SWOT analysis can be used in a variety of settings, including business planning, marketing, product development, and project management. In each case, the SWOT can help determine priorities and identify risks. The four factors that make up a SWOT analysis can be further broken down into subcategories.

Some examples in each category include:

- Strengths: financial resources, customer loyalty, brand recognition, and competitive advantage.
- Weaknesses: dependency on key suppliers, high customer turnover, and limited distribution channels.
- Opportunities: new markets, untapped customer segments, and positive industry trends.
- Threats: regulatory changes, economic conditions, and competition.

By taking the time to perform a SWOT analysis, businesses and individuals can gain a better understanding of their current situation and develop strategies for moving forward. I tend to think of strengths and weaknesses as being more internal while threats tend to be more external. Opportunities can be either internal or external. Some basic questions to ask for each area can be found on the SWOT template.

SWOT Analysis

Strengths (internal)	Weaknesses (internal)
What are the things that the company does well? What are your competitive differentiators? • • •	What does the company need to improve? If you're going to be beaten by a competitor, why? • • •
Opportunities (internal/external)	**Threats (external)**
What are the things that you could take advantage of in the market? What could you do to improve on your weaknesses? • • •	What could do significant damage to the business if not addressed? If you were out of business in 5 years, why? • • •

STRENGTHS (internal): What are the things that the company does well? What are your competitive differentiators?

WEAKNESSES (internal): What are the things that the company needs to improve? If you're going to be beaten by a competitor, what are the reasons why?

OPPORTUNITIES (internal/external): What are the things that you could take advantage of in the market? What could you do to improve on your weaknesses?

THREATS (external): What are the things that could do significant damage to the business if not addressed? If you were out of business in five years, what would be some likely reasons?

The End Goal: The One-Page Product Plan

Once you have the SWOT analysis done, you can map it over to your One-Page Product Plan template. I'm a big fan of this single-page view because it forces you to prioritize and edit. This will ultimately help you crisply communicate the plan with stakeholders. You might not have room for everything you've uncovered in your research, so hit the high points that you think will link to the rest of the information on the page. You can also pull in your north star vision statement that we worked on in the last chapter.

If it helps, you can think of the remaining sections in the one-pager like this:

- North star/Vision: What is your end goal?
- Goals/OKRs: What are your intermediate goals?
- Strategies: How will you achieve your goals?
- Tactics: What are the implementation details of your strategies?

To create good goals and OKRs (Objectives/Key Results), you need to first understand what you want to achieve. We'll spend an entire chapter on product metrics and OKRs later in the book. (See Chapter 20.) Do you want to increase revenue? Improve efficiency? Some combination of the two? Once you know what you want to do, you can start setting goals and objectives that will help you measure your progress. Here are a few tips:

1. *Set specific goals.* "Increase sales by 10% next quarter" is a specific goal that can be easily measured. "Improve customer satisfaction" is a bit vague, but can still be operationalized with specific measures, like Net Promoter Scores. These are the KRs in OKRs.
2. *Make sure your goals are relevant to your overall strategy.* If your goal is not in line with your company's mission or vision, it's not likely to be successful.
3. *Make sure your goals are challenging but achievable.* If a goal is too easy, you're not likely to see much progress. On the other hand, if a goal is too difficult, you'll quickly become discouraged.
4. *Set timelines for each goal.* This will help you stay on track and ensure that each goal is given the attention it deserves.
5. *Communicate your goals to all members of your team.* This will help ensure that everyone is on the same page and working towards the same goals.

The development of business strategies is essential for any company that wants to be successful. Keep them general. That's why I call them "Strategic Themes" on the template. Resist the urge to get too specific. That's what your tactics are for.

1-Page Product Plan

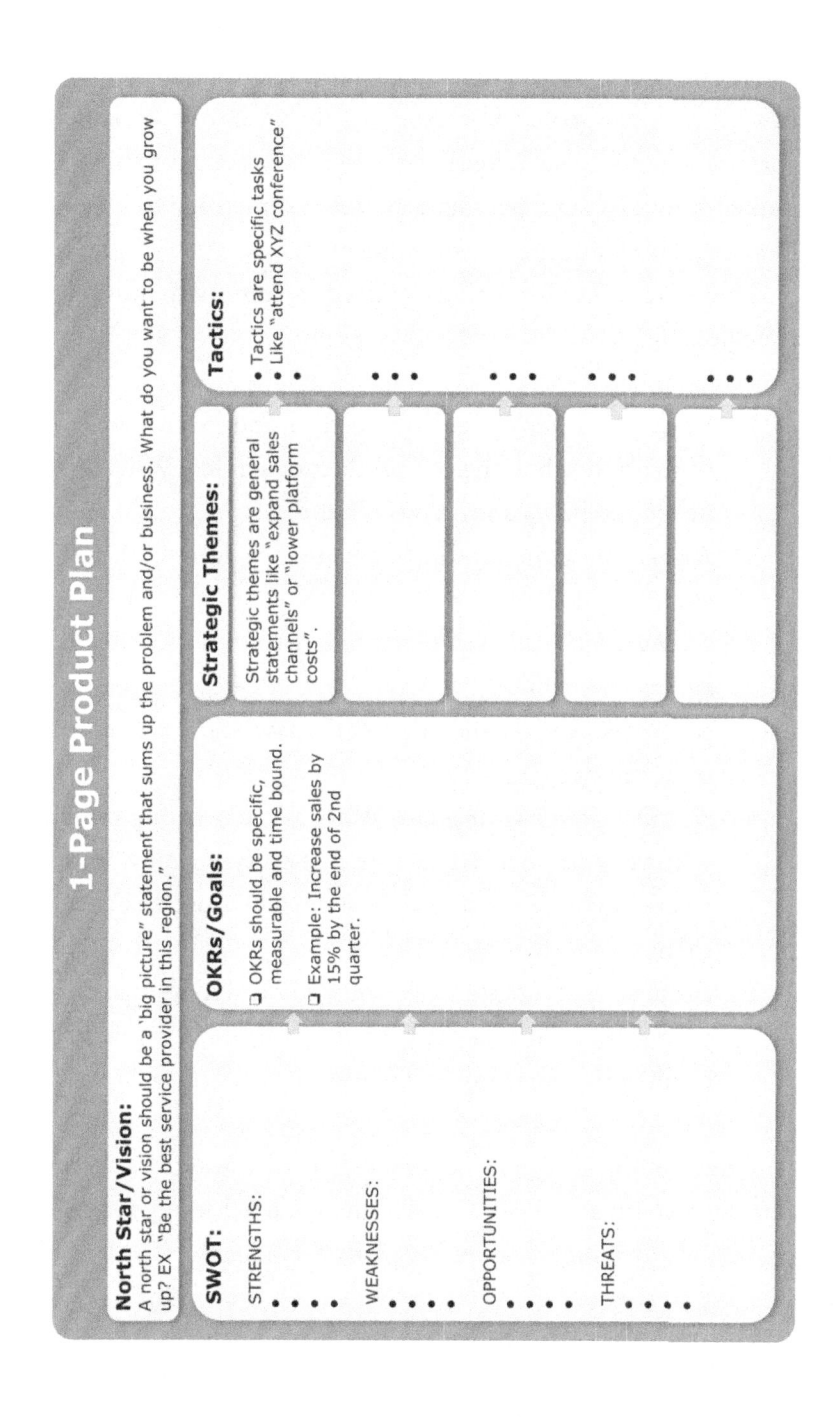

North Star/Vision:
A north star or vision should be a 'big picture" statement that sums up the problem and/or business. What do you want to be when you grow up? EX "Be the best service provider in this region."

SWOT:

STRENGTHS:
- ...

WEAKNESSES:
- ...

OPPORTUNITIES:
- ...

THREATS:
- ...

OKRs/Goals:
- OKRs should be specific, measurable and time bound.
- Example: Increase sales by 15% by the end of 2nd quarter.

Strategic Themes:
Strategic themes are general statements like "expand sales channels" or "lower platform costs".

Tactics:
- Tactics are specific tasks
- Like "attend XYZ conference"

WMGPG? Page 189

Ask yourself: "What are the high-level activities needed to move forward on your goals?" For example, if you have a revenue goal, what are you doing to increase revenues? Are you launching a new product line to expand the market? Doing something to incentivize the sales team? Planning a price increase?

There are a few key things to keep in mind when developing strategies:

1. *Know your audience.* You need to understand who you're trying to reach with your product or service. What are their needs and how can you meet them?
2. *Know your competition.* What are they doing well and what could you do better?
3. *Understand your strengths and weaknesses.* The SWOT again. This will help you develop strategies that play to your strengths and avoid those that would put you at a disadvantage.
4. *Be clear about your goals.* What are you trying to achieve with your strategy? Make sure that everyone on your team is aware of your goals so that they can work together to achieve them.
5. *Be flexible.* Things change and you need to be able to adjust your strategy as necessary. Don't be afraid to try new things or pivot if something isn't working.

Once you have a good understanding of these things, you can start developing strategies that will help you achieve your goals. If you're not sure where to start, here are a few ideas:

- Increase sales by targeting new markets or segments.
- Improve efficiency by streamlining processes or implementing new technology.
- Reduce costs by negotiating with suppliers or reducing waste.
- Enhance customer satisfaction by improving customer service or adding new features/products.
- Increase brand awareness by marketing more effectively or expanding into new channels.

These are just a few examples of strategies that can be used to achieve different goals. The important thing is to tailor your strategy to your specific situation and needs.

Tactics are the implementation details of your strategies. Here you're looking for specific actions and specific target dates that are focused on the execution of your strategy. They are the activities that will help you achieve your goals. When developing tactics, it's important to keep the following things in mind:

1. Tactics should be aligned with and flow from your strategies. If they're not, they're likely to be ineffective.
2. Tactics should be specific and actionable. Vague or general tactics are not likely to produce results.
3. The results from your tactics should be measurable and map to your OKRs. This will help you track progress and decide whether or not the tactic is working.
4. Tactics should have a timeline or deadline. You'll be coordinating actions across your team and potentially across multiple workflows. Knowing when deliverables need to be delivered will help with this planning and coordination of resources.

5. Make sure to communicate your tactics across your product team and stakeholders. No one likes surprises. If you're doing something that could cause a spike in call volume, giving that team a heads-up so that they can staff for it is just good collaboration and helps insure the tactics' success.

Here are a few examples of tactics that could be used to achieve the goals mentioned above:

- To increase sales, roll out a 10% discount coupon code in 1Q.
- To improve efficiency, review and revise the process for approving expenses in 2Q.
- To reduce costs, update volume forecasts and renegotiate deals with the top 3 vendors in 3Q.
- To enhance customer satisfaction, add a live chat feature to the website in 4Q.
- To increase brand awareness, launch a social media campaign in 1Q.

As you can see, tactics can be very different depending on the goal they're trying to achieve. The important thing is to make sure that they're well-thought-out and aligned with your overall strategy.

Strategic Add-ons For Product Plans

Product plans are the foundation for success, but they're not the only thing you need to consider when launching a new product or business. While we won't go into a great deal of detail on each of these, here are several other strategic add-ons to your product plan that can be included as needed:

1. Product Roadmap: This is a high-level overview of the major milestones and features that will be added to your product over time. It's useful for long-term planning and can help you communicate your vision to stakeholders. (For more on this, see Chapter 17.)
2. Resource Plans: What do you need to have to execute your product plan? This may include things like funding, personnel, platforms, and equipment.
3. Business Case and Financials: A business case is a document that justifies the investment in a new product or project. It should include an analysis of the costs, benefits, risks, and opportunities associated with the venture. Financials are an important part of any business case and should be included as well. (See Chapter 15 for more details.)
4. Pricing Strategy/Business Model Review: What pricing model will you use for your product? Will you charge a subscription fee, a one-time fee, or something else? How will this impact your overall business model? These are important questions to answer before launching your product.
5. Marketing Plan and/or Sales/Channel Plan: How will you generate demand for your product? What sales and marketing strategies will you use? Who will you sell through? These are all important questions that need to be answered in your go-to-market plan.
6. Operational Plan: How will you run your business on a day-to-day basis? What teams are involved? Manufacturing, fulfillment, customer service and others? How does the work flow?
7. Risk Management Plan: What risks are associated with your product or business? How will you mitigate them? A well-

considered risk management plan is critical for any new venture.
8. Implementation Timeline: When will each element of your product plan be implemented? This timeline should include milestones and deliverables for every team member.
9. Project Management Plan: How will you manage the development and launch of your product? This includes things like scheduling, milestones, and deliverables.
10. Communications Plan: How will you communicate with stakeholders throughout the life-cycle of your product? This should include things like press releases, blog posts, and customer emails.

Each of these add-ons can be critical to the success of your product or business, so make sure to include them in your planning as needed.

One Last Pass...

Before you're done with your product plan, there are a few more things that you need to do. First, check the alignment with your company's overall strategic plan. We'll talk about that more in Chapter 22. You should also revisit your north star and make sure it is still relevant. Are there new problem statements to consider? Has your "why" changed/evolved based upon your research and any new information you might have uncovered?

Second, make sure to check the alignment across your goals/OKRs and your SWOT. Do they align with the opportunities in your SWOT? Fix a weakness? Manage a threat? Exploit a strength?

Third, make sure every tactic connects clearly to a strategy or a goal and that these reach all the way back to your north star. If they do not, ask yourself, "Is this truly important?" Why or why not? If you have tactics that don't tie back to anything, why are you doing it? Did you miss something that should be listed as a strategy or goal? If you have goals/strategies without tactics, are they just wishes? How do you plan to execute them?

Once you've done these steps, you're ready to share with stakeholders. Assuming that you've been in contact with them along the way, there shouldn't be a lot of surprises. Now you can get their feedback to incorporate into the next iteration because your product plan should be a living document, regularly updated, rather than a one-and-done exercise tucked away in the cloud somewhere. Hopefully, you'll find that your plan becomes a key deliverable that shares your product narrative and drives positive action throughout your organization.

TL;DR

- Product plans are the primary tool for product leaders to turn wishes into goals and goals into reality. Elements of a product plan include research, situation assessment, vision setting, goal-setting strategies and tactics.
- Research is a critical first step in the product planning process; this includes market research, surveys, interviews, focus groups and deep dives on products/competitors online.
- Vision should be clear, concise and achievable; Goals should be SMART (specific, measurable, achievable relevant and time-bound); Strategies and Tactics need to be aligned with overall vision and strategy.

- SWOT analysis can help determine priorities by breaking down Strengths (internal), Weaknesses (internal), Opportunities (internal/external) and Threats (external).
- The One-Page Product Plan is a useful tool to help prioritize and crisply communicate the plan with stakeholders. It includes sections for North star/Vision, Goals/OKRs, Strategies and Tactics.
- To create good goals and OKRs (Objectives/Key Results), it's important to understand what you want to achieve, set specific achievable goals relevant to your overall strategy which are challenging but achievable, have timelines for each goal and communicate them across the team.
- Business strategies should be general while tactics should be specific actions with target dates focused on execution of strategy aligned with overall goal(s).
- Before finishing, product plan alignment must be checked against your company's strategic plan as well as your SWOT analysis; every tactic must connect clearly back up through each level from north star vision statement; the plan is a living document that must be updated regularly throughout organization for feedback purposes.
- Strategic add-ons such as a Product Roadmap can also help support product plans; these include Resource Plans, Business Case and Financials, Pricing Strategy/Business Model Review, Risk Management Plan, Implementation Timeline, Project Management Plan, Communications Plan, etc.

CHAPTER EXERCISES

1. Copy your North star/Vision into the One-Page Product Plan template. If you didn't do one in the previous chapter, go ahead and do one now.
2. How much time do you think you'd need to do a comprehensive job during the research phase of product

planning? A week? Whatever you come up with, let's reduce that to 20% of that amount and start putting blocks of time on your calendar to do the work. To get into a good flow and optimize this condensed research time, I'd recommend that the blocks be at least two hours long but not more than four.
3. Once you've completed the research phase, take what you've learned and complete the SWOT analysis. Distill the details down to key bullet points and put the results into the product plan template.
4. Come back and fill out the rest of the template after you've read the chapters on OKRs.
5. What are the high-level activities needed to move forward on your goals and hit your OKRs? Fill those into the "Strategic Themes" section.
6. Next, identify the implementation details of your strategies – specific actions and specific target dates that are focused on the execution of your strategy. Put those into the "Tactics" section. Congrats! You've got a One-Page Product Plan.

CHAPTER NOTES

CHAPTER 15: Getting To The Bottom Line - Building A Strong Business Case For Your Product

Different organizations have different takes on business cases. For a stretch, while I was at Sprint, there was a senior VP in charge of Product Innovation who decided that he only wanted to see potential project business cases with "B's not M's'" in them, as in billions of dollars and not "just" millions. This was around the time that Sprint was writing off that $29.7 billion loss from the 2005 purchase of Nextel, so maybe the hero approach was understandable, if ultimately misguided.

This just isn't how innovation works. It would be like a baseball team that's already behind by ten runs deciding that it's only going to try to hit grand slam home runs. Since you might not be a baseball fan, for context, a grand slam is a home run with runners on each of the three bases (also known as bases loaded), resulting in four runs scored. For this strategy, you'd need your players to load the bases with a few simple base hits before you could even think about hitting a grand slam. Even then, home runs are not just something you do on demand. Over the decade preceding the 2023 Major League Baseball season, teams averaged less than four grand slams over an entire one-hundred and sixty-two game season. Grand slams and billion dollar ideas don't come along every day.

Even if you don't have a billion dollar idea to pitch, you'll likely need to have a business case at some point to get internal or external investment in your product. As a product leader, it is critical to have a clear understanding of how to build a strong business case to get that funding. This chapter will show you how.

What Is A Business Case?

A business case is a crucial communications tool for new products, especially startups. It communicates the "why" for a specific project and can be essential for getting funding from both internal and external investors. A business case typically includes some kind of risk vs reward analysis and can be presented in either written or verbal form. Depending on the size and complexity of the project and the needs of your org, a business case can be one page or more than fifty pages long. It can also take anywhere from five minutes to hours to present.

Gatekeepers who control access to needed resources often review business cases before making decisions, so it's important to make sure that your business case is clear and concise. By taking the time to develop a strong business case, you'll increase your chances of success in getting the funding you need to get your product off the ground.

A business case helps to quantify the benefits and costs of a proposed project in a way that enables comparison between different projects. This level of detail can be essential in making decisions about which projects to prioritize and how to allocate resources. Furthermore, a business case forces you to anticipate future challenges and plan for them upfront. This can lead to improved implementation and fewer abandoned projects. By getting a business case in place, you'll level-set expectations across your team and leadership. This should eliminate future surprises by identifying them upfront and lead to improved implementation by ensuring that the team has the resources needed to execute.

Nine Things You Need For Your Business Case

When you're building out your business case, you can use the template we've included here. In that document, we've identified nine key elements that probably should be a part of your analysis.

1. *Problem Statement* - A problem statement is a clear description of the issue to be addressed by a project. It should include a summary of the current situation, the desired outcome of the project, and the main stakeholders involved. A well-crafted problem statement will help to keep the project focused and on track.
2. *Options Considered* - This might include things like doing nothing or build vs buy decisions like buying something off the shelf, custom in-house development, using external contractors, and so on. It's important to consider at least three options, evaluate the pros and cons of each option, and choose the best course of action. This demonstrates to decision-makers that you've done your homework. By considering multiple options, you can also avoid making a rash decision that could have negative consequences.
3. *Recommended Solution and Why* - From the list of options considered, you'll want to make a recommendation of the path to pursue. Your leaders will also want to understand the logic behind the decision you're suggesting.
4. *Business Benefits* - Business benefits are the positive outcomes that a company can expect to achieve by implementing a new project. These benefits can be financial, strategic, or operational. By quantifying the expected business benefits, you can make a stronger case for investing in a new project.

5. *Estimated Costs* - Estimated costs are the projected expenses for a new project. These costs can include materials, labor, and overhead. Knowing the estimated costs upfront can help you to decide whether or not a new project is feasible. It can also ensure that you have a clear understanding of the resources you'll need to get the project across the finish line. Be as realistic as possible. You're setting expectations that if the decision-makers give you the requested resources, you can deliver. You don't want to cash in your credibility by needing to go back and ask for more.
6. *Timeline* - The expected timeline is the period that a new project is expected to take. This timeline can be used to set expectations and ensure that the project stays on track. Essentially, you're establishing a de facto contract that says, "If you give us the resources needed, we can deliver this project by the milestones in the timeline."
7. *Risks and Key Assumptions* - Risks are potential problems that could occur during a project - that is, the known unknowns. Key assumptions are beliefs that are held to be true for a project to be successful. They may be the things you think you know about the known unknowns. By identifying risks and key assumptions up front, you can plan for them and minimize the likelihood of problems occurring.
8. *Financials* - Financials are the numbers that show how a project will impact a company's bottom line. This includes the expected return on investment (ROI) and the breakeven point. Financials are important because they show whether or not a project is worth investing in. For your resource gatekeepers, this is probably the most important element of your business case.

1-Page Business Case Template

Product Name:
Owner:
Sponsor:
Date:

Problem Statement:

Options Considered:
1)
2)
3)

Recommended Solution/Why?:

Expected Benefits/Revenues:

Cost Estimates:

Estimated Timeline:

Risks/Key Assumptions:

ROI/Payback/Financials:

Next Steps:

9. *Next Steps* - One of the more frequent elements that I've seen left out of a business case is the next steps. The next steps are the actions that need to be taken to move a project forward. By outlining the next steps, you can ensure that the project stays on track and that all stakeholders are aware of their roles and responsibilities. But more importantly, let's assume that you share all the rest of the information with a gatekeeper and they give you the thumbs up to proceed. They're going to want to see that you have a plan and know how to get started. So, act as if you're going to be successful and tell them what happens after they sign off on your business case.

Getting Started on Your Business Case

To get started on putting together your business case, just like building a product strategy, do your research. An important first step is problem definition. What is the problem you want to solve? How are people with this problem handling it today?

Take time to identify internal and external options for solving the problem. From an internal standpoint, has your organization ever done anything like this before? If so, what did you learn? For example, if there was a similar project that succeeded before, maybe you can look at that project to see what kind of resources they had and use that as a benchmark for the current project. You might also talk to the team members on the previous project to get insights on how best to proceed or any learning they might have gathered from the work that could shorten cycle time or improve resource efficiency.

You should be thinking about who the internal stakeholders and potential sponsors for the project might be. Getting that lined up early will help significantly as you move forward. Understand how your organization assigns project resources. For example, whether you have dedicated resources versus shared resources can have a big impact on the velocity of your project and the related timelines. Having a programmer split across two projects likely means you're getting less than half of a programmer because you're also losing some efficiency due to context switching as that programmer moves between projects.

Externally, you'll want to understand if there are enabling technologies that you might need to acquire or build. Figure out what the competitive landscape looks like and how those solutions compare to yours.

Financially, you'll likely want to at least take a best guess at possible pricing or business models. If appropriate, you're going to need to work on market estimates to quantify the revenue benefit for your organization. You'll also want to understand if there are any intellectual property claims or patents to be filed that could add to the quantification of business benefits. You should also know if there are standard financial metrics or OKRs that you need to make available so that decision-makers can do a comparison between potential projects.

Finally, if available, look at a business case that has been approved previously to see how it was put together. What are the expectations of decision-makers? What have they approved/killed before and why?

Eight Key Questions When You Think You're Done

When you think that you have a business case that's ready for prime time, here are some tough final questions to ask yourself before you engage the gatekeepers. Try to answer them as honestly and clear-eyed as you can.

1. Am I aligned with the current overall larger organizational business strategy?
2. Have I reviewed with stakeholders and incorporated their feedback?
3. Have I accurately identified the biggest risks and costs?
4. Are the timelines realistic?
5. Am I padding or overstating the incremental benefits of the product/project?
6. What questions should I expect? What would I ask?
7. What questions do you most NOT want to answer?
8. Who's most likely to support/block the project?

Those last two questions might be the most important of all. If you can, think ahead to come up with your best answers to the questions you don't want to answer, then you'll have a lot more confidence when you get in front of the decision-makers. It's just going to go a lot smoother if you know where the gaps are and how to talk through them. I've seen many confident presenters get blown up because they thought they could stay on their happy path and didn't have the answer to questions that seemed obvious to everyone in the room except them.

If you can identify who your most likely allies are going into the discussion, you can share key talking points in advance to make sure that you're all speaking from the same narrative. Equally important: if you know the most likely players who would block the project, meet with them in advance and give them a pre-read of the business case. You'll likely hear their objections one-on-one rather than in a room of decision-makers. This can give you the chance to persuade them during the pre-read and potentially turn them into allies on game day. But even if not, by hearing their objections ahead of time, you can prepare better responses for the group presentation.

It's critical that you take the time to build a strong business case for your product. The process will help you to identify and assess risks, quantify potential benefits, and develop realistic timelines. A well-crafted business case will make it much more likely that your product is given the green light by decision-makers. So don't skimp on this important step in the development process.

TL;DR

- A business case is a tool to get internal or external investment for a product and typically includes some kind of risk vs reward analysis.
- A business case helps to quantify the benefits and costs of a project in a way that enables comparison between different projects and helps to anticipate future challenges.
- There are nine key elements which should be part of every business case: Problem Statement, Options Considered, Recommended Solution and Why, Business Benefits, Estimated Cost, Timeline, Risks and Key Assumptions, Financials, and Next Steps.
- Research should be done first to define the problem, identify options (internal and external) to solve the problem and understand competitive solutions.
- When nearly done with the business case formulation process, review and answer our checklist of eight tough questions, which include "Am I aligned with the current larger business strategy?"; "Have I accurately identified the biggest risks and costs?"; and "Are timelines realistic?"

CHAPTER EXERCISES

1. What's a potential problem statement for a product or project that you think you might want to get funded? What's your solution and why do you think it's a winning idea?
2. Identify some key benefits and potential costs for this project. Document them in the One-Page Business Case template.
3. Think about the business assumptions you're making and any potential risks that you need to consider. Add them to your business case.
4. Who are the stakeholders or gatekeepers that you'd need to get on board for this project? How likely are they to support the project?
5. How well aligned is this idea with your organization's overall business strategy? Is there anything you could do to better position it within your company?

CHAPTER NOTES

CHAPTER 16: Writing Effective Product Requirements - It's Not Rocket Science

By creating a link between what the customer needs and what gets built by the developers/engineers, clear and well-defined product requirements are an essential element in the product building process. If you miscommunicate the requirements, at best, you'll fail to meet customers' needs. At worst, it could be dangerous, deadly or a waste of money.

On December 11, 1998, NASA launched a space probe designed to study the climate and weather patterns of Mars. The project was known as the Mars Climate Orbiter. Working with Lockheed Martin as the Orbiter's manufacturer, the project cost over $300M. Just over nine months from launch on September 23, 1999, the orbiter had reached Mars and prepared to enter orbit around the planet. As it began the pass behind the planet, it fell out of radio communications with the NASA team sooner than expected.

It never showed up again.

Post-mortem analysis suggested that the probe was likely destroyed because it entered the atmosphere at too low an altitude. The reason? Software created by Lockheed Martin generated output in US customary units, i.e., feet, while the inputs to NASA's flight control software required metric measurements.

Attempting to explain what happened, NASA assistant administrator Edward Weller said, "The problem here was not the error; it was the failure of NASA's system engineering and the checks and balances in our processes to detect the error. That's why we lost the spacecraft." Worse, it turns out that in tests, there was "unease" about source error estimates. Meetings were held to discuss. But the issues of concern were not pursued in part because, according to NASA's investigation, "they didn't use the existing formal process for such concerns." In other words, they didn't fill out the expected forms to document the issue. But while NASA might blame their Quality Assurance (QA) process, in large part this epic fail was due to unclear, poorly communicated and poorly executed product requirements. Without the initial error, there'd be nothing to find in QA. The root cause here was the misread requirement.

Lucky for the rest of us, it doesn't take a rocket scientist to write clear product requirements and properly communicate them. In this chapter, we'll discuss one of the key deliverables for most product managers, the product requirements document (PRD). We'll also talk about some of the best practices and finish up by looking at a unique approach used by Amazon for their requirements docs.

There are entire books written about managing product requirements, usually tied to software development concepts like Agile/Scrum. Some of the best books on this subject include Jeff Sutherland's *Scrum: The Art of Doing Twice the Work in Half the Time*, Jake Knapp's *Sprint* and Kenneth Rubin's *Essential Scrum*. You can also find several high-quality feature-rich software programs like Monday or Aha! that handle these requirements management needs very efficiently. I'd strongly urge you to check them out to go deeper in this area. We're going to just hit the high points here. Think of this chapter like learning to do basic math before you jump to using a calculator or spreadsheet.

Improving Team Communication With Your PRD

Product miscommunications can cause less tragic, but still undesirable or even comical consequences. In Japan, women give men chocolate on Valentine's Day due to a translation error by a chocolate company executive back in the 1950s. When Ford tried to launch the Ford Pinto in Brazil, sales stalled. It turns out that Pinto is Brazilian slang for "tiny male genitals."

In research published by The Economist in 2018, 44% of respondents said that poor communication had led to delays or failure to complete projects. I think this number is low.

Any good product leader knows that clear communication is essential to the success of any project. This is especially true when it comes to communicating exactly what product the team is creating. After all, if team members are not on the same page on what they're supposed to build, what are the chances that they can deliver on the expected experience?

One of the most important tools a PM has for ensuring clear communication is the product requirements doc (PRD), alternatively known as a product spec. It's a single document that provides a clear and concise overview and answers the who, what, why, when and how of the product. The PRD outlines key team roles and identifies the stakeholders and users. You'll find details around the problem being solved and definitions of what's in or out of scope. If there are any important assumptions or dependencies, they should be documented there.

Most importantly, it breaks down the key elements of the product into its individual component requirements, along with timelines for the delivery of key elements. A PRD translates your customers' needs into instructions for your engineers or developers to execute. It's a written blueprint of exactly what they need to build. By clearly defining the parameters of the project in as much detail as is available, the PRD helps to ensure that everyone is on the same page from the start.

A PRD Starts with Understanding Customer Needs

Building and maintaining the PRD is a primary job task for most product managers. But you can't really just jump straight to writing requirements. It's more of a sequential process.

To start, every business exists to solve a problem for its customers, and understanding their needs is paramount. *Customer needs* are the specific pain points that a potential customer has which might require a solution. Customer needs come in many forms - they can be functional, like the need for something that can move you from your home to your workplace, or emotional, such as the need for that transportation to be safe and secure. But no matter what form they take, customer needs are essential because they guide businesses in creating products and services that customers want to buy. Without understanding these needs, it would just be a lucky guess if you created a successful product or service that delivered on customer expectations.

Evaluating Product Ideas

After you understand your customer's needs, you can start identifying a potential *product solution*. We talk about ways to generate ideas in Chapter 26. Once you think you have a winning product idea, spend some time analyzing the concept for its viability and conducting thorough research and evaluation.

Here are some steps to consider before you move to the next phase:

1. Conduct market research: Since you know your customer's needs, you should be able to take a shot at determining the size of the potential market, identify your competition, and assess any existing products or services that are similar to your idea.
2. Evaluate the feasibility of producing the product: Consider whether you have access to the necessary resources, such as funding, materials, manufacturing facilities, and skilled labor to produce the product.
3. Assess regulatory requirements: Determine if there are any legal or regulatory barriers that may prevent you from bringing the product to market. Sometimes there's a good reason why a product doesn't exist.
4. Analyze financial viability: Keep it very high-level but think about the costs associated with production, marketing, distribution, sales, and other expenses along with a rough estimate of what kind of revenue you could expect to determine if the product can generate sufficient revenue to be profitable.

By following these steps, you can analyze a potential product concept for its viability more effectively before investing significant resources into it.

Defining The Product Feature Set

When you feel like you have a viable solution, it's time to start getting really clear on the *product features* in your build. You'll start with a hypothesis of what capabilities or features need to be in your Minimum Viable Prototype (see Chapter 19 for more on this). You might also brainstorm potential features with your potential customers, stakeholders and developers. After that, you should have a decent list of ideas. Next, you'll want to check each potential feature against your business or product strategy to make sure that they're generally aligned. For example, there's no reason to gold-plate everything if your business has a discount or value-centered strategy.

As part of the feature definition, take a look at the Product Feature Tracking Template that follows. This helps you define which features should be included in the prototype and which ones can wait.

The template gets the basic details you'll want to be able to identify the work that needs to be completed. These details would include:

- Name of feature
- Description
- Feature group/theme/customer need
- Relevant user stories
- Priority or targeted release
- Target completion date

When you start filling out this list, you might only have the feature name and description. We'll talk about user stories in a second, but for now, just know that you'll want to be able to track them back to the features here. For any other details that you might be missing, you can take a layered approach and add them to this document later as you get more information about the feature.

Product Feature Tracking Template

Feature Name	Description	Theme	Related User Stories	Priority	Release	Target Date
	A brief description of the feature	What theme or epic?	Number your stories & put that here	High, medium, or low	In which release is the feature targeted?	When's the expected date?
Feature 1						
Feature 2						
Feature 3						

Finally, you'll start prioritizing the list. When you're ready for this step, take a look at the different methodologies we offer in Chapter 18. We'll take a very basic approach here. For the most part, you're simply going to focus on getting the most "juice for the squeeze" with those initial builds — after you've identified the must-haves, go after the highest value that you can get with the least amount of effort. You can use something like the Value-to-Effort Matrix shown here. Think of the possible features as hypotheses that you can validate and gather information from actual prospective customers. Once you have your prioritized early stage features identified, you'll start working on the product requirements.

Value-to-Effort Matrix

High Value **Low Effort**	**High Value** **High Effort**
Low Value **Low Effort**	**Low Value** **High Effort**

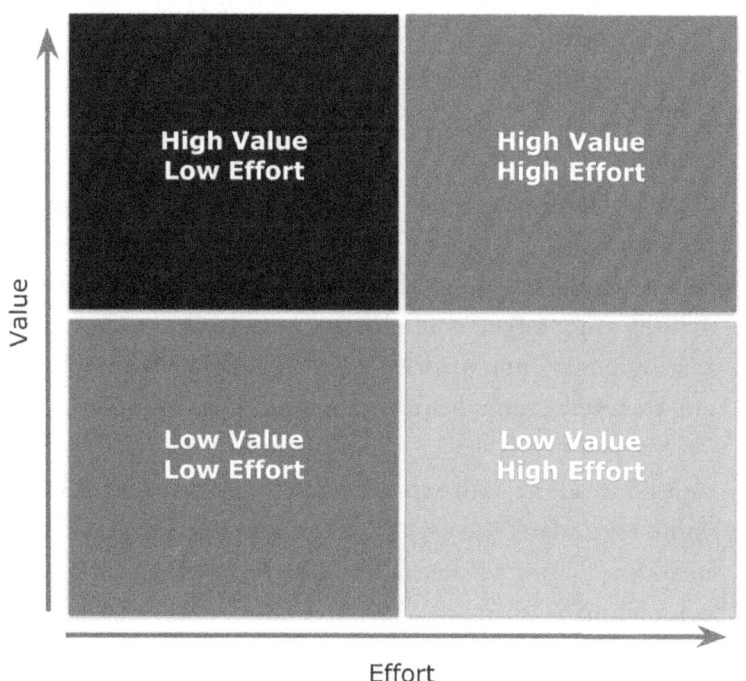

Value (y-axis) / Effort (x-axis)

What Goes Into A PRD?

So now that you're ready to write product requirements based on the features you've identified and prioritized, what exactly does that look like? Think of the finished PRD as capturing the who, what, why, how and when of the product or project.

- **Who** = The product team and roles involved, stakeholders, and target market.
- **What** = What problem are you trying to solve? Include a high-level description of the proposed solution, along with any key assumptions, resource constraints and dependencies. You might also include any boundaries around what's in or out of scope for the project.
- **Why** = Identify the business justification for the project. Ask "Why are we doing this?" Here's the place for the project's benefits, along with any high-level financial estimates.
- **How** = Here's the meat of the document – the product requirements. Tie them back to key themes, known as "epics" in the Scrum world. You'll include the user stories, priority and target date. In the template, we group the requirements into priority buckets (High/Medium/Low) and then stack rank the feature within those buckets.
- **When** = In this space, you'll identify the key project milestones along with expected duration, estimated start and completion date, the owner of the milestone. I also like to include a column to check off when the milestone is at 100% completion.

This might sound like a lot, but I've found that when your entire team, especially the product developers, understands some of the

1-Page Product Requirements Doc

Who
- Product/Project Name:
- Team Lead:
- Team Members:
- Stakeholders:
- Target Market:

What
- Problem Statement:
- Proposed Solution:
- Key Assumptions, Constraints & Dependencies:
- In/Out of Scope:

Why
- Justification/Why Are We Doing This?:
- Key Benefits/Financials:

How

Product Requirements:

#	Theme/Epic	Feature/User Story	Priority Bucket (HML)	Priority Rank in Bucket	Target Date

When

Timeline:

Milestone	Duration	Est Start Date	Est Finish Date	Owner	Complete (Y/N)

business elements behind what they're building, it improves both the quality of the output along with the energy, focus and morale of the team. When they know the reason why they're being asked to do certain things, they're less likely to take shortcuts. Execution improves as a result.

Writing User Stories

As part of putting together your PRD and the specific requirements, especially in the software or application development space, you're going to have to write user stories.

User stories are simple, brief descriptions of the functionality that users need to complete a task. They're the final step in translating customer needs into specific work that the developers need to complete. They are typically written from the stakeholder's perspective, and they detail what the user needs to be able to do. User stories are important because they help to explain the user's point of view and help ensure that the final product will meet those needs. By defining the functionality that users need, user stories help to guide the development process and ensure that the resulting product is usable and useful. In addition, user stories can help to identify potential areas of difficulty or confusion for users, allowing developers to address these issues before the product is released.

In the Scrum world, user stories have a defined structure that communicates roles, features, and benefits as follows:

As <role> I would like <feature> because <benefit>

For example, let's say that you're building an app for social media users. Your target market is Instagram influencers and you're thinking they might find value in a feature that makes it easy for their followers to try new products they're promoting. Your user story might look like this:

> As an Instagram influencer, I would like a way to invite my followers to simply try a new product because it would make it easier for me to share, promote and monetize my activities.

By writing user stories, you can ensure that the features and functionality of your product are clearly defined and meet the needs of your users. It's an important part of putting together a PRD, as well as developing successful software or applications.

Acceptance Criteria = The Definition of Done

After you have a user story written, you need to identify the story's *acceptance criteria* which are the specific conditions that must be met for a user story to be considered complete. In other words, acceptance criteria define how you'll know if the objective of the user story has been met. They're also one of the most frequently skipped steps in the development process, because people assume that it will be obvious if the story's objective isn't met. But don't give in to this temptation.

There are a few key reasons why acceptance criteria are so important. First, they help to ensure that everyone involved in a project understands what needs to be done and communicates what the definition of "done" is. By putting these statements in writing, you have a better chance that people will execute on them than if they're just mentioned in a meeting and never documented. By keeping everyone focused on the original goals of the user story, well-defined acceptance criteria can help to prevent scope creep –

the situation where a user story gets expanded into something more than its original intention.

Additionally, acceptance criteria provide a way to measure progress, so that you can see when the user story is complete. Finally, acceptance criteria can help to identify areas of risk and uncertainty early in the development process.

Acceptance criteria should be specific, measurable, achievable and testable. It's important to remember that these are not detailed design specifications, but rather an overview of the expectations for a user story. Checking that each acceptance criteria has been met is key to making sure the feature is functioning correctly and meeting the customer's needs.

If your product isn't software or an application, but rather a physical product, you'll still want to know what your acceptance criteria and test cases are. Let's say you're selling diamonds. You'd want to know the acceptable cut and color for a consumer-grade product versus something only good for industrial purposes. If you're selling milkshakes, you need to make sure that they have the right amount of flavoring and that they're the proper viscosity and temperature. No one wants to try to drink a flavorless milkshake that's frozen solid.

Test Cases: Don't Turn Customers Into QA

Before any feature is released, acceptance testing should be performed in order to ensure its quality and accuracy. The goal of this effort is to reduce or eliminate any defects in the launched product. This involves creating a set of scenarios or "test cases," which are based on the requirements and criteria that have been established by the customer or stakeholder.

Acceptance testing should be done by someone outside of the development team, such as a product owner or other stakeholder. This helps to ensure that the feature has been developed according to the customer's requirements and avoids any blind spots that the dev team might have had when they built the product. Test cases should be written after acceptance criteria have been established and used to verify that all user stories have been implemented correctly.

A *test case* is a set of conditions or variables under which a tester will decide whether an application, software system or one of its features is working as it should. This definition seems pretty simple, but there are a lot of different things that go into creating an effective test case. First, all the requirements for the feature being tested must be understood. Then, each potential scenario must be thought through to come up with every possible combination of inputs and outputs. Once all the scenarios have been identified, the test cases can be created.

Test cases are important because they help to ensure that software functions correctly before it is released to users. If there are bugs or errors in the code, they will be uncovered during testing and can be fixed before the software goes live. This can save a lot of time and money, as well as prevent frustration and disappointment for users. In short, taking the time to create thorough test cases is an essential part of developing high-quality software.

Please don't take the lazy route and let your customers be the primary QA for your product. I'm not saying that you should only release perfect products either. Just make sure that someone is doing a round of testing before a public release. You might not catch everything but hopefully you'll get the worst defects. When you miss an edge case, that's an opportunity to document it and add new test cases to future builds. Although the testing costs may seem high and an easy place to cut back, they can be easily recovered through a reduction in expenses from support calls and the revenue kept as a result of reduced customer churn.

Product Gaps and Feedback Loops

The long-term success of any product depends on its ability to continually solve your customer's problems. Once you have a basic product, it's important to start identifying product gaps. These will likely be the future requirements found in the next iteration of your PRD.

The best way to do this is to establish feedback loops with your customers. Like we discussed in Chapter 12, sales teams can provide valuable insights into which new features would help close or keep business. Support teams can help identify customer pain points and areas where the product needs improvement. It's critical to capture quality data from these feedback loops to continue improving the product. By constantly striving to close product gaps, you can ensure that your product remains relevant and solves the needs of your customers. This means that just like many of your other product documents, the PRD should become a frequently updated and maintained document that you share with your product team and stakeholders.

If you're not regularly getting feedback about your products, you're missing out on some of the most important data you could have about your business. Product analytics can tell you how customers are using your product and what features they value most, while competitive research can reveal what other products are available in the market and how your product stacks up. By incorporating feedback loops into your PRD that tie future product builds to real customer needs and market expectations, you can ensure that your product is always meeting the needs of your target audience.

Linking The PRD to Strategy

Just like you did in the product planning process in Chapter 14, you should be able to trace a logical thread from anything you're including in your PRD back to a specific customer need or strategic business objective. If not, why are you doing it? This is something I ask myself often, and it's a great litmus test for whether or not something is worth pursuing. If you can't see how it will help you achieve your goals, then it's probably not worth your time. This doesn't mean that every little thing needs to be justified in this way – sometimes it's important to do things just for the sake of learning or experimentation – but ultimately, when it comes to product requirements, if you can't link what you're doing back to a larger product strategic goal, it might be time to reconsider.

Similarly, it's important to think from the customer's perspective. What problem is it solving for them? How does it make their lives easier or better? If you can't answer these questions, then perhaps the feature isn't necessary, or maybe there are better ways of achieving your goals.

Amazon's Backwards Approach to Requirements

When it comes to product requirements, Amazon takes a unique approach – they start by working backward. Instead of starting with a list of features or a detailed roadmap, they begin by picturing the marketing doc they'll use for the product launch. This can include anything from a feature matrix in sales literature to writing the launch press release. From there, they develop a product FAQ and define the customer's user experience. They might even start writing the user manual. Only after answering all these questions are they ready to write the product requirements. This approach helps to ensure that everyone on the team has a clear and consistent vision for the product. As a result, it's no surprise that Amazon is known for launching high-quality products that customers love.

When writing your requirements, remember that the more detail you can provide, you improve the odds of a successful, on-time product launch. This is why the Amazon approach is so powerful. By doing all this customer and marketing work upfront, you're leaving much less open for the developers to have to interpret or take their time asking for constant clarification.

It's important to remember that product requirements are the link between the customers' needs and what gets built by the developers/engineers. If you don't take the time to write clear, concise, and detailed requirements, you run the risk of miscommunicating the needs of your customers. This could lead to a subpar product that doesn't meet their needs, or even worse, a dangerous or deadly product. By taking the time to write effective product requirements, you can ensure that your product is always meeting the needs of your target audience.

TL;DR

- Clear communication is essential to the success of any product-focused project.
- Product Requirements Documents (PRDs) are invaluable tools for ensuring clarity by providing an overview of key information such as team roles, problem being solved, stakeholders and users, feature details, assumptions, dependencies, and timelines.
- Before writing down requirements or generating ideas for a product, it's important to understand your customer's needs, analyze the financial viability and feasibility of producing the product, identify the target market and assess any legal or regulatory requirements.

- Writing user stories and acceptance criteria helps ensure that developers know exactly what they need to build and that their output meets customer needs.
- Test cases need to be written and performed in order to reduce or eliminate defects before releasing the product and avoid having customers serve as QA testers.
- Establish feedback loops with customers to identify product gaps and continuously improve the product.
- Incorporate feedback loops into PRD to tie future product builds to customer needs and market expectations.
- You should be able to trace a logical thread from anything included in the PRD back to a specific customer need or business objective.
- Amazon takes a unique "backwards" approach: they start by picturing their marketing doc, developing a user experience, and writing user manuals before writing product requirements.

CHAPTER EXERCISES

1. For a product that you manage or one that you're familiar with, identify what the specific customer need is for this product and write a problem statement that explains this need. If you don't already have this somewhere in writing, describe the potential product solution for the problem.
2. Brainstorm a short list of possible features for the product solution you just described.
3. Using the format "As <role> I would like <feature> because <benefit>" write the corresponding user stories for the features you just brainstormed.
4. For at least one of the features, suggest what the acceptance criteria would be for that user story. What is your definition of "done"?

CHAPTER NOTES

CHAPTER 17: Why Product Roadmaps Matter For Your Business (And How To Create One)

Imagine that you're leading a team of seventeen colleagues from around the world and you're putting together a face-to-face meeting with the team. You can tell them why you need the meeting by communicating a vision and a strategy for the session. But that's not enough, right? If they're going to execute by showing up somewhere, they need to know where they're going... a company retreat in Napa Valley, a family outing at Disney World, a casual meet-up at a bar in Barcelona called La Whiskeria? Still not enough though. Unless you want them to show up at the destination randomly over the next sixty days, they're going to need a date and time and maybe a map with a big red X to mark the location. To coordinate the team's activity, you need to communicate all the details with a plan and a timeline. Let's call it a ... roadmap.

Without a roadmap, you'll never get everyone at the same place and time except by happy coincidence. Each part of the team has specific tasks to deliver and as the product lead, part of your job is to coordinate everything by getting and keeping the team on the same page.

First, Some Product Roadmap Basics

In this chapter, we'll talk about how to build your roadmap. Product roadmaps serve as a planning tool for product managers and guide what features to build and when to build them. You should have linkages to the other planning elements via your themes and tactics. A roadmap takes your plans and adds a time element. It creates a visualization of your plan with a clear and understandable narrative for everyone.

A product roadmap is one of the most important tools in a product manager's toolkit. It provides a clear and shared vision for the product and gives everyone on the team a common understanding of where the product is going and why. It also helps to align strategy with execution and ensures that all stakeholders are aware of the product's direction. Finally, it can help to identify resource constraints and ensure that the right resources are allocated at the right time to the most important products.

Putting together a product roadmap is part of an integrated sequence. If you're doing this right, you're layering this work on top of other things we've talked about in previous chapters. Here's the typical layered workflow for getting to a roadmap.

1. Product Vision
2. Product Strategy
3. Product Plan
4. Product Roadmap

Your product vision is the big picture, while the product strategy starts defining goals and suggesting the paths for hitting them. The product plan combines these two views and adds a tactical layer. Finally, the roadmap is the communication vehicle that drives operational alignment and coordinates execution by telling everyone when. If you're planning a product launch, it should communicate your expected in-market dates. It should be the starting point for many cross-organization conversations as they sync to the roadmap. Because it's used for coordination across your org, it should be a living document and updated regularly rather than done once and forgotten. By keeping the roadmap updated regularly, you can ensure that everyone is on the same page and working towards the same goals.

Four Types of Product Roadmap

There are four main types of product roadmaps that you can apply depending on your needs and what you're trying to communicate: features, development, strategy, and portfolio.

1. Features - A *features roadmap* is focused on specific features and when they'll be market-ready. This type of roadmap is more detailed than a strategic roadmap but not as detailed as a development roadmap.
2. Development - A *development roadmap* is typically in sync with your development process (whether waterfall or Agile) and provides more details about epics and individual tasks. This type of roadmap can be helpful for teams that need to stay on track with their development process.
3. Strategic - A s*trategic roadmap* is more high-level, with themes instead of features. This type of roadmap can be helpful for teams that need to focus on big-picture items.
4. Portfolio - A *portfolio roadmap* can be appropriate if you have multiple products that use a common set of resources or are logically grouped from a market perspective. This type of roadmap can help you keep track of different products and initiatives.

Depending on your needs, one type of roadmap may be more appropriate than another. Choose the type of roadmap that will best help you achieve your goals.

While there are several different types of roadmaps, all share some common elements. The key elements of a roadmap include:

- Goals: What are the overall goals for the product?
- Objectives: What are the specific objectives that need to be achieved to reach the goals?
- Timeline: When do you plan to achieve the objectives?
- Scope: What themes, features, or functionality will be included in each release?
- Dependencies: What other factors could impact the delivery of the product?

Creating The Roadmap

In a blog post titled "How To Build A Product Roadmap Everyone Understands," writer Andrea Saez suggests a roadmap without a timeline called "Now Next Later" roadmap. Basically, the roadmap has three columns titled "Now," "Next" and "Later." You'll break your work down based on what you're working on currently, what you think you'll work on after that, and what you could be working on in the future. Saez recommends keeping it high-level and theme-based, especially as you go further out from a timeline perspective. I think this is a pretty reasonable approach, since it can be difficult to have a detailed view for activity more than six months out. Our slightly tweaked version, "Now, Soon, Future" follows. I like using "soon" instead of "next" because I think "next" implies a sequence or a work queue that might not really be an accurate depiction of how, when or in what order the work gets done.

	COMPLETED	NOW	SOON	FUTURE
Theme 1	• Feature 1.1 • Feature 1.2	• Feature 1.3 • Feature 2.1 • Feature 3.1	• Feature 1.4 • Feature 2.2	• Feature 2.3 • Feature 3.2 • Feature 3.3
Theme 2				
Theme 3				

STRATEGIES/ THEMES/ EPICS	TIMELINE >			
	Q1	Q2	Q3	Q4
Theme 1	• Feature 1.1 • Feature 1.2	• Feature 1.3	• Feature 1.4	
Theme 2		• Feature 2.1	• Feature 2.2	• Feature 2.3
Theme 3		• Feature 3.1		• Feature 3.2 • Feature 3.3

Creating a product roadmap can be helpful for businesses of all sizes, but it is especially important for startups. Startups often have to move quickly and make decisions with limited information. A product roadmap can help them focus on the most important features and make sure they are aligned with their overall goals.

If you're not sure where to start, we've created a roadmap template that you can use to create your own product roadmap. But no matter if you use it or not, there are a few basic steps that you'll need to complete the process:

1. Understand your product strategy and plan. If you've already built out those deliverables, you've got most of the building blocks you need for your roadmap.
2. Decide on your audience and the level of detail they need. There's no point in creating a roadmap that's too simple or too complex - it won't be helpful either way.
3. Cluster your initiatives/tactics into themes and prioritize them. This will help you focus on what's most important and make sure everything fits together coherently.
4. Create an estimate of the level of effort or time needed to complete each initiative. This will help you plan realistically and make sure you don't bite off more than you can chew.

A Backlog Is Not A Roadmap

One important distinction I'd like to offer as you build a roadmap: a development backlog does not equal a roadmap. A backlog is a list of tasks that need to be completed, and a roadmap is a plan for how to complete those tasks. Backlogs tend to be focused on relatively short-term user stories, while roadmaps usually have a longer-term focus.

A backlog will typically have both too much and not enough detail for most audiences. By too much detail we mean that, because backlogs have a very detailed view of the next month, you'll end up in the weeds for most conversations with anyone not on your dev team. But there's also such a thing as not enough detail, because outside of the well-groomed user stories for the next couple of iterations, you won't typically see a longer-term linkage to strategy, and the level of detail wanes.

Roadmaps help you understand the big picture and how all the pieces fit together. Roadmaps help build and contribute to your narrative, while your backlog is essentially a to-do list. Backlogs can be an input to the roadmap, but it's a pretty lazy take as a roadmap.

Communicating The Roadmap

Remember that your roadmap's primary job is to communicate with a variety of stakeholders. To make sure your document's message is aligned for the purpose, ask yourself:

- Who is the audience?
- What information do they need/want to see?
- What is the narrative I want to present?
- How granular do I need to be with my timeline for this audience?

No matter which type of roadmap you're creating, you're very likely to want to have different views of your roadmap for different audiences — customer, internal, sales, marketing, executives, developers, etc.

Be especially careful with the level of detail you share on the external roadmap and make sure that any internal audiences that might see the roadmap know what they should or shouldn't share with customers and prospects. There is often a great amount of pressure on the sales team from your customers or prospects to share the product roadmap with them. It's easy to understand why this happens. Some existing customers may have given feedback or requested new features and the sales team wants to let them know the customer's been heard. Other times, the sales team is trying to drive new revenue with a prospect that's rejected everything in the current product portfolio and sales is simply trying to get them excited about something.

But if you're selling futures instead of existing solutions, this is a big reason why you might want to have different views of the roadmap for different audiences. Frequently you may have things on your internal product roadmap that include proposed projects that haven't been funded or are even just early stage ideas that haven't been fully vetted. That can set dangerous expectations with stakeholders or customers that don't understand that the internal roadmap is not a contract to deliver those projects. Instead, show them the customer-facing roadmap that only has the projects you want to share.

Roadmapping software like Aha! or Monday can help you create different views of your roadmap, keep it up-to-date, and share it with others. Because a roadmap is primarily a communication tool, it's important to make sure it's easy to understand and share the right version with the right audience. Colors can be used to group or highlight different elements of the roadmap. By grouping themes and using colors to show how your roadmap elements tie back to your strategies and themes, you can make those visual connections easier for your audience. And making shareable versions of the roadmap ensures that everyone is on the same page and aware of the latest changes.

Some Final Roadmap Considerations

As you put together your product roadmap, it's important to keep in mind potential constraints on resources. Make sure you have a clear understanding of what dependencies exist between different features, and whether they'll be using the same limited resources. Does one set of features build on another? Are you using the same limited resources? A roadmap can often show potential future bottlenecks when you realize that you're running a couple of initiatives in parallel that have common resources. This identification can give you time to either get more resources onboard or set realistic expectations around the throughput of single-threaded resources.

It can also be helpful to establish separate queues and priorities for product fixes apart from other product development. That way, you can make sure that critical bugs are dealt with promptly, without sacrificing progress on larger initiatives. If you have shared resources working the separate queues, make sure to still set weekly hours limits for each queue. And finally, make sure you set up clear metrics for measuring progress. This will help you track your team's progress and adjust your roadmap as needed.

Wrapping up this chapter, product roadmaps are a crucial tool for product managers to align their teams and communicate the vision of the product. A well-crafted roadmap should answer the questions "what?", "when?", and "why?" by outlining the key features, development stages, and strategic initiatives that will guide product development. Effective roadmaps should be easy to understand and shared with all stakeholders, with clear connections between strategy and themes and adjustments made based on the information needs of your audience.

When creating a roadmap, it is important to keep potential resource constraints in mind. This involves balancing competing priorities such as new feature development versus technical debt reduction or bug fixes. Additionally, setting up clear metrics for measuring progress will help ensure that the roadmap remains on track towards achieving its goals.

A good roadmap can drive organizational alignment by supplying a shared understanding of the product's direction and priorities. It can also help teams stay focused on what matters most while working towards common goals. Ultimately, a well-designed roadmap can be a powerful tool for driving successful product development that meets customer needs while achieving business objectives.

TL;DR

- Product roadmaps are essential planning tools for product managers to guide the features to be built and when.
- Four types of roadmaps exist - features, development, strategy and portfolio - each tailored to specific needs.
- Creating a product roadmap involves understanding the product strategy and plan, deciding on the level of detail needed for the audience, clustering initiatives into themes, prioritizing those themes and creating an estimate of level of effort or time needed to complete each initiative.
- A "Now Next Later" or "Now Soon Future" type of roadmap can be put together with three columns showing current projects/tactics, upcoming ones and later iterations.
- Resource constraints should be considered when creating and updating the roadmap, as well as establishing metrics to measure progress.

- Roadmaps should be regularly updated rather than done once and forgotten.
- A backlog is not a roadmap, as it lacks connection to strategy and longer-term thinking.
- Set up separate queues and priorities for product fixes apart from other product development.
- Different views can be created for different audiences (customer/internal/sales/executives, etc.), depending on their level of detail needed. Be careful with sharing external views of the roadmap - some things may need to be internal only.
- Roadmapping software like Aha! or Monday can help create different views to make connections easier for audiences and keep updates consistent.

CHAPTER EXERCISES

1. Choose a product strategy and plan from your organization or one you are familiar with. Cluster initiatives into themes and prioritize those themes based on their importance to the overall strategy.
2. Using these prioritized themes, create a "Now Soon Future" roadmap. Include three columns showing current projects/tactics, upcoming ones, and later iterations. Prioritize each initiative and make a high-level estimate of the level of effort or time required to complete it.
3. Identify potential different audiences for the roadmap. What projects would you want to leave off of an externally-facing roadmap? What level of detail would you want to add for developers, if any?

CHAPTER NOTES

CHAPTER 18: Prioritization – Essential and Not as Hard as You Think

Prioritization can sometimes feel like a daunting task, especially when you are looking at an endless list of tasks and trying to decide which ones should take priority over the others. It's easy to feel overwhelmed and uncertain about where to start. But the truth is that prioritization isn't as hard as it seems; with a good understanding of the core principles and a bit of practice, anyone can become an expert in no time. In this chapter, we'll explore the essential concepts behind prioritization and discuss why it is so important for any successful project or goal. We'll also look at some helpful tips and techniques to make things easier and more effective.

Have you ever played *Overwatch*? For the uninitiated, *Overwatch* is a team-based first-person shooter video game developed and published by Blizzard Entertainment. It was released in May 2016 for Microsoft Windows, PlayStation 4, and Xbox One. The game centers around characters with special abilities fighting each other in a variety of game modes. The game has been very successful, generating $1B+ in revenue with tens of millions of players. The game has also become very popular in the e-sports world, with competitions that award millions of dollars to the best players and teams.

Overwatch is a game that also features virtually unlimited ammo. You just have to reload clips. It takes less than a second. The game's emphasis is on speed and action. Because of this, you never have to worry about running out of bullets. Whether you're taking on a team of enemy players or facing off against a powerful boss character, you can rest assured that you always have the firepower you need to come out on top.

By contrast, maybe you've played *The Last of Us* (TLOU) or its sequel *The Last of Us Part II* (TLOUP2). The Last of Us is a 2013 action-adventure game developed by Naughty Dog and published by Sony Computer Entertainment. An Emmy-nominated HBO TV series based on the show came out in early 2023. The narrative follows protagonists Joel and Ellie as they travel across the United States in an attempt to find a cure for a pandemic, an infection caused by the Cordyceps fungus that has caused the collapse of civilization. *The Last of Us* received critical acclaim, with critics praising its story, acting, graphics, music, and gameplay. TLOU has been hailed as one of the greatest video games of all time, winning over 200 Game of the Year awards. The sequel, TLOUP2, came out in 2020 to similar acclaim. Together the two titles have sold over thirty-seven million copies.

The Last of Us is a game that emphasizes stealth and planning. You are given limited resources – a handgun, maybe a long gun, or a shiv that always manages to break mid-fight if you overuse it. When you're out of ammo, you have to fight your way out of a situation with your fists or sneak away and find more supplies. The game's emphasis is on being a scavenger and topping off your resources ahead of time so you're ready for the next situation. You also learn to pick your battles, not rushing into a blazing bullet-sucking gun fight when you can do the same thing, albeit slower, with a bit more cunning and guile.

While we'd all love to live in an *Overwatch*-like world of abundance with unlimited resources, most of us find our personal and work reality more closely aligns with *The Last of Us*. That requires us to get really good at the art of ruthless prioritization. As former Meta Chief Operating Officer Sheryl Sandberg has suggested:

"I think the most important thing we've learned as we've grown is that we have to prioritize. We talk about it as ruthless prioritization. And by that what we mean is only do the very best of the ideas. Lots of times you have very good ideas. But they're not as good as the most important thing you could be doing. And you have to make the hard choices."

Almost all of us are restricted by something. Whether it's time, money, energy, or attention, we all have finite resources. And while it's tempting to think that those with more resources have an unfair advantage, the truth is that nearly everyone is limited in some way. The key is to find ways to work within those limitations.

Glass Balls, Brass Balls and Rubber Balls

At some point, everyone ends up juggling their to-do's, trying to manage themselves, their team, and their resources across a range of works-in-progress. As I've described this to my teams, I think it helps to visualize your juggling to-do's as juggling a set of glass balls, brass balls, and rubber balls.

Rubber balls are most of the things you manage each day. Routine things like non-urgent emails or maybe you have a daily standing status meeting that falls into this bucket. If you drop one of these balls, it'll bounce quietly on the floor. You can come back later and pick it up. No one notices or thinks much of it.

On the other hand, brass balls might be a bit more important and visible. Think of something like a missed deadline or a late report. If you drop one of these, it'll make a loud clatter. People will stop and look. It might even result in a slight dent to your reputation. But most of the time, you can still go over and pick it up and it hasn't caused much damage to the ball or anything else.

But then you have the glass balls. This is the really important "get-it-right" stuff. Product launches, maybe a high-visibility presentation or speaking engagement. If you screw up and drop one of these, it'll shatter into a thousand pieces and can't be put back together. Everyone notices. You've got a mess to clean up.

Having clear priorities can help make sure that you know which kind of ball you're juggling and give you the time needed to handle the brass and glass ones with some extra care.

Four Tips to Get You Ready to Set Priorities

I see a lot of people who struggle with setting priorities. They're constantly juggling a million things and they're never quite sure which one to focus on first. Sound familiar? Here are four tips that have helped me to improve my prioritization skills.

1. *Get clear on your goals.* What is it you're trying to achieve? If you don't know the answer to this, you can't move forward with much confidence. But once you have a clear number one goal in mind, it becomes much easier to prioritize the steps that will help you to reach that goal. Ask yourself, "Does doing this take me closer to one of my goals?" If the answer's "No," then there's probably something else you should be doing.
2. *Make a list of everything that you need to do.* This may seem like an obvious step, but it's important to get all of your tasks down on paper (or in your digital task manager of choice). This will help you to see exactly what needs to be done and will make it easier to prioritize. Do you have a lot of tasks that aren't connected to any of your goals? Do they really need to be on the list, or do you need to update your goals? Make a

list called "Parking Lot" and put the disconnected tasks there so you can pull them back onto your list if they become relevant.

3. *Break any oversized tasks down into small, manageable steps.* Once you have a list of everything that needs to be done, it can be overwhelming. To avoid this, break each task down into smaller steps. Let's say that you had "Throw a birthday party" on your to-do's. There's a lot of smaller tasks hidden in there. Instead, you want to have "Send invitations," "Buy a cake," "Put up decorations," etc. on the list. This will make it feel a little less daunting and will help you to see the progress you're making.

4. *Assign a priority level to each task.* This is where things can get tricky. A lot of times people will start with the tasks that are due soon and work their way down from there. But that can leave you constantly working on things that are urgent and not important. Remember the Eisenhower Matrix back in Chapter 5? You want to prioritize your time so that you're working on important things before they turn into a raging inferno of urgency. You'll need to use your best judgment to determine which tasks are more important than others, but since you've got your goals identified, start there. In the next section, we'll outline several basic ways that you can put your tasks in an order that aligns with your goals.

Eight Ways To Start Setting Your Priorities

Now that you have a list of tasks that you need to get done, let's take a look at a few ways that you can start setting your priorities a little more strategically without spending a bunch of time and energy on ruminative cycles.

1. *Priority or Eisenhower Matrix* - As we just mentioned, the Eisenhower Matrix (also known as the Urgent-Important Matrix) is a popular tool used to set clear priorities. To use the Eisenhower Matrix, take the task list we just created – for example "respond to emails," "schedule meeting" or "write a report." Then for each of these list items, assign it a ranking of either "urgent" or "not urgent" and "important" or "not important." Once all the tasks have been categorized accordingly, you can then place them inside the classic 2x2 matrix with "Urgent/Not Urgent" along one axis and "Important/Not Important" along the other.

    You'll handle each item based on where it lands in the matrix.

    - Low urgency/Low importance = Delete
    - High urgency/Low importance = Delegate
    - Low urgency/High importance = Decide/Schedule
    - High urgency/High importance = Do

2. *Value-to-Effort Matrix (or Cost-Benefit Matrix)* - Another classic 2x2 matrix option. This time you'll rank the options based on expected value (High/Low) and effort (High/Low). Value can be revenue, cost savings or some other metric. Effort can be actual physical effort, time or some other resource usage. You're essentially estimating the profitability of each project, looking for the High Value/Low Effort projects to do first and avoiding the Low Value/High Effort ones. I've also done this one as a 3x3

matrix and rated each project high, medium, or low on both estimates. Either one can give you important insights as you prioritize your projects. For example, what if the highest revenue-producing project is also going to be far and away the most expensive to build, such that it might not deliver profits for years? Might be good to understand and know if you have other better options before you divert all your resources onto the whale-sized project.

Value-to-Effort Matrix

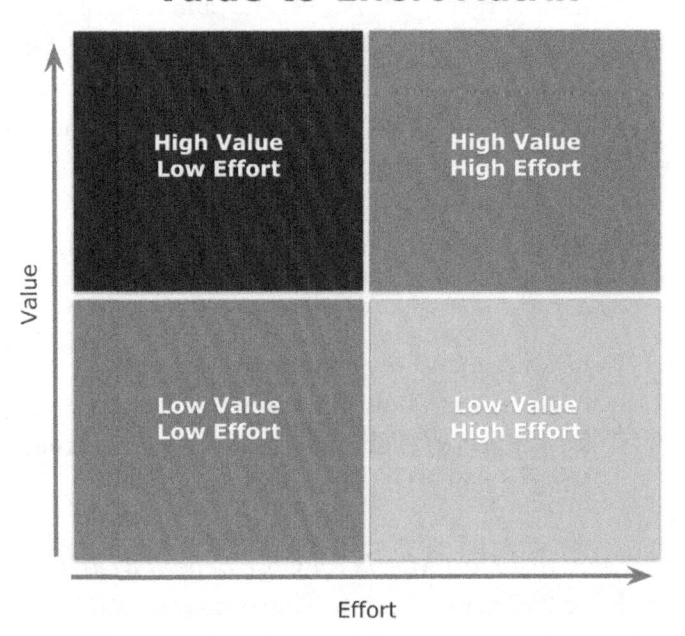

Value ↑	High Value Low Effort	High Value High Effort
	Low Value Low Effort	Low Value High Effort
	Effort →	

3. *Stack Ranking* - Stack Ranking is a simple way to prioritize tasks or goals, where items are placed in order of importance - with the most important item at the top. This allows for efficient addressing of key goals, as well as preventing procrastination.

To apply stack ranking, you must first decide on a single point of comparison that will be used to rank items. For example, if you have a list of ideas for your children's activities, "fun" could be used as the point of comparison; or if you have house projects, it could be how quickly each project can be completed or how much value they bring.

If "fun" was the goal and you had "paint the bathroom" and "bake cookies" on your list, it's probably time to preheat your oven. Once you establish the point of comparison and place items in the stack according to how well they score in that area, the most important tasks can be tackled first. If working within a team, it's possible to ask team members to provide stack rankings and then average them out to reduce any individual bias.

4. *Stack Rank plus Cost* - Similar to a regular stack ranking, this includes a cost estimate for each item on the to-do list as well as an estimate of resource capacity available. For example, let's say you have three things on your list and twenty units of resources available for the next cycle. Project A is estimated at thirty units and Projects B and C are each estimated at ten units. You can decide if you'd prefer to complete 2/3rd of Project A during the cycle or knock out both B and C with the available resources. With smaller projects on the list, you'll rank them in priority, then add up the resources until you hit your budget of twenty units and that's where you draw the line for the cycle. This is very similar to how Agile backlogs get managed as product owners determine what's getting built during each sprint.

5. *Pairwise Comparison* - Pairwise Comparison is a great way to sort and prioritize a long list of options. First, create a spreadsheet matrix of the list with all entries both across the top and also down the left axis. Then start comparing pairs 1-to-1 and decide which of the two is more important by

assigning a winner in each head-to-head pairing. Essentially, you're taking only Option A and comparing it to Option B and choosing between the two. Repeat this process until all pairings are compared – A vs C, A vs D, B vs C, B vs D, C vs D. Then tally up the total number of "wins" for each option and use this as a reference for ranking them. The options can be sorted in terms of the number of wins they have received, providing you with an easily stack-ranked list of prioritized items.

6. *Thematic Grouping* – With this way, you're building your priorities around a specific strategic theme as your goal. Ever done spring cleaning? That's a thematic grouping. Grouping similar tasks together and executing them usually results in some gains in efficiency and potentially lower switching costs as you move between tasks. For example, if you're doing your spring cleaning, once you get into a decluttering mindset, it can be much easier to move from room to room in your house. From a product standpoint, you'll still need to identify the most important work to include in the grouping. But in the end, you should find that this option helps with improved strategic alignment, internal communication, and building a marketing narrative.

7. *MoSCoW* - The MoSCoW method of determining product feature priorities is a technique used by product teams to quickly rank tasks and features according to importance. In this method, tasks are grouped into four main categories: Must Have, Should Have, Could Have, and Won't Have.

   Must Have (M) tasks or features are considered essential for the successful launch of a product or fulfillment of a customer request. These must be completed before anything else can be launched or carried out.

Should Have (S) tasks or features are important issues that need to be dealt with in order to have a successful product launch or customer request fulfilled. They may not be as time-sensitive as Must Haves but should still take priority over most other items.

Could Have (C) tasks or features include optional issues that could improve the customer experience but are not absolutely necessary for a successful outcome. These should generally take lower priority than Must Haves and Should Haves while still being taken into account during planning and decision-making processes.

Won't Have (W) features refer to tasks that will not be undertaken in the project timeline due to their lower priority and/or other constraints such as budget or time limitations. Decisions about Won't Haves should be revisited periodically in case conditions change and any of these can become useful later on in the process.

The MoSCoW method helps teams quickly assess which items require more urgency in order to achieve optimal results without getting bogged down by too much detail up front. It is an efficient way to prioritize tasks according to importance without sacrificing quality or letting things slip through the cracks.

8. *Weighted Scoring Matrix* - If you feel like some of these other methods are too simple, or maybe you need to include more than one or two criteria in your model, try a weighted scoring matrix. This is a tool used to prioritize products or features. It is typically used by organizations that have many products or features in development and need a way to objectively prioritize them.

To use a weighted scoring matrix, start by finding the different criteria you want to use in your model and the relative importance of those criteria. The criteria are then assigned weights, based on their importance. The products or features are then scored on each criterion, and the scores are multiplied by the weight assigned to that criterion. The resulting number is the product's or feature's weighted score. The products or features are then ranked from highest to lowest weighted score to determine their priority.

There are many different ways to weigh the criteria in a weighted scoring matrix. One common approach is to have a team of experts each weigh the criteria individually by assigning a common scale, say 100 points, across all the available criteria, and then take the average of all the weights. This helps to ensure that the final weights are objective and representative of the team's collective opinion.

Working Smart and Moving Quickly

At the end of the day, prioritization is all about working smarter and narrowing your focus to what matters most. It's easy to get bogged down by the day-to-day and lose sight of what's important. That's why prioritization is essential. By taking the time to prioritize, you can ensure that you're focusing on the things that matter most and getting them done quickly and efficiently. Many different techniques can be used to prioritize, and the best technique to use will vary depending on the situation.

But you don't have to make it a complicated, time-consuming process. Once you have your goals set and your task list identified, none of the processes we've mentioned will take more than thirty minutes, especially once you make it a routine. Start with something simple like a stack rank or one of the 2x2 matrices and spend fifteen minutes on it. Trust your gut and move quickly. Even that little bit of effort can help you make sure that you and your team are working smarter and working on the right things.

TL;DR

- Prioritization can often be a daunting task, especially when looking at an endless list of tasks. But because we almost always have limited resources, ruthless prioritization is an essential part of successful projects or goals, requiring a good understanding of the core principles and practice.
- Four tips to improve your prioritization skills: getting clear on goals, making a list of everything that needs to be done, breaking down big tasks into smaller ones and assigning a priority level to each task.
- Eight ways to start setting priorities include the Eisenhower Matrix, Value-to-Effort Matrix, Stack Ranking, Stack Ranking plus Cost Estimate, Pairwise Comparison, Thematic Grouping with MoSCoW method and Weighted Scoring Matrix.
- These methods allow for efficient addressing of key objectives with strategic alignment, internal communication and marketing narratives.
- Prioritization doesn't have to be complicated or take a lot of time. Almost every project can get a benefit from spending 30 minutes to align the work being done with the overall goals of the project or team.

CHAPTER EXERCISES

1. Find a project that you think could benefit from better priority setting. Write down the team or project's key goals. Don't have more than three.
2. Make a list of all the tasks that need to be completed to reach the goal. Break any big tasks into smaller ones. Put any tasks that aren't aligned with one of your goals on a list called "Parking Lot." Everything else goes on a "To-Do" list.
3. Choose one of the eight prioritization methods detailed in the chapter and use it to set the priorities for the tasks on your "To-Do" list.
4. If you didn't use the Value-Effort matrix in the last exercise, take just a few minutes and score each task high or low in terms of value and effort. Place them on the matrix in one of the four quadrants. Compare the results to your other method. Same result? Different?

CHAPTER NOTES

CHAPTER 19: The Real MVP = Minimum Viable Prototype

Austrian-born management consultant Peter Drucker was quoted as saying: "There is surely nothing quite so useless as doing with great efficiency what should not be done at all." This quote is particularly relevant to startups, since many end up failing due to a lack of market demand for their product or service. In fact, according to a CB Insights review of over 100 failed startups, 35% of the startups failed because of "No Market Need." Even if a startup has a great product or service, it will not be successful if there is a lack of sufficient demand for it.

So, while it is important to be efficient in all aspects of running a business, perhaps the simplest and most important is to make sure that you are working on something that people really want or need. Otherwise, you may find yourself wasting a lot of time and effort on something that will never go anywhere. Take the story of Juicero for example.

Juicero was a Silicon Valley startup that made a juicer and proprietary packets of pre-chopped fruits and vegetables. The idea was that you would buy these packets, insert them into the Juicero machine, and out would come a cold-pressed juice. The machine would do all the work for you, so all you had to do was drink the juice. The company attracted over $100 million in funding and launched with some decent buzz in March 2016. But by September 2017, the company had suspended all sales efforts and was out of business before the end of the year. What the hell happened?

Juicero failed for several reasons. First, the company significantly overestimated the demand for juicing machines. Juicers are notoriously messy and time-consuming to clean, so most people only use them occasionally. Only the hard-core juicers are regular juice machine types. A lot of would-be juicers just use an easier-to-clean blender and drink smoothies instead. Second, Juicero's packs were a lot more expensive than simply buying fruits and vegetables and juicing them yourself. Third, the Juicero machine was large and bulky, making it difficult to store in small kitchens. Finally, and the worst of all, many customers found that they could get just as much juice out of the packs by squeezing them with their bare hands, so the big bulky machine supplied little incremental benefit. In short, Juicero was a poorly designed product that did not meet the needs of consumers. Which makes you wonder how much of this could have been figured out by engaging those consumers earlier in the product development process - that is, before blowing through $100M?

In this chapter, we'll take a look at one of the most popular ways to engage customers early by launching a Minimum Viable Product (MVP). We'll review different kinds of product risk, explain why MVPs fail, and suggest an alternative solution.

A Minimum Viable Product Reduces Risk

A Minimum Viable Product, or MVP, is a version of a product with just enough features to be usable by early customers. The purpose of an MVP is to allow feedback for future product development. MVPs are popular in the tech world because they allow startups to test their assumptions and iterate quickly. This approach is seen as less risky than spending years developing a product that may not be successful.

Any new product faces three types of risk: product risk, customer risk, and market risk. *Product risk* is the uncertainty associated with whether the product will meet customer needs and expectations. *Customer risk* is the uncertainty associated with whether customers will actually purchase the product. And *market risk* is the uncertainty associated with whether the overall market for the product will be large enough to support sales. An MVP can help to reduce all three of these risks.

Product risk is reduced through the use of a Minimum Viable Product (MVP) because it allows for early testing and validation of the product's core features. By creating and releasing an MVP, the development team can gain valuable feedback from early adopters and adjust the product accordingly. This reduces uncertainty about whether or not the product will meet customer needs and expectations, as it allows for direct feedback from real users.

Customer risk is also mitigated by using an MVP because it gives an opportunity to test customer interest in the product before investing significant time and resources into its development. By releasing a basic version of the product, businesses can gauge customer interest and gather data on how potential customers interact with it. This helps to reduce uncertainty around whether or not customers will actually purchase the product, as businesses can make informed decisions based on real-world user data.

An MVP offers a solution to market risk by enabling businesses to evaluate their assumptions about market demand without investing substantial resources into full-scale production. By releasing a basic version of the product, companies can obtain valuable data on market demand and use this information to make informed decisions about future investments in production and marketing efforts. This approach reduces uncertainty around the size of the overall market for the product, as it empowers businesses to make evidence-based decisions supported by real-world data. With an MVP, companies can confidently enter new markets with a clear understanding of customer needs and preferences.

Nine Reasons Why MVPs Fail

Getting all this risk reduction is a good thing and MVPs have earned their place in the product manager's arsenal for a reason. But there is a downside to MVPs. Many MVP efforts have ended up with something that was neither viable nor a sellable product. Sometimes, product managers end up de-scoping key features to create an MVP that aligns with a launch timeline. Too much emphasis on "minimum" and not enough emphasis on "viable." MVP should only be used as a starting point for product development, not as the end goal. The MVP is both less and more than you think: less because you want your customers' reactions ASAP and so they need to see earlier cuts of the product; more because you'll probably need to build more than you think to get customers to actually cut you a check.

With that in mind, here are nine reasons why Minimum Viable Products fail:

1. *Unrealistic expectations — MVP instead of Minimum Sellable Product*

Language matters. One of the dangers of calling something a Minimum Viable Product is that people will believe you, especially your C-suite and sales team. They'll expect to be able to sell it immediately and generate revenue for the company. But the goal of your MVP might not be to get customers, but rather to get customer feedback. When it comes to product development, the goal should always be to create a product that is viable and will meet customer needs. However, too often the focus is on creating an MVP that barely meets the needs of customers. This can lead to problems down the road, as customers may be unhappy with the quality of the product or find that it doesn't fully meet their needs. You'll need to differentiate between an MVP and MSP (Minimum Sellable Product) and make sure that you are delivering an MSP if there are revenue expectations.

2. *Inability to gather or properly incorporate customer feedback.*

Another issue that can arise from MVP development is an inability to gather or properly incorporate customer feedback.

Because the focus is on creating a bare-bones product, there may not be enough functionality for customers to provide useful feedback. Additionally, even if customer feedback is gathered, it may not be successfully incorporated into future iterations of the product. Frequently, this is because the cost required to add the capability far exceeds the resources available or because existing technology won't support the feature at a high enough level of performance. This can lead to a disconnect between what customers want and what the product delivers, leading to frustration and ultimately poor sales.

3. *Solving a problem that doesn't have a sufficient market willing to pay enough for the solution to sustain a profitable business — no product-market fit.*

A third issue that can arise from MVP development is solving a basic problem that doesn't have a sufficient standalone market, one willing to pay enough for the solution, to help you sustain a profitable business. This can happen when the focus is on creating a Minimum *Viable* Product instead of a Minimum *Sellable* Product. We'll talk more about product-market fit in Chapter 21. Without a market willing to pay for the product, the business will not be sustainable in the long run. Of course, it's better to know this sooner rather than later so this kind of failure can save a lot of future pain.

4. *Didn't solve the problem — product doesn't work as expected.*

Another common issue with MVPs is that they simply don't work as expected. Customers may be disappointed when a product doesn't meet their needs or solve their problems. If you're lucky, you might find that there's a market for the problem you did manage to solve. But if the product is just broken and can't be fixed, there's probably not a happy ending in your future.

5. *Underbuilt product is missing key features.*

When a product is rushed to market, you will often find that you've underbaked your solution. Maybe you just guessed wrong about which features were needed for your initial release. But if there's not enough value in the features you built, you might not give the customer the needed justification for cutting you a check.

6. *Overbuilt product takes too long to get to market.*

The flip side of underbuilding. You can also spend too much time building features that don't add to the core value of the product. The extra time can cause a market window to close or narrow significantly, allowing competition to steal a first mover advantage that you can never get back.

7. *Poor user experience.*

In this case, the product's not broken. But the user experience just puts too many barriers between the user and getting value. Maybe your onboarding asks too many questions and potential users bail out during the initial set-up. Or maybe some of the key features are buried in an overly complex menu structure. Either way, there's too much friction in the product and if you're not getting that feedback incorporated, a lot of hard work could go to waste.

8. *Under-skilled team or poor execution.*

When you need a subject-matter expert in a particular skill and you don't have one, you might not have the horsepower you need to deliver your solution. Or maybe you've got the right team, but you're doing all the wrong things or getting bad direction from your leadership. If you need a rocket scientist, you're probably not going to make it work with a neighbor who's only real experience is flying drones in his backyard. Go get a rocket scientist.

9. *Product built for investors and not actual customers*

This one happens more than you'd think. The product is designed with the investors in mind. Frequently this is because there is a hot technology du jour that everyone's buzzing about... ChatGPT... cough... Blockchain... cough... Web3. So, you try to incorporate it into the design of your product because you know it'll get the attention of potential investors. But the investors rarely are the same as the target customers for your product. If the buzzy tech doesn't add significant value to your actual users, you might burn those investor dollars chasing the tech and never gain traction with real customers in the market.

Prototyping = A Better Path

Is there a better path? Simply releasing an MVP is not enough. You also need to have a plan for how you will use customer feedback to refine and improve your product. This is where prototyping comes in. Prototyping is the process of creating a simplified version of your product to test a specific hypothesis. By combining prototypes with the idea of a Minimum Sellable Product, you can quickly gather customer feedback and use it to iterate on your product. As a result, you can bring your product to market faster and with fewer resources.

In his book *The Lean Startup*, author Eric Ries suggests that you should be pursuing "the version of a product which allows a team to collect the maximum amount of validated learning about customers with the least effort." Product leaders frequently talk about time to market. But what about "speed to feedback"? What's the quickest path for you to start gathering customer insights about your solution?

When you have an idea for a new product, it can be tempting to rush into building it as quickly as possible. However, taking the time to create a prototype can save you a lot of time and money in the long run. A prototype is easier to discard or pivot from than a product that you've invested time and money to build. The goal is feedback, not just shaving a couple of weeks from product delivery by reducing features and scope. You can gain the insights from your prototype that you would have waited to gather from version 1.0 of the product. With that knowledge, you can launch your initial product with the customer input that effectively makes it the 2.0 version of the product. In the end, creating a prototype will save you time and money in the long run. You'll substantially increase the likelihood that you'll be launching with a Minimum Sellable Product.

Benefits to Prototyping

There are several other benefits to prototyping. It allows companies to test ideas quickly and cheaply, while also getting feedback from customers early on. This can help to reduce the risk of making costly mistakes further down the line. Prototyping can also help to reduce the impact of those mistakes by finding problems early on. As a result, prototyping can save businesses both time and money, while also helping to create better products.

Building prototypes to evaluate risky assumptions is a great way to reduce risk in any business venture. Again, here's Eric Ries:

> "When one is choosing among the many assumptions in a business plan, it makes sense to *test the riskiest assumptions first*. If you can't find a way to mitigate these risks toward the ideal that is required for a sustainable business, there is no point in testing the others."

By identifying the riskiest risks upfront and testing them through prototypes, you can save time and resources overall.

Additionally, this approach can help you to quickly find which assumptions are critical to the success of your venture and which can be safely ignored.

The biggest risk when launching a product is that you will spend time and money building a product or solution that no one is willing to pay for. This is why it's so important to validate your ideas with potential customers early on. Prototyping allows you to learn more about what customers want and need without having to make a full investment in development. This way, you can avoid wasting time and resources on features that don't meet customer expectations.

Some companies will incorporate *design thinking* into their prototyping process. Design thinking is a creative problem-solving process that can be used to develop new ideas or solutions. The process begins with a need or a problem that needs to be solved. Once the need is identified, the design thinker will generate a variety of possible solutions. These solutions are then studied and analyzed to decide which one is the most viable. After a solution is selected, it is then prototyped and tested. This iterative process allows for constant refinement and improvement until an optimal solution is found.

Design thinking is an effective way to solve complex problems, and it can also help to improve collaboration and communication among team members. Additionally, the use of prototypes can help to reduce the risk of failure by allowing for early testing and feedback. Ultimately, design thinking is a flexible and powerful tool that can be used to generate innovative solutions to a variety of challenges.

When you're ready to build your prototype, know that prototypes can take many different forms, from simple sketches to complex 3D prints. The most important thing is to choose the form that will best allow you to assess your hypotheses and gather the data you need. Sketches, for example, are great for exploring early ideas and getting a general sense of how something might look or work. UX/design mockups are more detailed and can be clickable, making them ideal for testing user flow. 3D printing can be used to create physical prototypes that can be used for user testing or trade shows. Service simulations, which use people instead of technology, are another possibility, though they are not scalable. Video prototypes, like the one Dropbox created (https://youtu.be/7QmCUDHpNzE), can be a great way to show how a product or service works in a real-world setting. And finally, storyboards and ads/landing pages can be used to test messaging and conversion rates. The bottom line is that there is no one right way to create a prototype - it all depends on your specific needs and goals.

Drawing on the words of Peter Drucker that started this chapter, startups should strive to be mindful of how they allocate resources to ensure efficiency and reduce risk. The Minimum Viable Product (MVP) approach allows businesses to reduce product, customer and market risk before making significant investments in production and marketing efforts. However, MVPs can also fail if they are not properly executed. The key to success is to identify the risks upfront and test them through prototyping. This way, you can avoid wasting time and resources on features that don't meet customer expectations. Ultimately, the goal is to create a prototype that will allow you to test your hypotheses and gather the data you need. With careful planning and execution, your Minimum Viable *Prototype* can help your organization move quickly and efficiently towards product success.

TL;DR

- Peter Drucker famously said that it is useless to do with great efficiency what should not be done at all; this concept is especially relevant to startups, as 35% of failed ventures cited "no market need" as the cause of their demise.
- The Minimum Viable Product (MVP) approach allows businesses to reduce product, customer, and market risk before making significant investments in the production and marketing of a product.
- However, MVPs may fail due to unrealistic expectations, difficulty incorporating feedback, lack of market demand for the product, poor execution or technical skill of the team, inadequate features, overly complex user experience, or building with investors instead of customers in mind.
- Prototyping is the process of creating a simplified version of a product to gather customer feedback and iterate on it. This enables companies to test ideas quickly and cheaply, while getting feedback from customers early on, resulting in a reducing the potential for costly mistakes later.
- Prototypes take many forms including sketches, UX/design mockups, 3D printing, service simulations, video prototypes, storyboards and ads/landing pages.
- Combining prototypes with the idea of a Minimum Sellable Product can help quickly gather customer feedback and use it to iterate on your product, resulting in a faster time to market.
- When done properly, Minimum Viable Prototypes can help validate ideas with potential customers while avoiding wasted time and resources on features that don't meet expectations.

CHAPTER EXERCISES

1. Think about either a new product or new features for an existing product. What are some risks or areas of uncertainty that could be tested by using a prototype?
2. Out of the risks you just identified, which one would you say is the biggest risk? How could you build a prototype to evaluate this risk?
3. Take a few minutes to sketch or storyboard a very basic product design. Show this very simple prototype to a friend or colleague and see what kind of feedback you get from them.

CHAPTER NOTES

CHAPTER 20: How To Know If You're Winning - Choosing The Right KPIs For Your Product

Over my desk as I write this book, I've got a few quotes and affirmations to keep me motivated. One of them is "Completion is perfection." I don't remember exactly where I got that, but I think it was my attempt to paraphrase a quote from Simon Sinek – "Progress is more important than perfection." When you're writing a book, it can get easy to get so caught up in trying to make every word perfect that you don't deliver on the big picture and get the book written.

To keep myself on target for completing the book, I came up with some metrics to help me know how I was performing day-to-day with the project and measure my progress towards completion rather than perfection. This included a daily word count goal of five hundred words and logging my daily work sessions with a phone app. Consistency matters. Thanks to the London Writers' Salon and the writing community there, as I write this, I've currently got a three-hundred-seventeen weekday streak of attending at least one writers' hour a day. And counting. Overall, I've tracked chapters completed through each iteration of the project on a whiteboard and monitored my total word count, now over one hundred thousand. And the book is in your hands now, so we'll call that progress and take the win.

As a product leader, one of your primary goals is to ensure that your team is meeting its targets and delivering value to the customer. We're not talking about perfection here, just making good steady progress towards completion. To do this, you need to have a clear understanding of what your team is working on and how it is performing. This is where KPIs come in.

As we've mentioned briefly elsewhere in the book, KPIs are *key performance indicators* that provide you with a quantitative measure of your team's progress. By tracking KPIs, you can show areas where your team is excelling and areas where improvement is needed. This data can then be used to inform decision-making and help your team to meet its goals. In short, KPIs are essential for product leaders who want to ensure that their team is making progress, staying on track and delivering results. We're going to go into much greater detail on them in this chapter. To get you started, we'll highlight thirteen metrics commonly used as KPIs, along with some basic steps to turn them into a product dashboard.

What Makes a KPI

The key differentiator between a KPI and just another metric is that your KPI is linked to a business strategy or objective. That's why you might also hear the term OKR used by some people. OKR stands for *Objective/Key Result*. This is the form that's heavily used by companies like Google. They link the goal or business objective to 3-5 KPIs that can be used to measure progress towards the goal. In this chapter, we're going to focus on the KPI side of the equation but, in either case, know that linking your measurements to your strategy is critical to overall success.

Every business has different goals, and those goals should be reflected in the KPIs used to measure success. Whether it's increasing revenue, improving customer satisfaction, or reducing costs, make sure that your KPIs are aligned with your company's overarching objectives. Otherwise, you risk chasing targets that don't lead your team where they want to go. By aligning your KPIs with your business goals, you can ensure that everyone in the organization is working towards the same objectives and that you're able to accurately measure progress.

Before you can choose the right KPIs for your product, you need to have a clear understanding of what your product is and what it's meant to do. Once you know that, you can start to look at the various aspects of your product and decide which ones are the most important to measure. For example, if you're selling a physical product, one important KPI might be how many units you're selling. But other factors, like product returns, customer satisfaction or how often people use your product, could also be important. The key is to choose KPIs that will give you the most insight into how well your product is performing. By doing so, you can make sure that your product is always on the right track.

There are many factors to consider when developing and launching a new product. To ensure that your product is on track, it is important to choose KPIs that will give you insight into its performance and help you manage it. Keep in mind that your product KPIs may evolve as your product goals change. For example, early in the product life-cycle, you might be focused on growth KPI to help build your business while later, as the product matures and you're seeking profitability, an emphasis on cost and efficiency metrics could emerge.

Before setting any KPIs, it's important to ask yourself whether or not they are actionable and measurable. Without actionable, measurable KPIs you could end up spinning your wheels without making any real progress. So before setting any KPIs, make sure they are actionable and measurable - otherwise, you'll just be wasting your time.

For example, let's say your goal is to increase sales by 20% this quarter. But how will you know if you've achieved this goal? What metric will you use to measure success? Sales revenue as a metric is a lagging indicator, so it might not be the best thing to measure to predict and manage team performance. It's also not actionable by itself. A better predictor might be to measure the number of sales calls made, as that could have a direct impact on sales revenue. You can take action by making your sales processes more efficient (more sales per person) or by adding salespeople to increase the volume of calls.

When selecting KPIs, it's also important to choose ones that are relevant to your business goals and that you can realistically track over time. For example, again, if your goal is to increase sales, you might track KPIs such as conversion rate, average order value, or customer lifetime value. If your goal is to improve customer satisfaction, you might track KPIs such as Net Promoter Score or customer retention rate.

Tracking the right KPIs might require you to collect additional data or keep a count on new things you didn't count before. You'll want to make sure that you're able to easily get access to the things you're tracking and that you're able to measure them consistently. Without accurate, consistent access to the KPI data, it can be difficult to measure them over time which makes them much less useful for tracking performance.

Thirteen Common KPIs

To help get you started, here are thirteen common KPIs that are frequently used to help manage products.

1. *Monthly recurring revenue (MRR)*: This is a good metric to track because it shows you how much revenue you can expect to receive every month. This figure is important for two main reasons. First, it provides a reliable indicator of future income, which can be used to make projections and budget for growth. Second, it helps to identify areas of success and potential areas for improvement. For example, if MRR is increasing month over month, it suggests that the company's marketing and sales efforts are effective. If MRR is stagnant or declining, it may be time to revisit the company's end-to-end user experience. One reason that the subscription business model is so popular is that if it's done well, it builds up a company's MRR.
2. *Customer Lifetime Value (CLV)*: Customer lifetime value is one of the most important metrics for any business. It

represents the total value that a customer will bring to your company throughout their relationship. This includes not only their initial purchase, but also any future purchases, referrals, and other forms of valuable behavior. Understanding CLV is essential for making smart marketing and sales decisions. It can help you distribute resources more effectively and make sure that you're focusing on acquiring and retaining the most valuable customers. In short, CLV is a key metric for any business that wants to grow and succeed.

3. *Customer Acquisition Cost (CAC)*: This measures how much it costs to acquire a new customer. This includes all marketing and sales expenses, as well as the costs of any customer success or support team. CAC is an important metric for businesses to track because it allows them to understand how much they need to spend to get new customers. Additionally, measuring CAC can help businesses to identify areas of inefficiency in their customer acquisition process. By understanding and reducing their CAC, businesses can improve their profitability and scale more effectively. It's important to track this metric so that you can assess the efficiency and impact of your marketing and sales efforts. It's also very important to know this in the context of your Customer's Lifetime Value. If you spend $100 to get a customer whose lifetime value is just $50, you're not going to be in business very long.

4. *Daily Active Users (DAU)*: Daily active users (DAU) is a measure of how many people use your product or service each day. Most times, "active user" simply means that the person has interacted with the product in some way and isn't really a measure of the degree of engagement. If you open an app for ten seconds or three hours, you're an active user. This metric is important because it helps you understand how well your product is being received by your target market and whether or not they are using it regularly. If you

have a large number of DAUs, it means that people are interested in what you're offering and are using it daily. This can be a good indicator of whether or not your product is successful and whether or not people are likely to continue using it in the future. Conversely, if you have a small number of DAUs, it may mean that people are not finding your product useful or interesting and are unlikely to continue using it. Therefore, measuring DAU can give you important insights into the success of your product and its product-market fit.

5. *Monthly Active Users (MAU)*: Monthly active users (MAU) is a measure of the number of people who use a particular digital service or application in a given month. This metric is important because it provides a snapshot of engagement and can be used to compare different services or apps. If you have a decent MAU but your DAU to MAU ratio is relatively low, this can indicate a growth opportunity if you can turn those infrequent monthly visitors into daily users by increasing the product's usefulness and encouraging a daily habit.

6. *Bounce rate*: If you're not familiar with the term "bounce rate," it simply refers to the percentage of visitors who land on your website and then immediately leave without taking any further action. While a certain amount of bouncing is to be expected, a high bounce rate can be a sign that something is wrong with your site. For example, if your content is not relevant to what users are looking for, they're likely to bounce. Or if your site is difficult to navigate, users may become frustrated and leave. Early in a product's life-cycle when you're still trying to build up your user base and convert visitors to customers, measuring your bounce rate can give you valuable insights into the effectiveness of your website. Armed with this information, you can then take steps to improve your site and reduce your bounce rate. As a

result, you'll be able to better engage users and encourage them to take the desired actions on your site.

7. *Retention rate*: Measuring retention rate is important for several reasons. First, it allows you to track whether your overall customer base is growing or shrinking. Second, it gives insights into which types of customers are most likely to stick around. And finally, it can help you find areas where you might need to improve your product or service offering, all of which can have a major impact on your bottom line. There are a few different ways to measure retention rate, but perhaps the most straightforward is simply to calculate the percentage of customers who remain active after a certain period. For example, if you have 100 customers and only eighty of them are still using your product after three months, then your retention rate would be 80%. While this method is fairly straightforward, it does have some limitations. For one thing, it doesn't take into account any customers who might have left but then came back later. Additionally, it doesn't provide any insights into why customers might have left in the first place. Nonetheless, measuring the retention rate is still a valuable exercise that can supply insights into the health of your business.

8. *Churn rate*: The flip side of retention is churn. Churn rate is one of the most important metrics for any business, yet it is often misunderstood. Put simply, the churn rate is the percentage of customers who cancel their subscription or stop using your product within a given timeframe. A high churn rate can suggest that people are not satisfied with your product or that it's not meeting their needs. While it may seem like a small number, even a slight increase in churn can have a major impact on your bottom line. That's why it's so important to measure the churn rate and take steps to reduce it. There are several ways to do this, but some of the most effective include offering discounts or incentives for loyalty,

improving customer service, and paying close attention to customer feedback. By taking these steps, you can help keep your customers happy and reduce the churn rate.

9. *Revenue churn*: Revenue churn is the percentage of recurring revenue that is lost each month due to customer attrition. While it is a relatively simple metric to calculate, it can give you valuable insights into the health of your business. For example, if you see a sudden increase in revenue churn, it could be a sign that your products are no longer meeting customer needs. Alternatively, it could be a sign that your sales team is not doing a good job of retaining customers. Revenue churn is different from the churn rate because it's weighted to give more impact to losing a high revenue customer, while a basic churn analysis treats each customer with the same impact whether they're spending $100 or $1M with you. Either way, measuring revenue churn is essential for understanding the health of your business. By tracking this metric over time, you can identify trends and take action to improve your retention rate.

10. *Total support calls*: Total support calls measures the number of customer service or support calls received by a company over a specific period. This metric is important because it provides insight into the volume of product issues your customers are experiencing. It can be used to find trends in customer satisfaction or dissatisfaction. For example, if the number of total support calls increases steadily over time, it may be indicative of lagging product design or some kind of user confusion you've introduced. A sudden spike in calls that happens at the same time as a new release is bad news. Should have tested that release more! Conversely, if the number of total support calls decreases over time, it may indicate that customers are satisfied with the product and the level of service they are receiving. Thus, measuring total support calls can be a valuable tool for understanding and

improving your product. In a growing market, you might also consider adjusting this into a ratio of support calls per 100 users so that the growth itself doesn't hide improvements you might be making on the product.

11. *Support escalations*: A support escalation is defined as a request for help from a higher level of technical knowledge within an organization. Typically, as it relates to your product's support process, it would mean that the support team has a problem that can't be handled through the tools they have like FAQs and troubleshooting guides. Frequently, this means that there's a defect that only a developer can resolve. Measuring the number of escalations can help give insight into your customer experience as well as your internal quality assurance and testing processes.

12. *Net Promoter Score (NPS)*: As I mentioned in Chapter 12, the Net Promoter Score (NPS) is a simple yet powerful tool for measuring customer satisfaction and loyalty. It is based on the principle that the best indicator of future behavior is past behavior. In other words, if a customer is satisfied with your product or service, they are likely to continue using it and recommend it to others. On the other hand, if a customer is unhappy, they are less likely to stay engaged, remain loyal or give positive word-of-mouth recommendations. The NPS can be used to gauge customer satisfaction with any type of product or service, and it has been shown to predict business growth. In addition, the NPS is easy to calculate and only requires a few minutes of survey data. For these reasons, the NPS has become one of the most popular measures of customer satisfaction worldwide.

13. *Customer Satisfaction Score (CSAT)*: The customer satisfaction score (CSAT) is a widely used metric for measuring customer satisfaction. It simply asks customers how satisfied they are with a product or service on a scale of 1-5, with 5 being very satisfied. The CSAT can be used to

measure satisfaction with a specific interaction or experience, or it can be used as a more general measure of customer satisfaction with a company or brand.

There are a few reasons why the CSAT is so important. First, it's a direct measure of customer satisfaction. This means that it can give you an immediate sign of whether or not customers are happy with your business. Secondly, the CSAT is highly correlated with other important measures of customer loyalty, such as purchase intent and brand loyalty. This means that if your customers are satisfied, they're more likely to do business with you again in the future. Finally, the CSAT can be used to benchmark your performance against other companies in your industry. This allows you to see where you need to improve to compete effectively for customers.

Building a Product Dashboard: Five Steps

Once you've identified your product's KPIs, the next task is to build out a product dashboard. A product dashboard is a visual display of all the key metrics and data related to your product. This can include everything from customer acquisition and retention rates to gross margin and revenue. By tracking these KPIs regularly, you can get a clear picture of how your product is performing and make necessary adjustments to ensure its continued success. By visualizing the data and sharing your dashboard with your team and maybe your org's leadership, you're setting expectations and communicating your progress towards the goals regularly.

So how do you go about creating a product dashboard? Here are five key steps.

1. *Set goals*: What do you want to learn from your dashboard? What strategies do you want to execute? What decisions do you want to be able to make? Be specific.
2. *Determine relevant KPIs*: Use the information we've provided in this chapter to identify key metrics that will help you achieve your goals. Again, be specific.
3. *Source and collect data*: Do you need real-time data? Operations tend to be real-time. Strategic and financial metrics tend to lag. Business analysis tends to compare the current view with historical trends. Data may come from internal sources like your accounting or CRM system, or external sources like market research firms. Make sure you have the data you need to answer your questions. Consistent access to quality data is key here.
4. *Create useful visualizations*: Data viz can be a bit of an art form, but it doesn't have to be that complex. For starters, just choose the right chart or graph for the data you're trying to communicate. Keep it simple and easy to understand. You can always add detail down the road if it brings additional value.
5. *Automate and publish*: Dashboards should be live and up-to-date. Automate data collection and updates so you can focus on using the dashboard, not maintaining it. There are several SaaS tools available to create, share and automate your dashboards, so you might consider that if you want something a little more sophisticated than a Google doc.

Creating a product dashboard may seem like a lot of work, but it's a significant value for any entrepreneur who wants to keep track of their product's progress on a regular basis.

Final Thoughts on KPIs

In conclusion, KPIs are an important tool for product leaders, but it's critical to choose the right KPIs for your product. There are a few things to keep in mind when choosing KPIs, such as making sure they're aligned with your business goals and that they're actionable and measurable. Common KPIs for products include the number daily of active users, churn rate and Customer Lifetime Value. You can use KPIs to measure success by tracking whether or not a product is on track to meet its goals, comparing a product's performance against competitors, or monitoring changes in a product over time.

When using KPIs, it's important to make sure your team is aware of them and understands their importance and uses data from your KPIs to drive action and improve your product. Sharing them on a dashboard can help in this area. Review your KPIs regularly and make changes as business needs evolve. By following these tips, you can choose the right KPIs for your product and use them effectively to measure success.

TL;DR

• KPIs are Key Performance Indicators that provide quantitative measure of team performance and help identify where improvement is needed.

• Before selecting KPIs, make sure they are actionable and measurable - otherwise no real progress can be made. Ensure that they align with business goals and that data is accessible for consistent tracking over time.

• Data must be consistently and accurately collected in order for KPIs to provide useful performance tracking.

• In the chapter, we identify thirteen common KPI used to measure product performance. These include Monthly Recurring Revenue

(MRR), Customer Lifetime Value (CLV), Customer Acquisition Cost (CAC), Daily Active Users (DAU), Monthly Active Users (MAU), Bounce Rate, Retention Rate, Churn Rate, Revenue Churn, Total Support Calls, Support Escalations, Net Promoter Score (NPS) and Customer Satisfaction Score (CSAT).

- A product dashboard is a visual display of all the key metrics and data related to your product.
- Five key steps to build a product dashboard are setting goals; determining the relevant KPIs; source and collect data; create visualizations; and finally, automate and publish.
- Consistent access to quality data is essential to establishing KPIs and displaying them on a dashboard.

CHAPTER EXERCISES

1. Identify one or two current goals for your product or organization. You can use one that you're familiar with if you don't have a current product. What are three KPIs that would align with these goals and effectively drive performance to meet them?
2. Think about these three KPIs and write down any options you can come up with for sourcing the required data so that they could be measured consistently over time.
3. Imagine a scenario in which one of the three KPIs changes significantly in a negative direction. What are some possible reasons for this change and what actions might you propose to restore them to expected levels?

CHAPTER NOTES

CHAPTER 21: Going Beyond Product-Market Fit

You probably know that Marc Andreessen is an American entrepreneur, investor, and software engineer. He co-authored the code for the first web browser, Mosaic. He is the co-founder of Netscape and Opsware, and a co-founder of Andreessen Horowitz, a venture capital firm. He also sits on the boards of directors for eBay, Facebook, and Hewlett-Packard. In his role as a venture capitalist, Andreessen has been an early investor in several companies, including Skype, Twitter, and Oculus VR. He was one of the six initial inductees into the World Wide Web Hall of Fame in 1994. Some would call him the Internet's GOAT or at least put him on the web's Mount Rushmore.

In 2007, Andreessen published a blog post called "The only thing that matters" in which he reflected on a term coined by Andy Rachleff – "product-market fit." According to Rachleff's law of startup success, "When a great team meets a great market, market wins. When a lousy team meets a great market, market wins." Andreessen concludes that "the only thing that matters is getting to product-market fit," which he defines as "being in a good market with a product that can satisfy that market."

As you might imagine, because of Andreessen's stature and strong declaration, product-market fit (PMF) became a cottage industry with books, blogs, and consultants swarming around it. You couldn't live in startup land without it dripping off the tongue of nearly every VC or investor. In this chapter, we'll try to get a better understanding of product-market fit, look at some ways to measure it and compare it to some other models to see if it's really the "only thing that matters."

Taking a Closer Look at PMF

It is certainly true that PMF is critical for any company to be successful. Simply put, PMF is the degree to which a product satisfies the needs of a particular market. For a company to be successful, its product must have PMF.

There are four main indicators of PMF:

1. The product is solving a problem that people in the market actually have.
2. There is a large enough market for the product.
3. The product can be differentiated from other products in the market.
4. The product is appealing to the target market.

If a company can create a product that hits all four of these indicators, it will be well on its way to success. However, it should be noted that even if a product has PMF, it is still possible for the company to fail if they are unable to execute it properly. Execution is key, and often it can be the difference between a successful company and one that fails. So, while having a product-market fit is important, it is only one piece of the puzzle. Companies need to make sure they can execute their vision to be truly successful.

A lot of people in startups think that PMF is important because they need to meet the needs of the market and, of course, that's true. But it also becomes a bit of a self-fulfilling concept because it's become so ingrained in the investor world. Since the people with the money have decided it's important, it's important. Full stop. Now I'm not arguing that a solution that has a clearly identified, robust market and meets that market's needs isn't important, just that maybe it's been given outsized importance relative to some other critical elements that can also make or break a business. It might not be the **only** thing that matters.

To find PMF, it's important to focus on the market first. There's a lot of debate about what makes a great market, but some experts say it's important to have 1000 true fans and it's definitely true that you need 1000 fans before you can get to 1M of them. Others say it's simply a large scalable market.

Trying to be all things to all people to grow your market is a recipe for disaster. If you do the things that grow your base of fans, you'll likely have product-market fit. But be careful — adding things that dilute your product for your core fans to try to attract more general customers can break your product-market fit. Imagine you've built a base of followers for your electronic dance music (EDM) playlist on Spotify. Adding Taylor Swift tracks to broaden your subscribers may temporarily boost your sub numbers. But you're likely to end up with a playlist that makes neither your old fans nor the new Swift-loving adds happy. The Swifties won't stay, and your old fans may abandon you, leaving you with lower numbers than you had before you made the ill-fated additions.

At some level, the size of your market depends on whether you're trying to build the next Facebook or a local shoe repair shop. But either way, it's helpful to start with a great market that you're already a part of. From there, you can start to identify problems that, if solved, would drive value to that market. Only then should you start thinking about product solutions.

Back to "the only thing that matters," Andreessen offers that "In a great market—a market with lots of real potential customers—the market pulls product out of the startup." In other words, in a truly massive and growing market, the most successful startups are those that can quickly adapt their products to meet the market needs of their customers. The one that most successfully does this the soonest is the likely market winner.

Please Don't "Fail Fast"

Of course, this is easier said than done. It requires a strong focus on the "build, measure, learn" cycle popularized by Eric Ries and known as the Lean Startup Methodology. We'll talk about that more elsewhere in the book. Startups need to constantly be testing and iterating their products, making small adjustments along the way until they find a product that resonates with users. Only then can they hope to scale up and achieve true success.

You might have heard someone call this iterative process "failing fast." The idea is that, to succeed, you need to be willing to fail – and fail quickly. This means that you need to put yourself out there and try new things, even if you're not sure you'll be successful. It also means that you need to be willing to accept failure when it happens and learn from your mistakes. By failing fast, you can quickly find what doesn't work and move on to something that does.

Andreessen's take here is better, in my opinion. "The goal is not to fail fast. The goal is to succeed over the long run. They are not the same thing." I'll add my addendum to this – "Don't fail, but if you must, please fail productively." Learn your lessons from the experience. Some of my best work was on projects that failed and sometimes the lessons I learned from that failure helped set up the next success. So don't be afraid of failing but don't make it your goal either.

How To Measure Product-Market Fit

There's no single agreed-upon definition or metric for product-market fit, but there are a few ways to think about it. One of the most common analogies is the dating relationship: when you meet someone and just "know" that they're the one for you, that's product-market fit. You have a strong feeling that this is the right thing for you and everything clicks. Not very scientific, though. Another way to think about it is whether your product solves a real, pressing need for your target market. If you've built something that people need and they're using it regularly, you probably have product-market fit. If you're making money, there's some degree of PMF for at least some part of your market.

Finally, you can measure it more concretely by looking at engagement and retention metrics. If people are using your product frequently and don't churn off into the void, that's usually a good sign that you've achieved PMF. The key here is to focus on frequent regular usage that drives your business model and generates revenue.

There are a few other common metrics that startups use to measure product-market fit, including the Pirate Metric and the Rule of 40:

The Pirate Metric, also known as AARRR, is a framework for measuring PMF that was popularized by startup advisor and investor Dave McClure. It stands for Acquisition, Activation, Retention, Referral, and Revenue. To measure product-market fit using this metric, startups need to track how many people they acquire as users, how many of those users become active (engage with the product), how many of them stick around long-term (retention), how many refer new users (virality), and finally, how much revenue they generate.

The Rule of 40 is another common metric. The rule states that at scale, a company's revenue growth plus profit margin should equal or exceed 40%. This metric was popularized by venture capitalist Peter Thiel and is often used by VC firms to assess whether a startup is on track to achieve product-market fit.

There are also more qualitative ways to measure PMF, like *user surveys*. User surveys can be a useful tool for measuring PMF, but it's important to keep in mind that they have their limitations. For one, user surveys can be susceptible to bias and may not always give an accurate picture of how people are feeling about a product. Additionally, in the Software-as-a-Service (SaaS) world, user surveys only measure actual users of the product. This means that they don't take into account people who have heard of the product but haven't tried it yet, which can be a significant portion of the potential market. We mentioned one popular tool for conducting user surveys in the last chapter – the Net Promoter Score or NPS. NPS surveys ask users how likely they are to recommend a product to a friend or colleague on a scale of 0 to 10. The results of NPS surveys can be helpful for startups to gauge how well their product is resonating with users and whether they've achieved PMF.

Retention and churn also are important metrics to measure product-market fit because they show whether users are using the product and sticking around long-term. A high retention rate suggests that users are finding value in the product and are less likely to churn (cancel their subscription or stop using the product). A low churn rate indicates that once people start using the product, they stick around and continue using it.

There are a few different ways to calculate retention and churn. The most common is to look at *cohort retention*, which measures the percentage of users that remain active in a given period (usually monthly or weekly). For example, if you have a cohort of one hundred users and sixty of them are still using the product after one month, your retention rate would be 60%.

Another way to measure retention is *stickiness*, which measures how often users come back to the product. This can be calculated by looking at the number of days between each user's logins. The higher the stickiness, the more likely it is that users are finding value in the product and are less likely to churn.

Churn, on the other hand, is the percentage of users that cancel their subscription or stop using the product. For example, if you have a cohort of one hundred users and ten of them cancel their subscription after one month, your churn rate would be 10%.

Churn and retention can be a big deal. One of Marc Andreessen's partners at Andreessen Horowitz, former Uber executive Andrew Chen, blogged about an analysis of Quettra's usage statistics from over 125 million Android mobile phones. There's a massive difference in the sixty-day retention rate between the top ten apps (55 percent), the next fifty (40 percent), the next 100 (21 percent), and the next 5,000 apps (11 percent). The average of all apps was just seven percent. So just one of 14 new users you get today will still be using your Android app in 60 days.

No one said this was going to be easy.

The Killer PMF Question

If you're not familiar with Sean Ellis, he's the guy who popularized the term "growth hacking." He also came up with this killer question to help companies measure product-market fit: "How would you feel if you could no longer use ___?" This question is so simple, but it's such a powerful way to gauge user sentiment. And it can be a leading indicator of success, improvement, or trouble.

Typically, the user is presented with multiple-choice answers. If most users answer "very disappointed," then you probably have a good product on your hands. If they answer "somewhat disappointed," then there's room for improvement. And if they answer "not disappointed," then you might have a problem. You can keep asking this question over time and use the change in responses to track your progress and improvements. SaaS products can ask this from time to time with a basic pop-up, making it easy to gather from users.

So, we said at the beginning of this chapter that PMF wasn't the only thing that matters, then we've spent the whole chapter so far talking about how to get it and measure it. What gives?

Problems With PMF

The problem with assessing PMF alone is that it's not enough for business success. Too often, entrepreneurs think that if they can just find the right market, everything will fall into place. But the reality is that even if you have a great product, it's not guaranteed to find a receptive audience. There are a lot of factors that go into making a successful business, and product/market fit is just one piece of the puzzle. To be successful, you need to have a deep understanding of your target market, a well-defined value proposition, and a go-to-market strategy that resonates with your audience. Without all of these pieces in place, it'll be very difficult to find long-term success.

Some people think that if they build a product that perfectly fits a market need, they will automatically be successful. But that's not always the case. Just because you have a great product that people love and you know the price that the market will pay, it doesn't mean you can sell it profitably at the price and volumes you need to be successful. This is a problem that Andreessen's framework seems to assume away.

What if, for example, the market is big but shrinking? Keep in mind that PMF isn't permanent, and competition can always enter or adjust. So even if you have a great product that perfectly fits the market, you need to constantly be aware of changes in the market and adjust your strategy accordingly. Remember that PMF was initially just a benchmark for investment. Those investments don't come with a money-back guarantee.

The Other Fits That Matter

In his blog post "Product-Market Fit Isn't Enough," Brian Balfour adds channel and business models fit to product and market, creating four "Fits."

Balfour's four Fit models are:

1. Product-Market Fit
2. Product-Channel Fit
3. Market-Business Model Fit
4. Business Model-Channel Fit

We've spent the rest of the chapter looking at the first one, PMF, so let's take a closer look at the other three now.

Product-Channel Fit - Product-channel fit is the concept of matching a product to the best channel for its distribution. This involves understanding the different channels available, such as retail stores or e-commerce sites, and selecting the ones most likely to be successful for the product. It also requires an understanding of how each channel works and what type of marketing tactics work best for it. Finally, a good product-channel fit will ensure that customers have easy access to the product in order to ensure its success.

Ask yourself whether the channel you're using to sell your product is the right one. If you're trying to sell a unique sensory experience like a specialty food product, maybe you should be sampling it at Costco instead of just selling it online. Think of situations where different products might be required based on different channels – for example, fast food versus sit-down high-end restaurants, or video games on a mobile device compared to a similar game on a PS5. In either case, the scaled-back product likely fails to impress on a premium channel.

Business Model-Channel Fit - When trying to create alignment between a product's business model and the channels used to sell the product, it is important to consider the differences between each channel. Each channel has its own unique advantages and challenges that must be understood in order to create successful alignment. Certain business models are better suited for certain channels than others.

For example, subscription-based businesses may find more success in e-commerce platforms than traditional retail stores. On the other hand, products with high price tags might be best suited for brick and mortar stores due to the potential customer interaction. Ultimately, understanding the strengths and weaknesses of each channel will help guide decisions on creating effective alignment between a product's business model and its sales channels.

Market-Business Model Fit - When creating alignment between a product's market and its business model, it is important to understand the customer needs in that market. If a product is being offered in a particular market, you must consider what needs it fulfills for that customer and how your business model helps satisfy those needs. Different business models can work better in different markets based on customer needs.

A "freemium" model may be more successful in digital markets with low barriers to entry where the users have sufficient resources to upgrade to a premium version of the service. In situations where the target market is cash-strapped, like say the student market, an ad-based model that requires no payment at all could be more successful. Similarly, a premium subscription model may be more popular in B2B markets where they can capture the full value of the service from the business customer. Ultimately, understanding the target market and their needs will help guide decisions when selecting a business model for success.

Of course, everyone's focused on PMF, but to increase the chances of success, it's important to also be aware of the other three Fits. Each Fit is equally important, and if any one of them is off, the product can fail to get traction. The best way to ensure all four Fits are in alignment is to have a clear understanding of the problem you're solving, your target market, your solution, and your business model. Once you have a clear vision for all four of these areas, you can then start to align your product with the right market, your business model with the right channel, and so on. By taking a holistic approach to the Fits, you can increase your chances of success and avoid the common pitfalls that often lead to failure.

In conclusion, product-market fit (PMF) is an essential part of a startup or product's success, but it is not the only factor that matters. For example, it doesn't guarantee that a product can be sold profitably at scale. Entrepreneurs need to consider not just whether their product fits a market, but also their go-to-market strategy, value proposition and target market. Additionally, entrepreneurs should be aware of Brian Balfour's four "Fits" – Product-Market Fit, Product-Channel Fit Market-Business Model Fit, and Business Model Channel Fit – which all contribute to the success of a product. Understanding each of these factors will help entrepreneurs better position their products and services for long-term success.

TL;DR

- In 2007, Marc Andreessen published a blog post called "The only thing that matters" which reflected on Andy Rachleff's law of startup success: "When a great team meets a great market, market wins. When a lousy team meets a great market, market wins." He concluded that product-market fit (PMF) was the only thing that mattered for startup success.

- Product-Market Fit (PMF) is defined as being in a good market with a product that can satisfy that market and it's critical for any company to be successful.
- There are four main indicators of PMF: 1) The product solves a problem people have; 2) There's enough demand; 3) It has differentiation from other products; 4) It appeals to its target audience.
- Execution plays just as important a role in success as having PMF—startups need to constantly test and iterate their products until they find something that resonates with users.
- Failing fast isn't necessarily helpful, but learning lessons from failure can be productive when done right, so don't be afraid of failing but make sure you fail productively if necessary!
- To measure PMF there are quantitative metrics such as Pirate Metric (AARRR), The Rule of 40 or qualitative methods like Net Promoter Score or user surveys. Retention and churn are also important ways to measure PMF.
- Sean Ellis popularized the term "growth hacking" and came up with a killer question to measure product-market fit: "How would you feel if you could no longer use _?" This question can be used as an indicator of success, improvement, or trouble. It is typically presented with multiple choice answers that gauge user sentiment.
- Product-market fit alone is not enough for business success; entrepreneurs need to understand their target market, value proposition and go-to-market strategy in order to find long-term success.
- Brian Balfour added channel and business models into the equation, creating a total of four "Fits" - Product-Market Fit, Product- Channel Fit, Market-Business Model Fit, and Business Model-

Channel Fit - which all must be considered along with PMF in order to increase chances of a product's success.

CHAPTER EXERCISES

1. Think about your product or a product you have used before. How well do you think it meets the four main indicators of PMF?
    a. The product is solving a problem that people in the market actually have
    b. There is a large enough market for the product
    c. The product can be differentiated from other products in the market
    d. The product is appealing to the target market
2. Have you ever used a product that isn't available anymore? Using Balfour's Four Fits, come up with a theory about why the product might have failed and what they might have done differently.

CHAPTER NOTES

CHAPTER 22: Achieving Long-Term Product-Business Strategy Alignment

Product-business strategy alignment is essential for any business that wants to succeed in the long term. By aligning your product strategy with the overall goal of the business, you can ensure that your work is focused and aligned with the company's goals. This can be a difficult task, but by following some of the suggestions in this chapter, you can improve your chances of success.

When I was at Sprint, it was rare that we had a clearly defined and widely communicated business strategy. But a couple of examples come to mind. In 1998, then-CEO Bill Esrey had the entire company focused on delivering Sprint ION. This ground-breaking service would use the emerging high-speed internet market to deliver converged data, voice, and video to the home. At the time, it was a product that the Yankee Group called "visionary."

However, the investment in building the infrastructure that ION needed proved to be too much, resulting in a $3 billion loss and 6000 people laid off in the fall of 2001. Worse, by shutting down this project and eliminating the core vision that the entire company was focused on executing without replacing it with something else, the entire company was set adrift for the next several years as they sorted through the wreckage.

Fast forward to December 2007, Sprint was struggling to integrate with Nextel, with whom they had merged in 2005. They brought on board new CEO Dan Hesse, who took one look at the financial fiasco on the books and, two months later in February 2008, Sprint wrote off $29.7 billion of the $36 billion spent on the merger. How'd you like to pull the trigger on that decision in your first two months in a new job?

After that, Hesse focused the company like a laser on retaining customers and reducing churn. Every company-wide meeting reinforced this message and performance goals were tied to it. The results were impressive. From Dan Hesse's Wikipedia page:

> "During Hesse's tenure, Sprint went from last place to first in the wireless industry in customer satisfaction according to JD Power and the American Customer Satisfaction Index (ACSI). During this period, Sprint was recognized 20 times for excellence in customer service by JD Power. In 2014, the ACSI recognized Sprint as the most improved US company in customer satisfaction over the previous six years among all 43 industries studied. During his last two full calendar years as CEO, Sprint's total shareholder return ranked #1 among all S&P 500 companies."

In 2016, Fierce Wireless named Hesse one of the "best turnaround CEOs of all time." This is the power of focusing your organization on a clear and compelling business-level strategy.

In large companies, like Sprint was then with 30,000 employees, business strategies tend to be simple — "Reduce churn!" — but they probably need to be. In a company that large, it can be tough to have a line of sight between your day-to-day work and the company's goals. Entire teams can work quietly on projects for months, even years, which have no real connection to the core business. If the business is making money overall and no one's looking too closely, they can afford to waste... uh... "invest" resources in a pet project.

But this isn't just a large company problem. Smaller companies have alignment issues too. Except, in this case, they can be company-killers. When you don't have a lot of resources available, you can't afford to waste them.

The Case for Product-Business Alignment

Every company has a story. It's the narrative that explains who they are, what they do, and why customers should care. When you're developing a new product, it's important to ask yourself how it contributes to the business's story. Does it fit with the overall narrative? Does it help to advance the story? If not, you might want to rethink your product. Ask yourself, "How is this product contributing to the business's success?" After all, every product should be working towards the same goal: helping the company succeed. By aligning your product with the company's story, you can ensure that it makes a valuable contribution to the business's success.

If you don't see alignment, ask yourself why. Are you gold-plating everything while your company is trying to be the low-cost solution? Or maybe you're building a stripped-down product while your org is positioning itself as a premium-priced brand?

Maybe you're wondering why other projects in your organization seem to get all the visibility. But if you're not well-aligned with the business strategy, you're going to be working a lot harder for everything you do, while the resources flow to other projects. Being aligned with the company's narrative helps you get prioritized for resources. Or maybe it's the other way. Being prioritized for resources helps get you aligned with the company's narrative. Or maybe it's both. Either way, your life will be a lot easier if you can show how your work helps contribute to the company's big picture.

Your team can sense when they're working on projects that aren't aligned with the business. They see other teams getting all the attention. Maybe they also see money and promotions going to other people too. This can be a huge source of stress and poor morale.

Misaligned projects and the people working on them are often first on the chopping block when budget cuts or layoffs happen.

But when people see how what they do daily contributes to the company's success, it can be a major motivator. Maybe you've seen it in your company. The employees who feel the most ownership of their work and who have the greatest sense of control over their destiny are also the ones who are the most engaged and produce the best results. When people have a clear understanding of how their efforts contribute to the success of the company, it gives them a sense of purpose and belonging that is hard to match.

This is one of the things that makes working at a startup so special. Because it's easier to align with others and see your direct impact in a smaller company, there's a shared sense of mission and purpose that is palpable in every interaction between employees. And it's one of the things that attracts top talent to startups in the first place. At its best, working at a startup is about being part of something mission-driven that feels larger than yourself, something that is constantly evolving and changing. It's an opportunity to be part of a team that is building something new and exciting, something that has the potential to change the world. And when you understand how your daily work contributes to that larger goal, it can be immensely motivating.

But whether you work in a large or small organization, there's one important thing that you should be taking the opportunity to do. Know how to communicate your alignment to others, especially the leaders in your company, and do it regularly. This helps everyone better understand your product's value and contribution to the company's success.

You're mirroring the company's strategic language back to your leadership. Something like this...

Company: "We want to do Thing A."
You: "Our product helps us do Thing A and here's how."

Goodness follows.

Some Tips to Help Communicate Alignment

How do you signal to others that you're aligned with the company's goals? In other words, how do you let them know that you're on the same page and working towards the same objectives? It's important to be able to communicate this alignment, especially to leaders in your company. Here are a few tips:

1. Be clear about your own goals and objectives. It's hard to be aligned with someone else if you're not clear about your direction. Take some time to think about what you want to achieve and the ways you might go about accomplishing those goals in your current role.
2. Make an effort to understand the company's goals. It's not enough to simply know what those goals are - you need to understand why they're important and how they fit into the big picture. Take some time to talk to your manager or other leaders in the company to get a better sense of the overall strategy.
3. Be proactive in aligning your work with the company's goals. Once you have a good understanding of the company's objectives, take the initiative in aligning your work with those goals. Seek out opportunities to contribute and look for ways to make a positive impact.
4. Keep communication channels open. Good communication is essential for maintaining alignment. Proper alignment is not a one-and-done event. Make sure that you're keeping lines of communication open with your manager and other key stakeholders. You can do this formally with regularly

scheduled meetings, status reports and one-on-one's or informally with coffees, lunches and happy hours. Either approach should help ensure that everyone is on the same page and working towards the same objectives.
5. Be flexible and adaptable. As the company's objectives change, so should your own. Stay limber and be prepared to adjust your goals as the company's needs evolve.

Alignment is not a static state - it's an ongoing process. By following these tips, you can ensure that you're always working towards the same goals as the rest of your company. But there's also a more literal level of alignment that you can achieve using the Strategy Alignment template included here.

Step one - Align the "whys" - First you're going to make sure that there's an alignment between your vision and the company's overall direction from a business standpoint. Note that from your side, all of these points of alignment can come from a completed One-Page Product Plan (see Chapter 14 for more detail).

Step two - Align the "hows" - Next, you'll make sure that there's an alignment between business strategies. A premium product strategy in a discount-focused business is going to struggle.

Step three - Align the "whats and whens" - Finally, you'll do the important step of aligning your goals and OKRs with the business. If the business is focused on revenues first, you'll want to consider that before making a product-level decision that would move resources away from that effort.

After completing each step, compare them side-by-side in the next template. They don't have to be identical, but they should feel to each other can be a real eye opener. If you have a lot of unaligned strategies, first ask yourself if you're missing anything. Frequently, the misalignment is just because you have some unstated or undocumented goals, so this is a chance to capture the missing items.

Strategy Alignment

	BUSINESS	PRODUCT
WHY?	**Vision:** Put your business's vision here.	**Vision:** Put your product's vision here and compare to the business vision.
HOW?	**Strategy:** Put one of your business's strategies here.	**Strategy:** Put one of your product's strategies here and compare to the business strategy.
	Strategy:	**Strategy:**
	Strategy:	**Strategy:**
	Strategy:	**Strategy:**
WHAT & WHEN?	**OKR/Goal:** Put one of your business's OKRs or goals here.	**OKR/Goal:** Put one of your product's OKRs or goals here and compare to the business OKR/goal.
	OKR/Goal:	**OKR/Goal:**
	OKR/Goal:	**OKR/Goal:**
	OKR/Goal:	**OKR/Goal:**

If it's not a matter of missing or undocumented goals, you have a decision to make — broaden your strategy to include the misaligned items, reprioritize your work to move the better-aligned work into your strategy, or put the deviating items into a parking lot for consideration at a future time when they might be a better fit.

In the end, there should be a clear logical thread from your company's overall vision and strategy to every tactical-level decision made for your product. If you can't see the thread, ask yourself if you need to do the project.

Business > Product Alignment

- Business Vision
- Business Goals & OKRs
- Business Strategies
- Product Vision
- Product Goals & OKRs
- Product Strategies
- Product Themes & Features
- Product Tactics
- Product Specs/User Stories

In some situations, you might answer that, despite the misalignment, yes, you do need to do the work. Maybe you're working on a stealth project that doesn't show up on the overall company radar yet. Or maybe you feel that the work needs to be done while you lobby your leadership to better align the company strategy with the product's strategy. Make your case to the decision-makers.

But apart from these exclusions, once you've completed this exercise, there should be alignment at the vision/strategy/OKRs level. If so, the product should be well-aligned to the business. Now it's time to circle back to the stakeholders to confirm this alignment. Doing this will strengthen your product's position and the leaders' perception of it organizationally.

What If There Is No Company Strategy?

As a product leader, you're likely always looking for new ways to optimize and grow your business. But what if your company doesn't have a formal business strategy? How can you align your product strategy in this case?

First, it's important to see if there is a formal business strategy in place that just isn't widely shared or well communicated. Maybe it's sitting on someone's laptop somewhere. If this is the case, you may be able to increase its visibility from the bottom up. But if there really is no formal business strategy in place, try to identify some typical or basic business strategies that your company could benefit from, such as increasing sales, expanding markets, reducing care calls, simplifying processes, improving user experience, and reducing costs, or becoming more efficient. By aligning your product strategy with these general business goals, you can help move your company forward even without a formal business strategy in place.

In conclusion, establishing alignment between a company's overall business strategy and product strategy is essential for optimizing resources and contributing to success. It requires a deep understanding of the company's narrative and objectives, clear communication channels with leadership, proactive efforts to connect work with strategic objectives, and flexibility in response to changes. The Strategy Alignment template included in this chapter can be used as a tool to align vision, strategies, goals, and timelines. In the absence of a formal business strategy, typical goals such as increasing sales or improving user experience can be used as a guide for product strategies. Following these guidelines, companies of all sizes can ensure that their products are contributing to the overall success of the organization.

TL;DR
- Companies of all sizes need to ensure their product strategy is aligned with the company's overall narrative and goals in order to maximize resources and contribution to success.
- To ensure alignment, it is essential to understand the company's story and narrative and how your product contributes to it.
- Communicating alignment with leadership is essential - mirror the company's language back to them and stay in frequent contact.
- Achieving alignment requires understanding your own goals, knowing the company's objectives, being proactive in connecting your work with strategic objectives, maintaining clear communication channels, and remaining flexible and adaptable in response to changes.
- The Strategy Alignment template helps to align "whys" (vision), "hows" (strategies), and "whats & whens" (goals).
- If there is no formal business strategy in place, align product strategies with typical goals such as increasing sales, expanding

markets, reducing care calls, simplifying processes, improving user experience, or reducing costs.

CHAPTER EXERCISES

1. Take some time to identify your goals and objectives for your product. If you did the One-Page Product Plan previously, you should have this done.
2. If you don't already have access to the company's overall strategy, start asking around. If needed, explain that you're trying to make sure that your product is aligned with the business strategy.
3. Fill out the Strategy Alignment template with both the product and business strategies and fine tune your product strategy to improve alignment.
4. Write down some ideas on the best language to communicate your product's overall alignment with the business so that you're ready the next time you have an opportunity to talk to someone at higher levels in the business.

CHAPTER NOTES

CHAPTER 23: Van Halen And (Not The) WHO – How To Use A Checklist For Your Next Product Launch

David Lee Roth is a legendary American rock musician, best known as the charismatic lead vocalist of Van Halen. During the 1980s, he dazzled audiences with his dynamic stage presence and athletic performances involving high kicks and acrobatics. In recognition of his contributions to music, Roth has been inducted into the Rock and Roll Hall of Fame, and Rolling Stone magazine ranked him among the 100 Greatest Singers of All Time. Aside from his musical prowess, Roth is also renowned for his offbeat sense of humor. One famous example is how he included a unique clause in Van Halen's concert contracts requiring that all brown M&M's be removed from a bowl provided to them backstage. If this seemingly frivolous request was not met, it would result in forfeiture of the show's revenue.

At the time, this request was held up as an example of the kind of ridiculous excess that only rock stars could get away with. But the reality behind the legend was a much more pragmatic one. Despite its absurdity, this quirky demand actually served as a clever way for Roth to ensure that promoters were carefully reading every detail of their contract rider to ensure safety requirements had also been met.

As Roth tells the story, "There would be no brown M&M's found in the backstage area or the promoter would forfeit the entire show at full pay. This was touted widely as simple rock star misdemeanor excess and abusive of others simply because we could. Who am I to get in the way of a good rumor?

"In fact, the reality was quite different. Van Halen was the first to take 850 par lamp lights — huge lights — around the country,"

Roth said. "At the time, it was the biggest production ever. Getting it in and out of older buildings like the Spectrum in Philadelphia where the hockey team played, these buildings were built in the 50s, 60s, and 70s and they didn't have even the doorways or the loading docks to accommodate a super forward-thinking Gigantor epic-sized Van Halen production.

"The promoters would frequently not read the contract rider and we would have structural and fiscal issues because, hey, there wasn't the proper electricity, load-bearing stress, etc. So in the middle of a huge contract rider — most bands were like a pamphlet, we had one that was like the phone book — and in the very middle of it, I had them place... that there would be no brown M&Ms found in the backstage area.

"What was the point? If I came backstage, having been one of the architects of this lighting and staging design, and I saw brown M&Ms on the catering table, then I guarantee the promoter had not read the contract rider, and we would have to do a serious line check."

Roth was using the rider as a quick mental checklist for making sure that they'd have a safe stage for their extravaganza. The provision ensured that promoters would take care of all the details needed to repeatedly set up and tear down all the equipment as they moved from city to city. Effectively, the band and crew were doing a new product launch in each arena in front of a new crowd each night. The brown M&M's were the canary in the coal mine as to whether they were likely to have any issues.

This chapter delves into the crucial role that checklists play in successful product launches. Checklists are an invaluable tool that can help maintain consistency and coordination throughout the entire product launch process. They offer a systematic approach to identifying key tasks, ensuring all necessary details are covered, and streamlining communication across teams. By using a checklist, product leaders can effectively track progress, identify potential roadblocks, and mitigate risks before they become bigger issues. Additionally, checklists provide a clear framework for quality control and can be easily updated as new information becomes available. With the implementation of a comprehensive checklist for your next product launch, you can significantly increase your chances of success by ensuring that no detail is overlooked, and every team member is aligned towards achieving the same goal.

How A Simple Checklist Saves Lives

In 2008, the World Health Organization (WHO, not the classic rock band *The* Who) called out a major problem with the safety of surgery around the world. Per their website:

"While surgical procedures are intended to save lives, unsafe surgical care can cause substantial harm. Given the ubiquity of surgery, this has significant implications:

- The reported crude mortality rate after major surgery is 0.5-5%;
- Complications after inpatient operations occur in up to 25% of patients;
- In industrialized countries, nearly half of all adverse events in hospitalized patients are related to surgical care;
- At least half of the cases in which surgery led to harm are considered preventable;
- Mortality from general anesthesia alone is reported to be as high as one in 150 in some parts of sub-Saharan Africa."

This WHO study had a profound impact on the medical community. Above all, the study found that a simple checklist, used during surgery, could dramatically reduce the rate of complications and death. In the wake of these findings, WHO created the Surgical Safety Checklist. The checklist is designed to be used during three key phases of surgery: before anesthesia is administered, before an incision is made, and before the patient leaves the operating room.

The checklist includes nineteen different items, such as verifying the patient's identity and confirming that all necessary equipment is available. It's a simple list and takes about two minutes to complete. To date, there have been over 100 studies evaluating the impact of the checklist. The findings are unequivocal: implementation of the checklist leads to safer surgery with fewer complications and lower mortality rates. Prior to the checklist, one survey estimated globally that 234 million surgeries were done annually with 1 million people dying due to surgical complications. Per the WHO website, there's been a thirty percent reduction in complications and mortality where the WHO Surgical Safety Checklist has been implemented. This list is saving hundreds of thousands of lives every year.

In any complex undertaking, whether it's putting on a rock concert, performing life-saving surgery, or launching a new product, it's important to have a checklist to help ensure that everything is taken care of. A checklist provides a framework for getting everything done and helps to ensure that no important tasks are forgotten. It can also be a useful tool for keeping track of progress and spotting potential problems early on.

Using a Product Checklist

The pressure to launch a product can be immense. Companies invest massive amounts of time and money into research and development, and they want to see a return on their investment as soon as possible. However, rushing a product to market can often lead to disastrous results. One reason why companies struggle with launches is that they don't get repeatable processes in place. Without a launch process, teams across the organization don't know what to expect as everyone's scrambling to hit the launch date and, frequently, the result is chaos.

If you're launching a new product, a checklist can be essential for making sure that all the necessary steps are taken and that nothing is left to chance. It can help to ensure that the product is developed on schedule, that marketing and sales plans are in place, and that all the necessary regulatory approvals have been obtained. A checklist can also help track progress and troubleshoot any problems that arise along the way. In short, using a checklist helps make launching a new product a smoother, more successful and repeatable process.

Checklists are a powerful tool for making sure that everything is taken care of before product launches. It's a complex undertaking with a lot of moving parts. A *product launch checklist* helps to make launches more consistent and ensure that everyone is on the same page. Often, a small detail, once missed, can end up having a big impact. Or maybe something's delayed because a key dependency slipped. By documenting everything you've learned in your checklist, you make sure that you don't forget something. If by chance something does manage to slip through the cracks, add it to the checklist and only make the mistake of omission or delay just once.

It can also help to communicate and coordinate across an organization, ensuring that everyone knows what needs to be done and when it needs to be done. By following a checklist, businesses can launch their products with confidence, knowing that they have everything under control.

Introducing the 58-Point Product Launch Checklist

Eventually, you'll want to develop your own product launch checklist, as you'll very likely have specific items that need to be done as part of your company's processes. But you can start with the 58-point checklist that we've included here, using it as a first pass. You might also move some of the items between required and optional status, but this is a good start.

Here's a quick walkthrough of our sample template with a little explanatory detail to give you a feel for the types of questions you should be answering:

REQUIRED:
- Clearly defined product user stories/use cases/business requirements - If you're building the product, you're going to need to know what to build, document the details and be able to share it with others.
- Business model(s) - How are you going to make money?
- Financial analysis/business case - Looking at the risk versus reward. How long can we expect until there's a profit?
- Competitive analysis - Are there other companies doing something similar and, if so, what are they doing?
- Product name (legal, marketing approvals) - What are you going to be calling the product? Do you need to get trademarks, domain names, etc? Are there internal approval processes required?
- Overall go-to-market plan, launch schedule and timelines - What are the launch plans and timelines? Do you have all the dependencies mapped?

Product Launch Checklist

REQUIRED:
- ❏ Clearly defined product user stories/use cases/business requirements
- ❏ Business model(s)
- ❏ Financial analysis/business case
- ❏ Competitive analysis
- ❏ Product Name (legal, marketing approvals)
- ❏ Overall GTM plan, launch schedule & timelines
- ❏ Marketing plan including PR, social, and launch campaigns
- ❏ Sales plan
- ❏ Capacity plan
- ❏ Data collection strategy & plan
- ❏ Security Compliance
- ❏ Privacy Compliance
- ❏ Product Test Plan developed and completed
- ❏ Data Validation Plan developed & completed
- ❏ Backup/Recovery/Product Continuity
- ❏ Validation that finished product meets user stories/use cases
- ❏ Product QA Review
- ❏ Product documentation (internal)
- ❏ Customer Onboarding Plan/Workflow
- ❏ Product support plan developed, reviewed, and signed off by the operations team
- ❏ Operational workflows defined
- ❏ Product Fulfillment Plan
- ❏ Invoicing/Payment

CUSTOMER COMMUNICATIONS:
- ❏ Product descriptions, functions and features list
- ❏ Sales presentation (with sales script)
- ❏ Sales contract
- ❏ Sales training
- ❏ Product data sheet
- ❏ Product documentation (customer)
- ❏ Product SLAs
- ❏ Pricing Schedule
- ❏ Sample pricing proposal
- ❏ Product training
- ❏ Plan for collecting customer/prospect feedback

OTHER (AS NEEDED):
- ❏ Product user trial
- ❏ Trial/demo contract
- ❏ Quick reference guide
- ❏ FAQ
- ❏ Press release(s)
- ❏ White paper(s)
- ❏ Sales demo
- ❏ Custom URL
- ❏ Website content updated
- ❏ UI Design & Testing plan
- ❏ Product user workflow & wireframes
- ❏ Product packaging
- ❏ User testimonials (from trials)
- ❏ Webinar(s)
- ❏ Lead generation plan
- ❏ Channel plan, including key partners and affiliates
- ❏ Product Sample(s)
- ❏ Patents filed
- ❏ Future releases roadmap
- ❏ Product performance reports (internal)
- ❏ Analytics dashboard
- ❏ KPIs/OKRs
- ❏ Trade shows/launch events
- ❏ Product in inventory (physical goods)

- Marketing plan including PR, social, and launch campaigns -- Is there a marketing plan? Doing any press releases? Social media plans? Are you going to try to go viral? Make YouTube how-to videos? Promote on LinkedIn?
- Sales plan - How are you planning to sell the product? Channels? Compensation – who's getting paid and how much? Incentives or contests tied to launch?
- Capacity plan - Do you need to build out network capacity to support the product? If you're building a physical product, this might be making sure you have warehouse space to store the pre-launch inventory or to handle any returns. You'll also want to know the maximum sales you can support with your current capacity and maybe consider how you could quickly expand your capacity if you blow out your sales estimates. A good problem to have if you know what to do.
- Data collection strategy and plan - What customer data do you want to capture? How will you do it?
- Security compliance - How do you secure the application or related assets? What are you doing to keep hackers at bay?
- Privacy compliance - If you're collecting customer data, how are you keeping it secure and private?
- Product test plan developed and completed - What are the test steps to make sure that the product meets the technical requirements? Have they been completed and signed off?
- Data validation plan developed and completed - Similar to the test plan, how are you validating that the data you're collecting is accurate and complete? Has the person responsible signed off that the work has been done?
- Backup/recovery/product continuity - What happens if disaster strikes? Do you have contingency plans in place for

a service outage? What's the plan for backing everything up and recovering if something happens?
- Validation that finished product meets user stories/use cases -- Has the product owner signed off that the use cases have met acceptance criteria?
- Product QA review - Who's doing quality assurance, what's the plan, and has it been completed?
- Product documentation (internal) - Have the developers written the documentation needed for supporting the product internally? Is it available to whoever is going to be doing support and do they understand it?
- Customer onboarding plan/workflow - When you get a new customer, what's the workflow for onboarding them? Don't underestimate the importance here. Every customer experiences your onboarding. Don't let it suck.
- Product support plan developed, reviewed, and signed off by the operations team - Is there a plan for how to support the customers if they have issues or identify problems with the product? Has the team that's actually doing the support work reviewed and agreed with the plan?
- Operational workflows defined - Just like with the support plan, if there are workflows needed for key aspects of product delivery, have they been identified and communicated to the teams doing the work? Do they agree?
- Product fulfillment plan - When an order comes in, how's the product getting to the customer?
- Invoicing/payment - Once a customer's bought the product, how are payments made and collected? If it's not through a credit card, is there a plan in place to get invoices generated, sent, and collected?

CUSTOMER/PROSPECT COMMUNICATIONS:

- Product descriptions, functions and features list - You're gonna need marketing brochures that describe what the product does, how it does it and what the key features are.
- Sales presentation (with sales script) - If the product has a direct sales team, they're likely to need to know how to sell it and what the pitch should be.
- Sales contract - To close the deal, you'll need terms and conditions, either on the website or in a physical document for the customer to sign.
- Sales training - Teaching the sales team all about the product, how to create interest and close deals.
- Product data sheet - Many products will need a technical data sheet or list of the specifications that might be relevant to a customer.
- Product documentation (customer) - Customer-facing documentation so that the customer can learn how to use the product, do some basic trouble-shooting, etc. Unless you want to answer all the questions all the time...
- Product SLAs - If your product includes some service aspects, you'll want to set expectations by establishing Service Level Agreements or SLAs.
- Pricing schedule - What does the pricing look like? Are there volume discounts or some kind of basic/premium levels? You might even need two of these – one for customers and another that shows volume tiers and discounts that your sales team can negotiate.
- Sample pricing proposal - It always helps the sales team if they can see a sample of what a price quote should look like. If the product is complex, this might even take the form of a configuration tool.

- Product training - Depending on the complexity of the product, you might need to have some product training for your customers.
- Plan for collecting customer/prospect feedback - How are you going to collect feedback from your customers and what's the plan for integrating that back into future development cycles?

OTHER (AS NEEDED):
- Product user trial - Maybe you're doing alpha or beta user trials or some kind of paid trials. If so, what does that look like and how does it happen?
- Trial/demo contract - If you're doing a demo/trial, is there a more basic agreement you want to have in place? You might want to have some liability waivers at a minimum, in case your demo breaks and causes some problems for the trial users. I'd also consider a confidentiality agreement so that your trial doesn't get widely shared before you're officially in the market.
- Quick reference guide - Picture something like the quickstart guide you get when you buy a new laptop or television.
- FAQ - Not essential, but always a good idea. This can help offload some basic support questions as your customers can help themselves.
- Press release(s) - A short news-ish story that can be sent to targeted media to announce the availability of the product.
- White paper(s) - Maybe there's a technical aspect to your product that you'd like to educate customers as to why it's important.

- Sales demo - This is different from the product trial or demo. More focused on something that your sales team can easily use to show a prospect how the product works. Could be a trial log-in or something specifically designed for sales.
- Custom URL - Is there going to be a special landing page for the product on your company website? Or maybe a landing page associated with a product promotion?
- Website content updated - If you're not building a specific website or landing page, you might still need to update an existing website to include your new product.
- UI design and testing plan - Not always required depending on the type of product, but essential for many. Do you want to A-B test different designs?
- Product user workflow and wireframes - Understanding the end-to-end use case and how a customer engages with your product. Basic blueprint for your dev and UX teams.
- Product packaging - Is there a box, a wrapper or some kind of shrink-wrap or plastic around the product? Note: something like toilet paper is going to be easier to open than some electronics in a securely sealed plastic clamshell.
- User testimonials (from trials) - Are the customers saying positive things? If so, do you want to capture that and share them in your marketing?
- Webinar - Something for customer acquisition, onboarding or training?
- Lead generation plan - How are you going to find prospects and get them into your sales funnel?
- Channel plan, including key partners and affiliates - If you work with distributors, partners or affiliates, this is the plan for them. It should include the compensation and some aspects of the sales plan too.

- Product sample(s) - If you have a physical product, does it lend itself to sampling? When people experience the product, does it significantly increase their desire to buy?
- Patents filed - Is there intellectual property associated with the product? If so, make sure that patents are filed before the product launches and everyone sees what you're doing.
- Future releases roadmap - Again, not essential. But sometimes with a new product that requires a significant investment, customers will want to feel comfortable that there's a long-term plan before making a commitment.
- Product performance reports (internal) - Help show other teams how the product is performing by getting the internal reporting done before launch.
- Analytics dashboard - A dashboard for your leadership team can help them quickly understand where the product stands.
- KPIs/OKRs - Know how you want to measure the product's performance before you launch and make sure that if there's data you need, that you're collecting it.
- Trade shows/launch events - Frequently, new products are announced around big trade shows or conventions. Are you going to have a special launch event?
- Product in inventory (physical goods) - If you've got a physical product and are anticipating strong initial demand, you may want to build up a little inventory before launch unless you're ok with the occasional shortage.

Whew. Now, that's a list. This is why you need a product manager *and* a checklist for the product manager to execute. While everything on the list doesn't have to be done by the PM, they need to make sure that all relevant items are on someone's to-do list and that they get done.

Don't leave this stuff to chance. Before you're launched, walk through the checklist item by item — you might not think that a particular item is relevant for your specific product, and it might not be. But giving each checklist item a moment's consideration before you launch is essential to make sure that you don't miss something important. Every item should either be checked off as complete or "considered but not applicable."

You may also want to add new items that are specific to your particular industry or situation. If you've done previous launches, look back and consider any "gotchas" that might have caused delays or other issues. The launch checklist can become the place for the collected wisdom of the teams that came before you.

As you can see, using a checklist for your product launch can help ensure that you don't forget anything important. It can also help you coordinate better across teams and make your launches more consistent. It'll also make you and your team look smarter and better organized. Don't launch without one.

TL;DR

- Checklists are an invaluable tool for successful product launches. They help maintain consistency, track progress, and identify potential roadblocks. By utilizing a comprehensive checklist, product leaders can significantly increase their chances of success by ensuring that no detail is overlooked, and every team member is aligned towards the same goal.
- David Lee Roth included a unique clause in Van Halen's concert contracts requiring that all brown M&M's be removed from a bowl provided to them backstage. This seemingly frivolous request served as a clever way for Roth to ensure that promoters were carefully

reading every detail of their contract rider to ensure safety requirements were also met.
- The World Health Organization (WHO) identified a major problem with the safety of surgery and created the Surgical Safety Checklist, which has reduced complications and mortality rates around the world by 30%.
- Using a product launch checklist helps ensure that all necessary steps have been taken before releasing a new product to market, increases communication across teams and proves invaluable for keeping track of progress and mitigating risks.

CHAPTER EXERCISES

1. Think about the work tasks that you perform on a regular basis. Take 15 minutes and do a brainstorming session, writing them all down. You can also include things that you should do but often don't have the time.
2. After you have the list from your brain dump, start organizing them into groups. You can do this by the type of task (administrative work, product tasks, personal development), the day of the week you do them, the frequency (daily, weekly, monthly, annually). Whatever makes sense to you based on your personal workflow and rhythms.
3. Are there some tasks that are "must do" and some that are "nice to have"? Within your groupings, put your tasks in some kind of priority.
4. Congrats! You now have a prioritized checklist of your work. Put it somewhere visible and use it!

CHAPTER NOTES

CHAPTER 24: What Makes Great Products Great? The Magic Of A Customer Journey

When a magician creates an illusion, what they're really doing is controlling what you see and experience and making sure that you only see exactly what they want you to see and nothing else. Some of the same basic techniques that a magician uses to visually misdirect your attention away from what they don't want you to see towards what they want you to focus on are also used by user experience and design teams to grab and channel your attention on their web pages and apps. Using movement and color, and understanding how people's eyes track, both the magician and the designer create a very specific encounter for their audience.

A great product experience should feel like magic. Every customer touchpoint should be intuitive, user-friendly, and seamlessly integrated with the others. But in reality, creating a truly seamless end-to-end product experience is hard work. It requires a deep understanding of your customer's needs and wants, as well as a willingness to constantly iterate and improve. Like a good magic trick, you have to see the entire experience through your audience's eyes. But the effort is worth it. When done right, a seamless end-to-end product experience can give your customers a bit of "Wow!" that keeps them coming back for more.

We'll call this end-to-end experience the *customer journey*. This chapter will focus on understanding the six stages of the customer journey. The customer journey is the path that a customer takes from awareness of a problem or need, through research and purchase of a solution, to post-purchase support and, hopefully, long-term customer loyalty.

Within each stage, we'll take a closer look at different options and tactics that you might use to create a compelling customer experience. When creating a product, it's important to consider the customer's journey and how they will interact with the product at each stage. These interactions are called *customer touchpoints*. Customer touchpoints are any physical, human or online interaction between a company and its customers which can influence the customer's experience and lead them to brand loyalty.

A great product doesn't have to be a premium product. It can be expensive (a BMW) or relatively cheap (a bottle of Coke). What really sets a great product apart is solving a customer problem in a way that delivers a well-designed and thoughtful experience from beginning to end across all aspects of the customer's journey. The product manager should drive the end to end experience across all the touchpoints and parts of your organization involved in delivering it to customers.

A great end-to-end product experience considers all of the customer touchpoints and ensures that the experience is consistent. It should also make sense in the context of that stage but also create a frictionless flow across all the stages. If a prospect or customer becomes frustrated or confused at any point, they are likely to abandon their journey. As a product leader, a key part of your job is to smooth out the bumps and rough edges and keep them on the right path. While this entire book should give you the knowledge you need to build a great product, if I had to focus on a single area as the key to that goal, it would be perfecting the customer journey across all touchpoints and making it feel magical.

The Six Stages of the Customer Journey

Here are the six stages of a typical customer journey:

1. Awareness - when the prospective customer first becomes aware of the company and its products or services; this might also include their initial awareness of a problem that your product is designed to solve.
2. Consideration - the prospect starts to do some research on potential solutions and evaluates whether or not your product can meet their needs.
3. Purchase - the prospect converts to a customer and buys the solution from you.
4. Fulfillment - the product or service is delivered and/or the customer is onboarded and gets started with their initial usage.
5. Support - because when the customer has a problem or a question, they'll need to get answers somehow or they'll abandon your product.
6. Loyalty - consistently choosing your product over time as a result of a positive customer experience that creates an emotional connection between the customer and the brand.

Having a clear picture of the entire customer journey is essential because it helps companies understand what customers want and need, how they can improve their products and services to meet those needs, how to communicate the value of the solution and how to reinforce the brand experience to turn one-time customers into loyal fans.

Building a Service Blueprint

To begin understanding your customer's end-to-end experience with your product, you might want to start by establishing a service blueprint. A service blueprint, sometimes also known as a product delivery blueprint, is a diagram or workflow tool that can be used to visualize all of the steps involved in providing a product or service.

It's helpful for understanding how a product works and identifying all the processes required to deliver that product to a customer. The blueprint includes three key parts: the customer journey and touchpoints as we've already discussed, the product operations tasks that happen behind-the-scenes in support of all customer-facing activities, and the user interactions between the customer and the actual product.

We'll be returning to the customer journey a bit later in this chapter so let's focus on the other two components of the service blueprint. The product operations activities are all of the detailed support processes that need to happen in order for the product or service to be provided. This includes everything from stocking inventory to packing orders to training employees.

It is important to have a clear understanding of all of the steps involved so that you can identify any bottlenecks or areas of improvement. When an order comes in, who needs to do something to make sure that the customer gets served and what exactly do they need to do? Who are the people working in support of those efforts and what do they do? In the end, most people in your org have some kind of connection to the product even if they never talk to a customer directly. If you want your customers to receive a consistent high-quality experience, you'll want to know what needs to happen to deliver the goods and who's on point to do it.

Understanding how the user interacts with your product is also a part of the service blueprint. If they click a button in the app, what's supposed to happen? Is there a help screen somewhere? Does the help button go to product documentation, an FAQ, or maybe a live chat? Is someone responsible for maintaining the documentation or FAQ? Who gets the live chat request? Who's keeping track of what customers are using and making sure that those encounters are meeting expectations? Again, knowing the person or system that needs to take an action when the customer interacts with the product is critical to delivering a dependable experience.

Digging in at this level of detail isn't easy. Service delivery is often very complicated. That means that putting together a service blueprint can be a challenging process itself. But think about it this way. If you can't actually document what's supposed to happen at each step, how can you ever expect your teams to execute those steps to deliver your product or service with any quality or consistency? By taking the time to create a service blueprint, you have a much better likelihood that your service is delivering a positive experience for everyone involved.

Now that we've had a high-level review of the service blueprint, let's dig in on the customer journey in more detail.

Customer Journey > Stage One: Awareness

At the start of the customer journey lies the crucial first step of *awareness*, where potential customers are introduced to a company's products or services. This initial stage can be triggered by various means, such as advertising, word-of-mouth recommendations, or online discoveries. It is vital for companies to ensure that they have a strong online presence and offer solutions that meet their target audience's needs.

To achieve this, businesses must focus on tactics that make their brand visible and stand out in a crowded market. Whether it is through targeted advertising campaigns or creating engaging content on social media platforms, companies must employ effective strategies to attract potential customers' attention and leave a lasting impression. By prioritizing awareness-building efforts, businesses can set themselves up for long-term success and growth in today's competitive marketplace.

We've identified several potential touchpoints for the awareness stage in the following grid.

Category	Touchpoint	Role/Owner
Awareness	Advertising	Marketing
	Press Coverage/PR	PR
	Events/Tradeshows	PR/Product/Sales
	Online Lead Generation	Web/Marketing
	Webinars	PR/Product
	Word of Mouth	Marketing/PR
	Direct Mail	Marketing
	Social Media	PR
	Cold Calls	Sales
	Paid & Organic Search/SEO	Web/Marketing
	Blog/Digital Content/Videos	Web/Marketing
	Email	Marketing

There are several ways to create awareness for your company and its products or services. Advertising is one way to reach potential customers and make them aware of your company. This can be done through traditional channels like television, radio, and print, or newer channels like online ads, social media, and native advertising. Word of mouth is another powerful way to create awareness. This happens when customers tell their friends and family about your company and its products or services. Finally, customers can also stumble upon your company online through search engines, social media, or simply by browsing the web. It's important to make sure your website is optimized for all of these channels so that potential customers can easily find you.

Among the above, SEO (Search Engine Optimization) is particularly important for companies because it helps them to be visible in search engines like Google and Bing. When potential customers search for keywords related to your company, you want your website to appear as high up in the results as possible. People are far more likely to click on the first few results that appear. How many times have you gone to the second or third screen of search results? Many factors go into SEO, but some of the most important ones are keywords, website structure, and content. Because the SEO algorithms are constantly evolving, this can be a good place to engage an external resource with a strong history of delivering results.

As you can see, there are many different touchpoints that can be used to reach potential customers and create awareness for your company. It's important to consider all of these when planning your marketing strategy. You'll also want to think about who will be responsible for each touchpoint. In some cases, it will make sense for multiple people or departments to oversee different touchpoints. For example, PR may manage press coverage and events, while marketing handles paid search and social media.

Once you've identified the touchpoints you want to use, the next step is to create a plan for how you'll reach potential customers through each one. This will involve creating content, designing campaigns, and setting budgets. It's important to remember that not all touchpoints will be equally effective for every business. You'll need to experiment and see what works best for your company. Once you have their attention, you can move on to the next step.

Customer Journey > Stage Two: Consideration

Moving along the customer journey, the second critical step is consideration. At this stage, customers recognize a problem they need to solve and begin evaluating whether your solution can address their needs. This phase holds immense significance as it lays the foundation for a potential purchase. In today's selling environment, customers seek social proof that your offering is trustworthy, effective and can deliver on its promises. They conduct thorough research on your company and its products/services by reading reviews, comparing prices, and seeking recommendations from friends and family.

Category	Touchpoint	Role/Owner
Consideration	Direct Sales	Sales
	Sales Presentation	Product/Marketing
	Sales Literature	Product/Marketing
	Product Demos/ Samples/ Trials	Product
	Pricing/Business Model	Product
	Portal	Web/Marketing
	Chat Bots	Product/Web
	Online Reviews	Product/Marketing
	White Papers	Product/Marketing
	Search	Web/Marketing
	Customer References	Sales
	Case Study	Product/Marketing

It is crucial for businesses to ensure that they are easily discoverable online and that their products or services offer unique value propositions that appeal to potential customers. During the consideration phase, companies must focus on tactics that help potential customers gain a better understanding of their product's features and benefits. By using engaging visuals or interactive demos, businesses can effectively communicate how their solution meets customer needs while building trust in their brand.

There are several ways to help customers consider your company and its products or services. Again, it's important to make sure your company is easy to find online so that potential customers can research you. But once they find you, you need to provide them with compelling information if you're going to stand out in the crowd. It's not just about a sales pitch, even if that's important. If they can't get all their questions answered in a clear way, they'll just bounce over to a competitor. Uncertainty is a business killer.

Pricing and business model are also important considerations for potential customers. They will want to know how much your product or service costs and what the terms of service are. It's important to have this information readily available so that potential customers can make an informed decision. Innovation in pricing and business models can be a big differentiator but be careful. They can also become a source of customer confusion if the customer finds your pricing too complicated or significantly different from what they've experienced in the past. If you have to spend much time explaining your business model to customers, you're adding a barrier that could keep them from moving on to purchase.

Customer Journey > Stage Three: Purchase

The third and most crucial step in the customer journey is the moment of purchase. Time to ring the cash register. This is where prospects transition into paying customers, making it a critical point that directly impacts your business's bottom line. Failure to convert interest into a purchase can determine your company's survival chances in today's competitive market. Therefore, it is essential to ensure that this stage is as seamless as possible for the customer.

Once the prospect has made up their mind to buy, businesses must streamline the purchasing process by cutting any unnecessary obstacles or complications. From user-friendly checkout processes to multiple payment options, every detail must be carefully considered to make sure that customers complete their purchase with frictionless ease. A hassle-free purchasing experience will drive sustained revenue growth over time.

To meet this goal, companies must make sure their products or services are easy to buy and that they offer a good value for the price. We've identified several potential touchpoints for the purchase stage in the grid below.

Category	Touchpoint	Role/Owner
Purchase	Direct Sales Negotiation	Product/Sales
	Contract Terms	Product/Sales
	Online Ordering	Product/Web
	Coupon Code	Product/Marketing
	Product Bundles	Product/Marketing
	Product Cross-sell/Upsell	Marketing
	3rd Party Product Integrations	Product
	Order Confirmation/Thank You	Product/Sales/Ops
	Partnerships/Channels	Product/Sales

There are several ways to make it easy for customers to buy your products or services. For example, Amazon has made a lot of money by removing the friction from ordering using the 1-Click "Buy Now" buttons. You can also offer a variety of payment options, make sure your website is easy to use, and delivers good customer service. Of course, you'll also want to make sure you're offering a competitive price. If you've got a sales contract for the buyer to sign, making the agreement as simple and easy to understand as possible can also eliminate delays in purchasing your solution. After the purchase is made, it's time to deliver the goods.

Customer Journey > Stage Four: Fulfillment

The fourth step in the customer journey is fulfillment, which involves delivering the purchased product or service to the customer. At this point, customers eagerly anticipate receiving their order and expect it to arrive on time and in perfect condition. Therefore, businesses must ensure that their fulfillment process is efficient and reliable, with timely communication about shipping status and delivery updates.

This stage also presents an opportunity for companies to differentiate themselves by including personalized touches, such as handwritten notes or special packaging. By exceeding customer expectations during fulfillment, businesses can foster a positive impression of their brand and increase the likelihood of repeat purchases by creating long-term loyalty among customers and establishing a reputation for reliability and quality.

Onboarding is one of the most important aspects of fulfillment, if not the entire customer journey. This is the process where the customer initially engages with your product and gets set up for their first use. Keep in mind that, when they decided to buy your solution, they may have had some apprehension about whether to make the purchase. Your onboarding process can either reassure that they made a good decision or reinforce their reasons for apprehension and give them a case of buyer's remorse. A bad onboarding experience will significantly increase the likelihood of future customer churn while a positive one stacks chips on the side of long-term customer retention. Onboarding is likely to be the one common experience that all your customers will have along their customer journey. After making sure your purchase process is frictionless in Stage Three, if there's one more thing to make sure you get right, this is it.

Category	Touchpoint	Role/Owner
Fulfillment	Onboarding Process	Product/Ops/Sales
	Electronic data file/feed	Product/Web
	PDF	Product/Marketing
	Product Packaging	Product/Marketing
	Quick Start Guide	Product/Marketing
	Product Documentation	Product/Marketing
	Shipping Notification	Product/Ops
	Delivery Tracking	Product/Ops
	Customer Portal	Product/Web
	Application Download	Product/Web

Customer Journey > Stage Five: Support

Step number five in the customer journey is support. Regardless of how user-friendly and seamless your product or service may be, customers will inevitably have questions or concerns that require help. Therefore, it's essential to provide reliable and accessible customer support channels to address their needs promptly. Customers expect companies to be available when they need help, whether through phone calls, emails, chatbots or social media platforms. Providing excellent customer service is particularly vital for businesses that rely on recurring revenue from subscriptions or repeat purchases, as poor support can negatively impact customer lifetime value.

Moreover, exceptional customer service can positively affect brand reputation and foster long-term loyalty among customers. Businesses should strive to go above and beyond by anticipating potential issues and proactively addressing them before they become problems. This approach can turn a negative experience into a positive one that builds trust and strengthens relationships with customers.

In contrast, poor customer service can lead to negative reviews and word-of-mouth feedback that drives away potential customers. Therefore, investing in high-quality support services should be a top priority for businesses seeking sustained growth in today's competitive market. By providing attentive and personalized support throughout the entire customer journey, businesses can increase retention rates and drive lasting success over time. Getting customers is hard enough. Don't lose them to indifferent delivery of your support.

The support phase is not just about having someone to take phone calls, as important as that might be. It's also important to provide training and documentation so that customers can help themselves. This can be done through online tutorials, FAQs, and user manuals. Customers will appreciate being able to find the answers to their questions on their own, and they will be more likely to continue using your product or service if they feel confident in their ability to use it.

Category	Touchpoint	Role/Owner
Support	Customer Support - Phone	Sales/Product/Ops
	Customer Support - Online	Web/Product/Ops
	Product FAQs	Web/Product
	In-Product Help Screens	Product
	Invoice/Billing - Manual	Product/Finance/Ops
	Invoice/Billing - Auto	Product/Finance/Ops
	User Training	Product
	Video Tutorials	Product/Marketing
	Online Chat/Chat Bots	Product/Ops
	User Forum	Product/Ops
	Knowledge Base	Product/Ops
	Trouble Tickets	Product/Ops

Customer Journey > Stage Six: Loyalty

The final step in the customer journey is loyalty. This phase is crucial as it involves converting one-time buyers into loyal customers who become devoted fans and repeat buyers. Building a strong base of loyal customers can be much more cost-effective than constantly acquiring new ones, which can significantly impact a business's profit margins. In addition to this, a loyal customer base can serve as a launching pad for additional products and services that drive revenue growth.

You've probably noticed that each of the stages build on the previous stages, and that's definitely true with loyalty. To build customer loyalty, businesses need to focus on creating engaging relationships with their customers by delivering exceptional experiences at every touchpoint. This could include personalized communications, exclusive offers, loyalty programs or excellent after-sales support. By making customers feel valued and appreciated, businesses can foster long-term brand loyalty that translates into increased lifetime value.

Moreover, loyal customers are more likely to recommend your brand to others through word-of-mouth marketing, which can drive new customer acquisition at little or no cost. Therefore, building a community of happy and satisfied customers should be a top priority for any business seeking sustained growth in today's competitive market.

User groups also can be a valuable part of the loyalty phase of the customer journey. Customers who are members of a user group will feel more connected to the company and they will be more likely to continue doing business with the company. In addition, user groups also provide valuable feedback to the company about their products or services. If your product lends itself to the idea of a user group, and most products do, you'll likely find that it's well worth the investment when you end up with happily engaged customers who buy from you over and over.

Category	Touchpoint	Role/Owner
Loyalty	Customer Feedback - Sales	Product/Sales
	Customer Feedback - Ops/Care	Product/Ops
	Customer Feedback - Online	Product/Web
	Rewards Program	Product/Marketing
	Newsletters	Marketing
	Product Renewals	Product/Sales/Marketing
	Product/Feature Updates	Product/Marketing
	User Study	Product/Marketing
	Online Review Program	Marketing
	Customer Referrals	Product/Sales/Marketing
	User Groups/Events	Product
	Advisory Board	Product

Those happy repeat customers are also more likely to share their experiences with others. Customer referrals are another key part of the loyalty phase. Customers who are happy with your product or service will be more likely to tell their friends about it. This can lead to new customers and hopefully the next wave of future fans for your company. Finally, referrals are another way to lower your customer acquisition costs. Make sure that you have a plan to ask for referrals from your best customers.

Final Considerations

Across all the stages of the customer's journey, each touchpoint presents an opportunity to deliver a positive, consistent experience to the customer. However, coordinating touchpoints can be difficult, as different parts of the organization may "own" different touchpoints. For example, marketing may own the touchpoint of a website, while product development owns the touchpoint of the product itself. To deliver a seamless, consistent experience to the customer, it is important to coordinate all touchpoints. This can be done by developing a shared understanding of the customer journey and aligning goals across all touchpoints. By doing so, you can ensure that every interaction leaves a positive impression on the customer. As a product leader, if you're not thinking through your experience and owning it end-to-end, who is?

Another important thing to keep in mind is that not all touchpoints are equally effective at every stage of the cycle. For example, PR may be more effective in the early stages, when a product is new and generating buzz. User groups, on the other hand, may be more effective when a product is more mature and has a loyal following. The key is to understand the strengths and weaknesses of each touchpoint and to use them accordingly. By doing so, you can ensure that your product reaches its full potential.

In conclusion, companies must understand the value of cultivating long-term relationships with customers to ensure sustained success in the future. Just as a magician can captivate and surprise an audience with a dazzling performance, businesses can create an engaging experience that fosters a deep emotional bond with their customers. By delivering a consistently magical experience, they can position themselves as dependable long-term partners in their customer's journey and stand out from companies that prioritize short-term gains.

TL;DR

- Customer touchpoints are any interactions between company and customers that can influence their experience and lead to brand loyalty.
- A service blueprint visualizes all steps involved in providing a service including the stages of the customer journey, product operations tasks in support of the product and direct user interactions with the product itself.
- Companies must consider all customer touchpoints in order to provide consistent and frictionless product experiences.
- Companies can create a compelling customer experience by understanding and improving the customer journey, which has six stages. The stages are Awareness, Consideration, Purchase, Fulfillment, Support, and Loyalty.
- Stage One: Awareness - Businesses must focus on tactics that make their brand visible and stand out in a crowded market, such as targeted advertising campaigns or creating engaging content on social media platforms.
- Stage Two: Consideration - Companies must ensure they are easily discoverable online, provide compelling information that answer customer questions, and ensure that pricing and business models are easily understandable.
- Stage Three: Purchase - Make sure the purchasing process is as seamless as possible by providing customer-friendly checkout processes and multiple payment options.

- Stage Four: Fulfillment - Ensure timely communication about shipping status and delivery updates and provide customers with a positive onboarding experience to reduce customer churn.
- Stage Five: Support - Provide reliable customer support channels such as phone calls, emails, chatbots etc., and also include self-help resources such as online tutorials, FAQs, and user manuals. Go above and beyond by anticipating potential issues and proactively addressing them before they become problems.
- Stage Six: Loyalty - Focus on creating engaging relationships with customers by providing exceptional experiences at every touchpoint, converting one-time buyers into loyal customers with exclusive offers and loyalty programs; word-of-mouth and referrals from your best customers can drive new customer acquisition at little or no cost.

CHAPTER EXERCISES

1. Start with a product you're working on or a process outside of work that you're reasonably familiar with – maybe something like ordering food online. Write down the tactics that are used to create awareness and get you to consider this product.
2. When you're ready to buy, what are some of the key elements used to make the purchase process as frictionless as possible?
3. From a product operations standpoint, what are some of the steps behind the scenes that help get the product or service delivered to you?
4. Think about a product or brand that you use frequently. What is it about the product or brand that inspires you to keep buying it again and again?

CHAPTER NOTES

CHAPTER 25: Getting More Productive by Taking Control of Your Time and Fighting Interruption Culture

We all know that feeling. The never-ending to-do lists. The constant interruptions. The projects always seem to take longer than we think they will. Barely manageable chaos. If this sounds like your life, you're not alone. This problem exists in nearly all businesses today. Productivity inefficiencies cost US businesses almost $600B a year.

The good news is that there are plenty of proven methods to help you take back control of your time and be more productive. In this chapter, we will take a look at the negative impact of multitasking and interruption culture on projects. We'll also talk about methods and tools to reduce interruptions and improve time management.

Time management is always a hot topic. As far back as the 1700s, American founding father Benjamin Franklin kept a daily calendar with six focused time blocks designed to improve his productivity. Now with the advent of always-on mobile technology within arms' reach along with wearable sensors and activity trackers in our watches actually strapped to our arms, we are now literally connected 24/7. It can be difficult to disconnect and focus on one thing at a time. This constant connection can lead to information overload, and it can be hard to know how to manage our time effectively.

The Problem With Multitasking

Imagine a "productivity" tool that...

- Reduces your productivity by as much as 40%
- Increases stress levels and gives you the feeling that you're surrounded by chaos

- Increases the likelihood that you'll make mistakes
- Reduces your ability to meet deadlines
- Makes you work harder to think slower
- Makes it increasingly harder in the future to adopt other productivity methods
- All while believing that the opposite is true

Welcome to multitasking.

Multitasking is often lauded as a necessary skill in today's fast-paced world. But what exactly is it? Multitasking simply means working on several things at the same time. This can be anything from trying to carry on a conversation while also checking your phone, to writing an email while also on a conference call. While it may seem like you're getting more done by multitasking, research has shown that it can be detrimental to your productivity. When you try to focus on multiple tasks at once, your brain has to switch back and forth between them, which can lead to errors and mental fatigue.

In his book *Thinking, Fast and Slow*, Daniel Kahneman explains we all have two systems of thinking – System 1 and System 2 – and explores how they can affect our decision-making. System 1 is fast, instinctive, and emotional. It's the thinking that happens automatically, with very little effort or conscious thought. We use System 1 thinking when we're quickly reacting to something. System 2 is slower, more deliberate, and more logical. It's the thinking we have to put effort into, like when we're driving or navigating. We can't do multiple System 2 things at the same time – that's why distracted driving is so dangerous. As Kahneman says, "Distractions are everywhere ... [and] our minds are not built to handle them." When we're trying to do multiple things at once, our brains get overloaded and we make mistakes.

It's no secret that productivity levels tend to drop when we switch between tasks. Whether we're trying to juggle work and personal obligations, or simply trying to get things done around the house, it can be hard to stay focused when we're constantly changing gears. But why does this happen?

Simply put, it takes time and energy to adjust to new tasks, especially if they are complex or unfamiliar. Every time we switch tasks, our brains have to adapt to the new demands placed on them. This process takes time and effort, which means that it's inevitable that some level of productivity will be lost in the process.

Are you still thinking we must be talking about someone else and that you're an effective multitasker? It's unlikely. According to research by Jason Watson and David Strayer, only 2.5% of people can effectively multitask. In a room of forty people, that's just one good multitasker. Odds are you're not the one. The other 97.5% of us show significant performance impacts when trying to do more than one thing at a time. This research has big implications for how we live and work. In today's world, we are constantly bombarded with distractions and demands on our attention. We feel like we have to be available 24/7, responding to emails, texts, and phone calls as soon as they come in.

What is the impact of all this multitasking? According to research by Saraswathi Bellur, Kristine Novak, and Kyle Hull, multitasking can have negative consequences for both intellectual pursuit and work efficiency. In their study, "Make it our time: In-class multitaskers have lower academic performance," they found that students who engaged in multitasking during class had lower GPAs than those who didn't. Additionally, they found that students who multitasked while doing homework took longer to complete their assignments. And finally, they found that multitasking can cost up to 40% of your work time.

The truth is, this constant multitasking is taking a toll on our productivity, our relationships, and our health. It's time to rethink our approach to multitasking and learn to focus on one thing at a time. When we do, we'll be happier, healthier, and more productive.

The Cost of Interruption Culture

In the 2007 paper "Information Overload: We Have Met the Enemy and He Is Us," Jonathan Spira and David Goldes wrote that ineffective management of productivity tools, like email and instant messaging, drive interruptions which cost US businesses $588B each year. That number has only gotten bigger, probably much bigger, in the years since then.

More recently, *The Economist* article "In Search of Lost Focus" estimates that 28% of the time spent on knowledge work is lost to interruptions and that increased focus and decreasing distractions could have a $1.2 trillion impact on the US economy alone. 71% of workers spend at least an hour a day on email and nearly 20% spend more than three hours. For those working in an office setting, 34% said that interruptions from their colleagues are their number one distraction.

Not only can an interruption take you away from important work, but the impact can linger to make you less productive and more error-prone long after the interrupter has moved on to other interruptions. A University of California - Irvine study showed that it takes an average of 23 minutes and 15 seconds to get back on task after an interruption. And a Michigan State study found that just a three-second interruption can double the error rate on a task.

Employees who are constantly interrupted are also more likely to create shortcuts to try to make up for lost time, which can lead to even more errors and lower quality work. Interruptions also increase work stress, contribute to an overall feeling of chaos, and lower morale due to a feeling of loss of control.

In a world where we are constantly bombarded with notifications, it can be hard to focus on any one task for more than a few minutes at a time. According to a Loughborough University study, the average work email alert got a reaction in just six seconds. That's the average and this explains a lot about our work expectations. This interruption culture has become so ingrained in our lives that it can be hard to imagine working any other way. But there are some things you can do.

Fighting Interruptions

So what can be done about the interruption culture that's become rampant in the business world? Here are a few ideas:

1. One way to fight back against interruption culture is to batch your interruptions. That is, set aside specific times throughout the day to check your email, return phone calls, and scroll through social media. That way, you can minimize the number of times you're interrupted during the day, and maximize the amount of time you have to focus on truly important tasks. Some productivity experts recommend checking email only twice per day: once in the morning and once in the evening. Of course, this won't work for everyone; some jobs require more frequent communication.

   But if you can batch your interruptions, even just partially, you'll likely find it much easier to focus on the task at hand. If you struggle with this, especially on your phone, take a look at Google's Digital Wellbeing initiative on their Android devices. By turning on Focus mode and scheduling it to automatically start at specific times, you can keep distracting apps and notifications at bay.
2. Another way to fight back against interruption culture is to implement company-wide or team-wide time blocks for deeper work. During these time blocks, everyone is off-limits for interruptions. No one can schedule meetings or send emails. This allows everyone to have uninterrupted time to focus on their work. Time blocks could be

implemented for an entire day, like "No Meeting Fridays," although this may not be realistic for every organization. Do you really only want to be able to focus one day a week? Alternatively, mornings before 10 or afternoons after 3 can be set aside as uninterrupted time. Find something that works for your team or organization and stick to it.

3. One effective way to optimize your work schedule and boost productivity is by using themed time blocks or time boxing. This technique involves scheduling specific blocks of time for different tasks throughout the day, such as answering emails, writing reports or meeting with colleagues. By intentionally blocking off these periods on your calendar, you create a sense of structure and set clear boundaries around each task. This helps minimize distractions and interruptions, allowing you to focus fully on each activity. It also ensures that important tasks are not overlooked or pushed aside in favor of less pressing matters.

   To make the most out of themed time blocks, it's important to group similar tasks together. For instance, if you have a few reports to write or emails to answer, schedule a two-hour block specifically for those activities. By doing this, you can get into a state of flow more quickly and efficiently complete those tasks. Themed time blocks can be especially helpful when working remotely or from home where there may be more distractions compared to an office setting. By creating a clear structure for your workday, you can maintain focus and stay on track toward achieving your goals.

4. A slightly longer-term approach would be to focus on our focus — building our focus "muscle." Just as we exercise our bodies to stay physically fit, we need to exercise our attention span if we want to be able to focus in the face of distractions. One way to do this is to set aside some time each day for "deep work" where you turn off all distractions and focus on

a single task. As you build up your ability to focus, you'll find it easier to tune out distractions for longer periods and get more done.
5. A simple but practical option for dealing with distractions that I've used pretty successfully is to keep a columned sheet of paper next to you as you work. When you hit a distracting task, quickly write it down on this parking lot list rather than switching over to it right then. Now that the thought is documented, you can stay in the flow. You'll deal with the items on the list during your next block of time for that kind of work.
6. Identify a DTF (Do This First) task and set aside a block of time to work on this at the beginning of your day. This will help you to focus on the most important task at hand and get it done before you get pulled into the rabbit hole of email, social media, and other distractions. Of course, this isn't always easy. But if you can commit to doing it just a few minutes first thing each day, you'll be surprised at how much more productive you can be. And as you get better at it, you can gradually increase the amount of time you devote to your DTF task until it becomes a daily habit. When I wrote this book, I set aside an hour every morning from 7 to 8 AM specifically for writing in London Writers' Salon.
7. Another way to fight interruption culture in the workplace is to establish "no interruption" zones where people can go physically to do deep work. This could be a specific room or area in the office that is designated for quiet work. If you find that people are already "escaping" the office to go to a coffee shop, this approach can save time and increase productivity, as well as reduce stress levels.

By implementing some or all of these ideas, we can begin to shift the culture of interruption and create a more productive and respectful work environment. Remember, changing ingrained habits takes time and effort, but the benefits are well worth it. Stick with it. By prioritizing focused work, reducing distractions, and respecting others' time and attention, we can pave the way for greater success and fulfillment in our professional lives.

What Does A Tomato Have to Do with Time Management?

Besides handling interruptions, a lot of what we're talking about boils down to managing your time productively. One of my favorite time management techniques is named after a tomato. I'm using it to keep myself on task as I write this book.

The *Pomodoro Technique* is a time management method developed by Francesco Cirillo in the 1980s. Cirillo used a tomato-shaped timer to manage his work blocks — "pomodoro" is the Italian word for tomato. The technique is based on the idea that breaking down work into timed intervals (called "pomodoros") followed by short breaks can improve focus and productivity.

The basic Pomodoro Technique involves working for twenty-five minutes followed by a five-minute break. This cycle is then repeated four times, after which a longer break of fifteen minutes is taken. The Pomodoro Technique has been shown to reduce task reluctance and improve focus, as well as fight distractions and interruptions. The Pomodoro Techniqueki can also be a helpful way to structure your work and make sure you are taking breaks throughout the day.

The Pomodoro Technique helps to measure your work in smaller units of time, rather than hours or days, which can make it easier to stay focused and avoid getting bogged down in a task. Additionally, the interval structure provides much-needed mental breaks that can help you avoid burnout. There are a ton of apps that can help you implement the Pomodoro Technique, but I used the Productivity Challenge Timer while I was writing this book. I probably would have been able to finish the book without the timer and the technique, but I know it would have taken me much longer.

The Pomodoro Technique also pairs well with timeboxing, mentioned earlier, another time management technique that uses short bursts of focus to increase productivity. *Timeboxing* is a time management technique that involves setting a fixed amount of time for an activity, and then working on that activity until the time is up. The benefit of timeboxing is that it can help you to focus on a task and get it done within a set timeframe. This can be helpful if you have trouble staying focused on tasks or if you tend to procrastinate.

You can also use timeboxing as part of your prioritization process. You've probably heard Parkinson's Law before. Simply put, "work expands to fill the time available for its completion." I once had a boss that suggested that another use of the Pareto Principle was that 80 percent of the work happened in the last 20 percent of a project's timeline. By setting a goal and timeboxing it, you can often keep your work from taking longer than it needs to.

The process of timeboxing with the Pomodoro Technique is pretty straightforward.

1. Choose the task you want to work on.
2. Decide how many pomodoros you want to spend on the task.
3. Set a timer for twenty-five minutes.
4. Work on the task until the timer goes off.
5. Take a break, and then repeat the process until you reach the amount of time you have decided to spend on the task.
6. Stop working on the task and move on to the next thing.

Timeboxing can be a helpful way to get things done. However, it is important to remember that not every task will be able to be completed within a set time frame. And that's okay! The goal is to work on the task for the amount of time you have set and then move on to something else. Timeboxing can be especially helpful when gamifying your productivity. For example, you could give yourself a certain number of points for every task you complete within the time limit. Or you could simply count the number of pomodoros you're able to complete each day and compare your daily performance to your best efforts. This can help to add an element of fun and competition to your work, and it may even help you to get more done than you would without the time limit.

Setting Up A Time Budget

There are 168 hours in a week – if you sleep eight hours a day and work forty hours a week, you still have 72 hours or three full days to do everything else you need to get done during a week. If you're not getting it all done, do you have a time problem? Everyone starts each week with the same number of hours, right? Maybe it's a productivity problem? For a lot of people, it's a "saying no" problem. No matter the reason, putting together a time budget should help you get a better handle on your bandwidth.

Using the time budget template we've included, start with the time audit. A *time audit* is simply a tool that helps you understand how you're currently spending your time, so you can make adjustments accordingly — what are you doing and how much time do you spend doing each task? Start this process out by writing down your top three to five priorities, whatever they might be — health, family, spiritual, business, etc.

Next, make a list of all the things you do on a daily basis. Feel free to group tasks where it makes sense. For example, you probably don't need to break out taking a shower or brushing your teeth separately, but you'd want to have an overall block of time for your grooming. Your friends and co-workers will thank you for that.

Time Budget Worksheet

	What are your overall top 3 to 5 priorities?
1	
2	
3	
4	
5	

Column A: What I'm Doing Today	Est Hrs	Column B: What I'm Not Doing But Should Be	Est Hrs

Priority	A+B: Prioritized List of What I Will Be Doing	Est Hrs
1		
2		
3		
4		
5		
6		
7		
8		
9		
10		
11		
12		
13		
14		
15		
16		
17		
18		
19		
20		
	TOTAL HOURS IN ONE WEEK =	168

As you look at the time you spend on tasks, don't forget to capture the transition time in-between tasks. That's real time too. If you have a face-to-face meeting somewhere, you can't forget your prep time or drive time. Include your sleep time, exercise time, and so on. If you go to a gym for your workouts, the workouts might be an hour but you should also include the fifteen-minute drive each way in your total. That makes your total "workout" time 90 minutes, which is a 50% increase than the hour you thought you were spending. Be realistic. A big part of this process is about being honest with yourself about what you can do in the time you have each week.

When you're done, you should have a list of everything you do in a week along with the hours spent on the task and the total hours should add up to 168. Then, identify any things you think you should be doing but aren't and estimate how much time you'd like to have for it. Now go back to your list of priorities and use them to create a stack-ranked list of all your activities based on those priorities.

Now that you can see the list of everything you do and everything you want to do, ranked by what's most important to you, start adding up the hours associated with each task. When you hit 168 hours, draw a line. That's it. That's everything you can actually do in a single week.

Are there important things that didn't make the cut? How does your stack ranking align with those overall priorities? Time to negotiate with yourself. What are you saying "No" to? Is there something that you could delegate to someone else? Maybe you'd like to get eight hours of sleep but decide to cut it to seven so you have time for a morning workout. Or perhaps there are lower priority things that you'd like to do weekly, but you can pair them with other things and shift them to every other week so that they still happen but just less frequently.

Once you have a final cut of your 168 hours, draw them out on a weekly calendar view. You know you want to spend five hours a week on a particular task, but which five hours is it? A lot of times, this will be where reality smacks you in the face because you'll realize that you need more buffer or transition time. Maybe you forgot that you really should spend thirty minutes showering and cleaning up in the morning after your workout and before you start work. It's not real until you've completed this step of writing it all out on a calendar.

All along the way, keep your priorities at the front of your mind. Many of us struggle with saying no, whether it's to a coworker asking for help or a friend requesting our time. However, saying yes to everything can lead to overcommitment and ultimately, burnout. By setting clear priorities and learning when to say no, we can better manage our workload and keep a healthy work-life balance.

In conclusion, multitasking and interruption culture have become pervasive in today's fast-paced work environment, but the negative effects on productivity, health, and relationships cannot be ignored. Research has shown that focusing on one task at a time is not only more efficient but also leads to higher quality work. By implementing strategies such as batching interruptions, creating no-interruption zones, and using time boxing with the Pomodoro Technique or making a time budget, we can take control of our time and improve our productivity. It's time to break free from the cycle of interruption and prioritize focused work in order to achieve greater success and fulfillment in both our personal and professional lives.

TL;DR

- Multitasking is often touted as a necessary skill, but in reality, it reduces productivity by up to 40%, increases stress levels, and leads to mistakes.
- Only 2.5% of people can effectively multitask while the remaining 97.5% experience significant reductions in performance when trying to do multiple tasks at once.
- Research has shown that multitasking has negative consequences for both intellectual pursuits and work efficiency in students as it

leads to lower GPAs and longer completion times for homework assignments.
• Constant multitasking takes a toll on productivity, relationships, and health; it's time to rethink our approach and learn to focus on one thing at a time.
• Interruption Culture can lead to loss of productivity, errors, stress, chaos, and low morale in the workplace. Interruptions are estimated to have a $1.2 trillion impact on the US economy alone.
• It takes an average of 23 minutes and 15 seconds to resume focus after an interruption;
• Strategies for fighting Interruption Culture include batching interruptions, implementing company-wide/team-wide time blocks for focused work, building focus muscle through deep work, identifying DTF (Do-This-First) tasks, creating no interruption zones.
• The Pomodoro Technique is a time management method developed by Francesco Cirillo to help improve focus and productivity. It involves working for twenty-five minutes followed by a five-minute break, repeated four times with a fifteen minute break after each cycle.
• Timeboxing pairs well with the Pomodoro Technique and is based on setting a fixed amount of time for an activity and then working on that activity until the time is up. It helps with task focus and avoiding procrastination.
• A time budget can be set up to help maximize productivity; it includes completing a time audit to understand how one's current time is spent, setting priorities and stack ranking them to better manage one's 168 hours per week.

CHAPTER EXERCISES

1. For the next week, be very aware of when you're multitasking. Do your best to stay focused and present on

one thing at a time. Are there certain situations or environments where you notice that you slip into multitask mode?
2. Start preparing for your time audit by making notes about what you're doing during the day and how much time you're spending. When you sit down to do the audit, then you'll have real captured data to use for your estimates.
3. Do the time budget exercise in this chapter. What did you have to say "No" to? Can you delegate any of that to someone else?
4. Take a look at this completed time budget. Pick out a couple of the most important tasks and schedule time now on your calendar for them. Are there timeboxes that you could set up on a recurring basis to make sure they happen each week?

CHAPTER NOTES

CHAPTER 26: The Art of Innovation – What You Need to Know to Get and Stay Ahead

Henry Ford didn't invent the car. The automobile was invented by German entrepreneur Carl Benz in 1886. Henry Ford didn't invent the assembly line either. Ford and his team originally saw the idea of an assembly line in a Chicago meat packing plant. Ford found that there was a significant gain in efficiency from keeping the workers stationary and flowing the work through them with a focus on each individual worker doing small repeatable processes.

Ultimately, Ford's Model-T car assembly line would have eighty-four individual processes. It reduced chassis assembly times from twelve and a half hours to ninety minutes, an 8X reduction in labor. Before the Model-T and assembly line, cars were a luxury item reserved for the wealthy. However, Ford's innovation of the assembly line changed that by enabling mass production reduced production costs to make cars more affordable and accessible to the growing American middle class. As a result, Ford's car assembly line innovation changed the world.

Beyond the automobile, the innovation of assembly lines was a revolution in manufacturing and its benefits were far-reaching and nearly immeasurable. Job creation, cost reduction, and increased efficiency were just some of the advantages that factories saw almost immediately. Workforce specialization increased quality, eventually leading to further refinements brought by Six Sigma. Increased efficiency would also result in higher wages, as some part of the new value and higher profits each worker created came back to them. This in turn led to more money being available for consumer purchases, driving even more growth. It's hard to overstate how important the innovation of the assembly line was to the development of the modern society we know today.

While Ford didn't invent the car or the assembly line, he generated all this value by bringing the two ideas together as an innovation. Ford's innovation was a process innovation. Process innovation is one of the three areas where businesses most often innovate. The other two areas are product innovation and business model innovation.

In this chapter we're going to take a closer look at innovation. We'll examine those three areas of business innovation just mentioned. We'll look at an interesting brainstorming technique to drive new ideation. You'll also hear about incremental and exponential innovation. Then we'll finish up with a couple of ideas that can make sure that you're getting and staying out in front of your competition. Let's take a closer look.

Generate New Ideas with 20/50 Brainstorming

As previously mentioned, the first step in any innovation process is generating new ideas. There are several different ways to do this, but one of the most popular is simple brainstorming. Brainstorming is a technique that is often used to generate new ideas by a group of people. The goal of brainstorming is to come up with as many ideas as possible, without judgment or criticism. This allows people to think outside the box and come up with ideas that they might not have thought of otherwise.

To generate a ton of new ideas, I use something I call 20/50 Brainstorming. This technique is a great way to get everyone in a group to engage and come up with new ideas. Challenge everyone in the brainstorming session to come up with twenty ideas of their own and write them down. When done, use these separate lists to come up with a list of at least fifty ideas as a team. Start by going around the room and asking each person to give their best and worst ideas.

This forces each individual to engage, which doesn't always happen when you brainstorm out loud as a group. It gives a vehicle for quieter members — who are often the most creative and thoughtful — to participate. Setting high individual and group goals forces you to dig deep, think out of the box and not just trot out the same ten dog-eared ideas every time the team brainstorms.

The next part is important. Reward the worst idea with some kind of positive prize like a gift card and tell people ahead of time that you're doing it. Intentionally trying to come up with bad ideas might seem counterproductive, but it can actually help you to find more creative solutions to problems. When we only focus on coming up with good ideas, we often get trapped in a limited way of thinking. By encouraging ourselves to think of bad ideas, we force ourselves to change the lens through that we're looking at the problem. This can lead to more out-of-the-box thinking and eventually to differentiated solutions. In addition, intentionally coming up with bad ideas can also help to break down barriers between people. When we share our "dumb" ideas, we are more likely to be open to others' suggestions and feedback. Removing the desire to judge and filter our ideas also removes a huge block to our imagination. As a result, this exercise can help to foster collaboration and creativity.

Now that you've got some ideas, you're ready to put them into action. Don't be afraid to experiment with different approaches. Remember, the goal of brainstorming is to expand your thinking and explore new ways of looking at a problem. The next step is to prioritize the ideas. While developing a range of ideas is important, it's also necessary to focus on the most promising ones.

As a method of trimming the list of fifty ideas down to an actionable list, I usually do the following. Take the list of fifty and cut it in half down to twenty-five. This cut is usually pretty easy, eliminating or combining similar ideas to get the list pared down.

The next cuts are harder. Take your list of twenty-five and now cut it down to ten. People will start to get serious as some favorite ideas end up on a parking lot list. But you're not done. One final cut from ten down to five. You can't do everything. You're not saying the ideas you've cut will never happen, just not yet. Once you're down to five, stack rank them from one to five. Now you're ready to execute. If you'd like to see some other ways to prioritize your ideas, check out the chapter on prioritization. (See Chapter 18.)

Next, we'll dig into the three general categories of business innovation: process, business model and product.

Getting Efficient With Process Innovation

Process innovation is all about finding new ways to build or deliver a product or service. It can involve implementing a new support system, changing how you fulfill orders or anything else that streamlines the way you do business. The goal is to make your process more efficient and effective so that you can improve your bottom line. As mentioned, the Ford Model-T assembly line is one of the GOATs of process innovation.

Another example of process innovation is the evolution of video delivery. In the early days of home video, customers had to travel to their local Blockbuster store to rent a movie. This was convenient if the store was nearby but often resulted in long lines on the weekend and late fees if the movie was not returned on time. Plus, if the store was out of copies of *Top Gun*, then you had to watch something else. Then along came Netflix, which allowed customers to borrow DVDs by mail. This was a major innovation at the time and made it much easier to rent movies from the comfort of home. You still might have to wait for certain videos, but they'd send you the next choice in your queue while you waited.

However, the arrival of streaming video has changed the landscape once again. Today, there are many options for streaming movies and TV shows, with new services launching all the time. This has made it easier than ever to watch whatever you want, whenever you want. And while there have been some setbacks (such as the closure of over 9000 Blockbuster video stores), it's clear that the process innovation of streaming video is here to stay, at least until the next idea arrives. Petabytes of holographic video stored locally in your home and managed with predictive algorithms?

Of course, process innovation is not without its challenges. Striking the right balance between efficiency and quality can be difficult, and there is always the risk of disruptions to your business if something goes wrong. However, if you can successfully navigate these challenges, process innovation can give you a major competitive advantage.

Getting to Revenue with Business Model Innovation

Business model innovation is all about coming up with new ways to create value for customers, consolidate portions of your value chain, and drive revenues. It can be difficult for your competition to copy process and business model innovations because they often happen behind the scenes and are less obvious than the product innovations you're likely to tout in your marketing efforts. The rewards can be great. Business model innovation can help you to tap into new markets, reduce costs, and boost profits.

There have been many different examples of business model innovation over the years, but some of the most commonly used today are:

- Subscription services
- Flat rate pricing
- Marketplace platform
- Software-as-a-service
- Freemium
- Ad/data subsidized

Each of these business models can offer something unique to customers, allowing them to access products and services in a way that's more convenient or cost-effective. Maybe you'll come up with a fresh idea to add to this list.

> Subscription Services

Subscription services, like Netflix or Spotify, provide customers with access to a range of content or products for a monthly fee. This type of business model has become increasingly popular in recent years, as it supplies several advantages for both businesses and customers.

For businesses, the subscription service model offers a more predictable and consistent stream of revenue. This can help the company plan for growth and ensure that the business can sustain itself over the long-term. It also allows businesses to build trusting relationships with their customers, as they are counting on them to return each month or year. And, because customers are typically locked in for at least a period, businesses can feel confident that they will not be churning through new customers constantly.

For customers, the subscriptions offer convenience and flexibility. They know they will always have access to the service and they can cancel at any time if they are not happy with it. There's a sense of community and a brand relationship that can come from being a subscriber. This type of arrangement often provides discounts or other perks for loyal subscribers. Overall, the subscription services business model is a win-win for both businesses and customers.

> Flat Rate Pricing

Charging a single price for unlimited use of a product or service is what's known as the *flat rate pricing* or all-you-can-eat business model. The main advantage of this pricing model for customers is that it allows them to use the product or service as much as they want without having to worry about incurring other costs. From the business's perspective, this can result in increased customer satisfaction and loyalty. Additionally, flat rate pricing can help to simplify the billing process and make it more streamlined operationally for companies. Complex pricing models can be a drag on sales if people can't understand what they're paying for. Flat rate pricing makes things about as simple as it gets.

However, it is important to note that this pricing model is not without its challenges. For example, customers who only use the product or service occasionally may feel that they are overpaying. On the other side of the usage curve, flat rate pricing can encourage high levels of usage which may drive significant costs into the business, especially if it exceeds the volume assumptions that the original pricing was based upon. This can be dangerous if your business can't find cost savings as you scale. As such, it is important to carefully consider whether flat rate pricing is right for your business before implementing it.

> Marketplace Platforms

Marketplace platforms have emerged as a popular business model in recent years. The idea is simple: create an online platform where two sides of a market can connect and generate revenue by taking a percentage of each transaction.

One major advantage of this model is that it can be highly scalable. As the platform grows, it can become more valuable to both buyers and sellers, creating a virtuous cycle of growth. Additionally, the marketplace takes on less risk than traditional retailers, since they don't have to carry inventory or manage fulfillment.

However, there are also challenges with marketplace platforms. One of the biggest is getting the platform to critical mass, balancing buyers and sellers. If you don't have enough of one or the other, then you risk people coming there to do business and finding no one to do business with. Another major issue is ensuring trust between buyers and sellers. This can be particularly difficult when dealing with high-value or sensitive items.

Some examples of successful marketplace platforms include Airbnb and Uber. Airbnb has disrupted the traditional hotel industry by allowing homeowners to rent out their homes to travelers. Uber has done the same with the taxi industry, allowing drivers to use their own cars to provide rides to passengers. On the other hand, there are also examples of marketplace platforms that have failed, such as Shyp and Beepi. Shyp was an Uber-like on-demand courier service to pick up and transport packages but it over-estimated market demand and over-built its infrastructure. Beepi was a marketplace platform for used cars but found that consumers were unwilling to trust a third-party platform to buy a used car sight unseen.

> Software-as-a-Service (SaaS)

The *software-as-a-service (SaaS)* business model has revolutionized the way software is delivered and consumed. As an evolution of subscription models, with SaaS, businesses can subscribe to a software application on a pay-as-you-go basis, eliminating the need to install and maintain software on their premises. This model has many benefits for both businesses and customers. For businesses, SaaS reduces the up-front costs of buying and deploying software. It also simplifies the IT infrastructure, which can result in lower IT costs. For customers, SaaS provides a convenient way to access software applications from any location with an Internet connection. In addition, customers only pay for what they use, which can save money compared to traditional licensing models. The SaaS business model has been a major driver of growth in the software industry, and it is poised to continue its rapid expansion in the years ahead.

> Freemium

When a company offers a basic version of its product or service for free and then charges the user for premium features or add-ons, that's known as the *freemium* business model. The goal is to attract a large number of users with the free offering and then upsell them on the paid features. This model has become increasingly popular in recent years, as it allows companies to reach a wide audience with minimal marketing costs. However, it can be difficult to generate revenue from a free product, and some freemium companies have failed to monetize their add-ons effectively. Nonetheless, the freemium model has proven to be successful for many organizations, and it still is a popular option for startups and established businesses alike.

Just because you've found a winning business model, it doesn't mean that you're good-to-go forever. In 1901, King Camp Gillette invented the modern safety razor, and with it, he established the first freemium business model. The idea was simple: give away the razor at cost and sell the blades for profit. This model proved to be highly successful, and in the following years, Gillette dominated the market for razor blades. However, in recent years, this hegemony has been challenged by a new wave of razor subscription services. Dollar Shave Club, Harry's, and others have disrupted the market by offering cheaper blades and more flexible subscription plans. As a result, Gillette has been forced to rethink its business model. In response, the company has launched its own subscription service and introduced a new line of multi-blade razors. It remains to be seen whether these changes will be enough to keep Gillette on top of the razor market.

> Ad/Data Subsidized

Ad or data-based business models have become a key path to revenue in the digital age. Both models are similar to the freemium model, but where a freemium model tries to upgrade customers from free to premium levels of services, these alternative models are monetized in other ways. *Ad-based business models* generate revenue by displaying in-product advertisements to users, while *data-monetization business models* rely on collecting, analyzing and selling user data to provide valuable insights to businesses.

One of the most popular models for mobile and web apps is to make money by displaying ads in their app and then charging customers for ad-free versions of the product. You'll see this model in almost any mobile game you download. Ads can be a great source of revenue, but they can also negatively affect user experience. They can also generate a significant revenue stream for the owners of the ad platform (Google, Facebook, etc.).

Another way to make money with apps is to monetize the data they collect from their users. Companies that collect user data are able to provide valuable insights to businesses, who in turn use this information to inform marketing decisions and strategies. An example of a data-subsidized business model is Google. By collecting user data, such as search queries and location information, Google is able to provide advertisers with valuable insights into consumer behavior. This information allows advertisers to better target their Google ads to specific audiences, so Google makes their dime on both sides of this business model. You might not want to stand up a business to compete with Google, but if you're able to collect rich high-value data in sufficient volume, there's likely a data broker out there looking to pay you something for it.

Business model innovation can be a powerful tool for companies looking to stay ahead of the competition. By thinking creatively about how they generate revenue or combining these models in unique ways, businesses can tap into new markets and find new paths to grow their bottom line.

Getting Creative with Product Innovation

In today's ever-changing market, *product innovation* is crucial for businesses looking to stay ahead of the competition. It involves creating new value for customers by developing innovative features, products or services that offer better performance, convenience, or functionality at a lower cost. It can also be about finding new ways to increase engagement or simplify usage. When done successfully, product innovation can lead to increased revenue and customer loyalty.

However, achieving successful product innovation requires a deep understanding of customer needs and desires. This involves asking questions such as: What are customers looking for that they cannot find in the current market? What would make their lives easier or better? What are their unmet needs? By answering these questions, businesses can identify gaps in the market and develop solutions that meet those needs.

The process of product innovation can be complex and challenging, but it is also incredibly rewarding for businesses that execute it successfully. By understanding customer needs and developing new products and services to meet those needs, businesses can create significant new value for their customers – and themselves. Moreover, consistent and successful product innovation can help businesses establish themselves as industry leaders while building brand reputation and customer loyalty.

In the next section, we'll discuss two key types of product innovation - incremental and exponential.

Incremental vs Exponential Innovation

"Our intuition about the future is linear. But the reality of information technology is exponential, and that makes a profound difference. If I take 30 steps linearly, I get to 30. If I take 30 steps exponentially, I get to a billion." - Ray Kurzweil

Ray Kurzweil is an American author, computer scientist, and inventor. He is best known for his work on artificial intelligence (AI) and Singularity theory. Kurzweil has written extensively on the future of technology and its impact on society. He is a proponent of the view that the Singularity—the point at which technology becomes so advanced that it surpasses human intelligence—is inevitable and will have profound implications for the future of humanity. In recent years, Kurzweil has become increasingly involved in the development of AI technologies. He is currently a director of engineering at Google, where he is working on projects related to machine learning and natural language processing. Kurzweil is also a co-founder of several startups, including Singularity University and Neuralink.

Kurzweil is suggesting two types of innovation here, incremental innovation and exponential innovation. Exponential innovation is when an innovative company takes a big leap forward in its industry by developing new technology or ideas that are orders of magnitude better than what currently exists. This type of innovation is often game-changing and can lead to the incumbent companies being disrupted or even replaced entirely. Venture capitalists call these companies "unicorns" because they are so rare and hard to find.

Incremental innovation, on the other hand, is when a company makes small improvements to its existing products or services. While this type of innovation may not be as earth-shattering as exponential innovation, it can still be important for helping businesses to stay competitive. Additionally, incremental innovation often leads to exponential innovation, as it allows companies to gradually improve their offerings until they reach a point where they can make a breakthrough. When a Ph.D. spends years researching a subject, going deeper and deeper and then eventually adding a small bit to the canon of knowledge about that subject, that's incremental or additive. But sometimes along the way, they can discover that a process or cognitive model used in an entirely different arena can apply to their work and by doing so, creates a unique perspective and a solution that no one's ever considered before. This can be an exponential opportunity.

One is not necessarily better than the other. Most innovations are incremental, and they sustain the vast number of businesses. Incremental innovation is important for the evolution of existing products to meet new customer needs. This type of innovation tends to lower risk and is less expensive to develop since it builds on an existing product. Exponential innovation can carry a lot of risks since you're frequently building a solution that just didn't exist before. Get it right and maybe you'll find a new growth market that is waiting for your product. Get it wrong and... well, you might end up with a laser razor.

In 2015, a company called Skarp Technologies raised over $4 million on Kickstarter to fund the development of a new razor that would use laser technology to cut hair. The idea was that the razor would eliminate the need to buy blades and be able to provide a close shave without causing any irritation. However, the Skarp razor did not live up to the hype. The company was unable to perfect the laser technology to cut more than a single hair at a time and since the average human face has around 30,000 hairs that's gonna take a little while. Ultimately, Skarp had to refund all of its Kickstarter backers. As of the writing of this book, laser razors are still at least a few whiskers out of reach.

The Exponential Innovation Mashup Matrix

While you might want to take a hard pass on the laser razor idea, if you want to encourage exponential innovation on your team, I've come up with something I call the Exponential Innovation Mashup

Matrix (EIMM). It's a pretty simple premise. You can use the template included or make one of your own in a spreadsheet. To start, create a grid with ideas, product concepts, markets, and emerging tech down the first column, one per line. Then copy the same list across the top of the page, one per column.

Now, consider each intersection of two items and briefly brainstorm what kinds of problems and solutions would come from the combination. To see how this might work, let's roll back the clock a few years and say that your first column had "Social Media" in it. As you work your way down the list of tech and consider the intersection of...

> Social media + texting = Twitter
> Social media + pictures = Instagram
> Social media + video = Snapchat/TikTok/Vine

Exponential Innovation Mashup Matrix

	Social Media	5G	Blockchain	Video	Texting	Pictures	Email	Cloud
Social Media				TikTok	Twitter	Instagram		
5G								
Blockchain								
Video								
Texting								
Pictures								
Email								
Cloud								

Not everything is going to be a perfect fit together, but you will find some that come together in very interesting ways. You might even become the next YouTube star.

Will It... Innovate?

When Rhett McLaughlin and Link Neal met in the first grade, they knew they were destined to become friends. They bonded over their shared love of making videos and often spent hours after school working on their latest project. In 2012, they decided to take their passion to the next level by launching a YouTube channel called Good Mythical Morning. The show quickly gained a loyal following, thanks to the duo's hilarious antics and creativity. Today, Rhett and Link are two of the most popular YouTubers in the world, with over eighteen million subscribers tuning in to Good Mythical Morning (GMM) every week as I'm writing this.

On Cinco de Mayo in 2014, Rhett and Link would introduce one of their signature bits with their "Will It Taco?" video. In the video, the pair try different combinations of food in taco shells, tasting each combination and declaring whether they believe that the combination "tacos." The results:

> Taco shell + Broccoli & cheese = No
> Taco shell + Peanut butter & jelly = Yes
> Taco shell + Chicken pot pie = Yes
> Taco shell + A burger = Yes
> Taco shell + A second soft taco = Yes
> Taco shell + Grocery store sushi = No
> Taco shell + Pine needles = No
> Taco shell + Baby shampoo = No
> Taco shell + Biodegradable packing peanuts = Yes (!?!)
> Taco shell + Congealed pork blood = No

"Will It?" videos have become a staple of GMM since then. Now there are over 100 "Will It?" videos with more than 40M views asking questions like "Will It Hot Pocket?" (French toast "Yes!", flowers "No!") and "Will It Ice Cream Cake?" (popcorn "yes!", KFC "No!"). And they are a perfect example of exponentially innovative thinking.

The Callan Curve

"I'm an inventor. I became interested in long-term trends because an invention has to make sense in the world in which it is finished, not the world in which it is started... Launching a breakthrough idea is like shooting skeet. People's needs change, so you must aim well ahead of the target to hit it." — Kurzweil

This quote from Kurzweil perfectly sums up a problem my teams and I have been discussing for years in the context of building new and innovative products. In order to create truly breakthrough products, you need to anticipate future trends and make your build decisions accordingly. This is a major challenge since you can't always know the best path forward in advance. It's even more difficult when you're in a competitive environment where other players in the space have a headstart, because you don't know what your competition is going to do and what their timelines look like.

But if you don't anticipate correctly, you're going to constantly be playing catch-up. To explain how difficult it can be when you find yourself in this situation, I came up with something that I call the Callan Curve. What is the Callan Curve? (See diagram on the next page.) Here's what it's describing. Note that in this situation, you're the lower of the two curves shown.

When you're building a product that has competition, you're likely to be looking at the competition and analyzing its features and using that feature list in part as a roadmap for your product. Then you build those features and launch them, only to find out that... surprise! During that same time, your competition has been improving their product and building new features too. They've also presumably benefitted in the market from already having the features you've been building, driving new sales, making money and using those resources to push themselves out further ahead of you on the development curve again.

Callan Curve

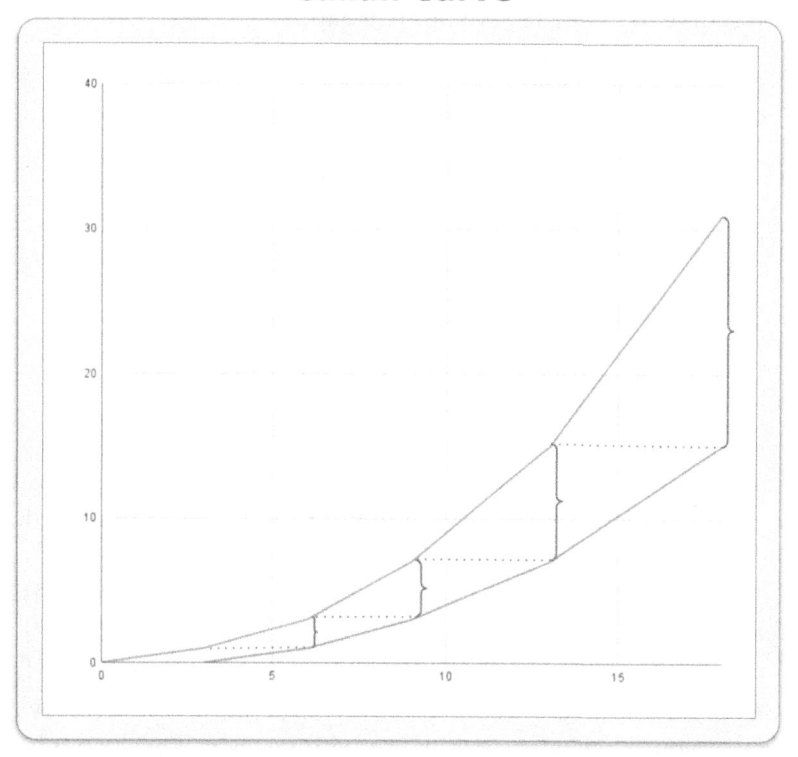

So, you start building the next set of features and launch those, only to find that the targets moved again, maybe even farther away as they've taken advantage again of the added resources they gained from having more customers than you. You're not getting closer. They're actually accelerating away from you with each development cycle. That's the Callan Curve.

When you realize that you're on the bottom line of the curve, you might ask "How do I accelerate my curve or jump up from my curve to the competitor's curve?" Is it a lost cause? Can you ever catch your competition once they have a lead? If you just build what they have, you'll only fall further behind. You've gotta do something else. I'm not saying it's going to be easy, but I've identified five ways to jump up the curve to close the development gap:

1. Out-innovate
2. Partner
3. Acquire
4. Accelerate resources
5. Better process/execution

Let's take a closer look at each of these options.

> Out-Innovate

Everyone tends to initially land on the first idea, to out-innovate the competition, as what they're going to do. They like this idea because it can often require the least initial investment.

"We'll just be smarter and more clever," you tell yourself. But ideas are the easy part.

Closing a product gap by being smarter or more creative is far from a sure bet. Your competition isn't stupid. After all, they're ahead of you. They must be doing something right. They're not lazy either. They're working hard to stay ahead. Don't underestimate them. That's not to say that you shouldn't spend time innovating. Absolutely please do. This chapter's all about how to do that successfully. But you might not want to put all your eggs in this basket.

> Partner

Option #2 is to find a partner that can move you out further on the curve. It could be those smart competitors that we were just talking about. It might be someone who has a useful technology that could be integrated into your product. Maybe it's access to new third-party data that can give you an edge. The main barrier to partnering can be having the vision to see how the two pieces can come together and create synergy and then negotiating with a potential partner who may not share in that vision. But partnering, especially if you can land an exclusive deal, can give you a quick boost on the curve and create a sustainable advantage. Many times this can happen without driving a lot of new costs into the business too, which helps a lot.

> Acquire

Depending on your company's size and resources, you might consider option #3. You might be able to buy your way up the curve by acquiring a competitor. This can be an expensive proposition, but if you have the resources, it can be a quick way to gain a foothold in the market. For example, Google/Alphabet has acquired over 250 companies as of this writing. YouTube was originally an acquisition that accelerated Google into the video space. It doesn't always work. For every YouTube, there are several new entries on the killedbygoogle.com website. See Picasa, Zync Render, Timely and others.

Another example, Amazon's 2017 purchase of Whole Foods was met with equal parts excitement and trepidation. For many, the $13 billion acquisition suggested that Amazon was poised to take over the entire grocery industry. And, given Amazon's history of upending established businesses, it's not hard to see why. Five years later, it hasn't happened yet. But it clearly accelerated Amazon on the Callan Curve.

Of course, this strategy is not without its risks. If the market is already saturated, or if there are other well-established competitors, you might find it difficult to turn a profit. But if you do your homework and choose your target wisely, buying up a competitor can be a great way to jump the Curve and expand your business.

> Accelerate Resources

A similar but potentially less-expensive path would be to try option #4 and accelerate access to resources within your organization. Companies that can move quickly to take advantage of new opportunities or respond effectively to threats are often the ones that come out ahead in the end. If your competition has five developers, can you close the gap by getting five more?

Or maybe you're trying to close the gap and know you need a rocket scientist to do it. Go get a rocket scientist. At least a fractional one. Or acknowledge that you're not really serious about getting the resources you need and closing this gap.

One of the key factors in a company's ability to move quickly is its ability to attract and retain top talent. People with the skills and experience that your company needs to succeed can be difficult to find, and once you have them onboard, you need to keep them motivated and engaged. An effective way to close the development gap with your competition is to invest in a talent management system that will help you identify, attract, and retain the best employees. With the right system in place, you'll be able to get the resources you need onboard faster and keep them engaged and motivated so that they can help your company succeed.

> Better Process/Execution

Finally, option #5, the last path to closing a development gap, is to have better, more efficient processes and crisper execution. Shorten your cycle times. Don't waste precious bandwidth on things that don't add value to the customer-facing product. Eliminate distractions. Look for ways to cut waste and process busywork and make things run faster and more smoothly.

This could involve automating tasks by integrating tech like AI or machine learning into your work plans, streamlining communication, or improving project management. By having a clear plan, staying organized and communicating crisply, you will execute your projects more effectively. But it also means being nimble and adapting to changes as they come up. By being efficient and effective in your execution, you'll be able to get more done with the same resources in a shorter period and close the gap between where you are and where you want to be. You might not be able to land more resources to accelerate along the Callan Curve, but you can almost always work a little smarter with what you have.

No matter what methods you use, the key to closing the development gap is to pick a path (or a combination of approaches) and keep moving forward. By consistently making progress and being persistent, you'll eventually reach your goals. So don't let the development gap stop you from reaching your potential - with the right strategy in place, it can be narrowed or even eliminated over time.

Sprint ION and the WOW-NOW Matrix

"I realize that most inventions fail not because the R&D department can't get them to work, but because the timing is wrong—not all of the enabling factors are at play where they are needed. Inventing is a lot like surfing: you have to anticipate and catch the wave at just the right moment." – Kurzweil

Getting the timing right on product innovation involving new technology isn't easy. As I mentioned back in Chapter 22, in 1998 I moved to Overland Park, Kansas from Cincinnati to work on a massive project called Sprint ION. The basic idea was to deliver phone, internet, and video services over a high-speed internet connection and distribute it throughout the home. Sound familiar?

ION stood for Integrated On-demand Network. The product required a high-speed DSL internet connection to the home. DSL stands for Digital Subscriber Line and was installed by the local phone company in each market. That was how broadband internet was delivered in the days before cable, fiber and 5G. The high-speed connection was connected to our Residential Gateway (called the RISH or Residential Integrated Services Hub) and was distributed to the rest of the house from there.

You got four phone lines and high-speed data. There were field reports of 6 MB downloads, which was ridiculously fast at the time. But installations were really hard. First, you had to coordinate with the local service provider, and they were still sorting out their reluctant wholesaling of consumer data services on their network to other resellers. Then, there was the trick of wiring the home with ethernet because the Wi-Fi Alliance wouldn't be formed until 1999 and the wireless standard we've come to take for granted now just didn't exist.

We also created a product that didn't exist then with the RISH. We tackled the perceived problem of keeping the phone lines hot in case of a power failure because we were trying to offer parity with the existing local phone service. This resulted in us incorporating a battery backup that was spec'd to last up to eighteen hours. At the time, my team felt a ton of responsibility to get this right because we knew that if people lost phone services during an outage, lives could be lost.

Early prototypes were ugly desktop PC-sized beasts from Cisco. But they couldn't or wouldn't get the costs down so we found an alternative source and launched with a much smaller plastic modem-like hub not much bigger than the wi-fi routers you have at home today.

So why did the product fail? Well, the installation nightmare was a big part of it. Installs were rescheduled over and again because the local phone company hadn't turned up broadband service at the house. Established and standardized home networking over wi-fi would have helped. A lot. The ethernet wiring situation in each home drove installation costs higher. We had recommended a BYOB (Bring Your Own Broadband) version of the product my team called ION Lite which would have sidestepped those local phone company installation issues, but the company was focused on the additional revenue we'd get from reselling that high-speed connection and didn't want to give that up.

In 2001, as the plug was being pulled on ION, Vonage would emerge in the home VOIP space but with a product you could install on any internet connection just like ION Lite. Today, you have the kind of integrated services we envisioned over fiber connections and can buy phone/internet/video services. We were in the right spot with ION, just a few years too soon.

WOW-NOW Matrix

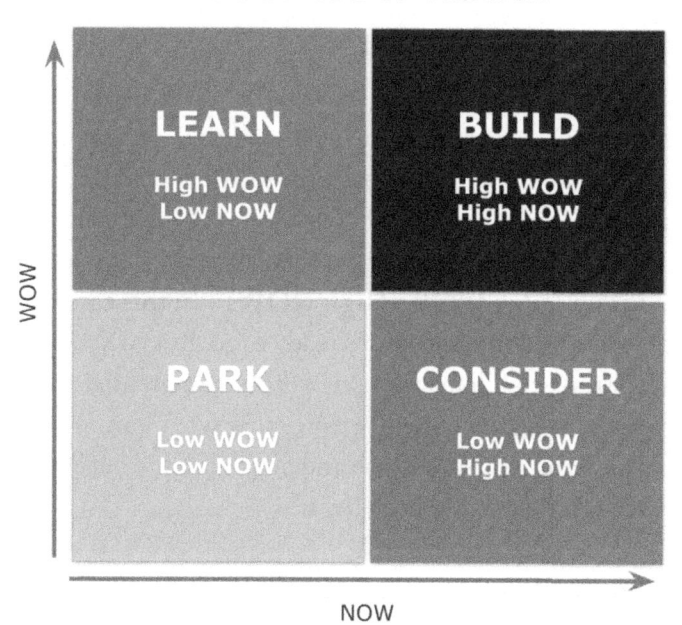

	Low NOW	High NOW
High WOW	LEARN (High WOW, Low NOW)	BUILD (High WOW, High NOW)
Low WOW	PARK (Low WOW, Low NOW)	CONSIDER (Low WOW, High NOW)

With this experience in the rearview mirror and to address concerns like Kurzweil's market timing, I came up with something I call the Wow-Now Matrix. It's a way to prioritize development based on aligning the product with market timing using a 2x2 matrix with the "Wow" factor on one side and the "Now" factor on the other. I define "Wow" as the concept's innovative value. You could also see it as differentiation. Some might simplify that to just revenue, but that's really a different metric. Then I define "Now" as how quickly it can be delivered. Does the tech for it exist in a working form today or does it require some R&D and tech advances? Does it require a lot of resources to develop or is it a quick build?

Score each project from 1 (low) to 10 (high) and chart them on your matrix. The target quadrant is finding High Wow/High Now projects. Those will be your best bets to avoid your very own Sprint ION story.

What action do you take in each quadrant of the Matrix? Let's take a look.

- **Build (High WOW/High NOW)** - This is the desired situation where people have a strong positive value for your solution and the technology is ready for building your product. You're in your market window. Go like the wind.

- **Consider (Low WOW/High NOW)** - In this case, you've got tech that you can use. It's ready to go. But you're not sure how strong the demand/value is for the potential solution. Do some research here, to ensure that what you're creating is something people will use and pay for. If the business case looks viable, consider building it.

- **Learn (High WOW/Low NOW)** - For products in this quadrant, you know that people are interested in the solution. But the tech's just not ready yet. Invest in learning, by researching the market's needs and exploring how to develop your product. Consider if an alternative tech could get you there with a modified solution to gain customer learnings. If you own the tech you're trying to use, keep evolving it and learning from each iteration.

- **Park (Low WOW/Low NOW)** - In this situation, neither the technology nor the demand for a solution is available. Sometimes these situations change with time, so don't throw away the idea. Park it for now and move on. But check back from time to time to see if either the WOW or NOW have shifted.

The WOW/NOW framework is designed to help you evaluate where your projects fit within the innovation process. By considering both the "WOW" (impact and market potential) and "NOW" (feasibility and readiness), you can gain a better understanding of when it makes sense to invest in certain projects. Keep in mind that the WOW/NOW framework is just one tool to help prioritize your innovation ideas. Other criteria such as team skills, resources, etc. are also important when considering which projects to take on.

With Innovation Comes Some Failures

Innovation is the lifeline of any company that aims to stay ahead of the curve. However, innovation is not a bed of roses. With innovation comes failure, and sometimes a lot of it. A sizable part of innovative efforts and investments go down the drain. But that doesn't mean the efforts are a waste of resources. As famed inventor

Thomas Edison once said, "I have not failed. I've just found 10,000 ways that won't work." Failure is another source of innovation. One learns from their mistakes and comes back stronger and wiser. Like I mentioned earlier, don't try to fail but if you do, fail productively.

All too often, good ideas never make it to market. This is because the journey from concept to commercialization can be long, arduous, and fraught with peril. To succeed in innovation, companies must invest in an innovation culture that promotes risk-taking, experimentation, and learning from failures. This chapter has outlined some of the best practices for building and nurturing an innovative culture that will drive creativity while minimizing the risks. Embracing these ideas and implementing them systematically will not completely shield a company from innovation failure, but it will tip the scales in favor of more wins than losses.

TL;DR

- Henry Ford didn't invent the car or the assembly line, but he innovated by combining them and creating the Model-T car assembly line. This reduced chassis assembly times from twelve and a half hours to ninety minutes, making cars more accessible and affordable for the growing middle class.
- There are three general categories of business innovation: process, business model, and product.
- Generating new ideas for innovation can be done through 20/50 brainstorming where each person is challenged to come up with individual ideas and then collectively refine them into a list of at least fifty ideas.
- Business model innovation helps businesses tap into new markets and reduce costs; examples include subscription services, flat rate

pricing, marketplace platforms, software-as-a-service, freemium and ad/data subsidized models.
• Process innovation is about finding new ways to build or deliver a product or service that are efficient and effective such as Netflix's streaming video delivery model.
• Product innovation involves creating new value for customers through improved performance, convenience and/or functionality. To achieve successful product innovation, one must have a deep understanding of customer needs and desires.
• There are two types of product innovation – incremental and exponential. Incremental innovation involves making small improvements to existing products while exponential innovation involves making breakthroughs in the industry through emerging technology or ideas.
• The Callan Curve illustrates how competing businesses can find themselves repeatedly playing catch-up if they do not anticipate future trends to move ahead of the competition. To close the development gap, companies can out-innovate, partner, acquire, accelerate resources, or adopt a better process/execution strategy.

CHAPTER EXERCISES

1. Think about an innovation you've seen in a product or service that you use. What type of innovation was it – process, business model or product? How did the innovation change or improve the customer's value proposition?
2. Find an area where you'd like to generate some new ideas. If you have available team members, invite them to take part in a 20/50 brainstorming exercise with you. If you're flying solo, go through the process of coming up with your twenty

ideas. Then cut them down to ten and then a stack-ranked list of five.
3. Take a look at the Exponential Innovation Mashup Matrix. Make a list of interesting technologies or other business opportunities and put them in the appropriate columns. Now look at the intersections of these opportunities and see what solutions you can identify at the intersections.
4. Using the list of potential exponentially innovative ideas that you just made, score them on the WOW-NOW scale from 1-10. Do you have any ideas that fall in the Build category?
5. Go back and look at the Callan Curve. Think about a product you're working on or one you're familiar with. Are you on the upper or lower curve? If you're on the lower curve, which of the five paths to jump the curve feels like the most viable alternative?

CHAPTER NOTES

CHAPTER 27: How to Build A Product-Focused Culture

There have been a lot of words written in the business world about the importance of workplace culture and as I bring this book in for a landing, I'd like to throw my two cents in. What exactly is workplace culture? Put simply, culture is the set of values and behaviors that dictate how a company's employees interact with each other and with the outside world. And while it may seem like culture is something that develops organically over time, the truth is that there are many opportunities to shape it as it evolves. I think this is one of the most important jobs of a company's leadership.

Because this is a product-focused book, I'll assume that if you've made it this far, you're at least a little bit interested in having a product-focused business. And if you want to build a product-focused business, you need to start by creating a product-focused culture. In this final chapter, we'll take a look at what that means and how to take steps towards making it a reality.

Building a product-focused culture (PFC) starts with defining your organization's core values. These are the guiding principles that will shape every decision your team makes—from the products you build to the way you treat your customers and each other. We've talked about knowing your "why" (Chapter 8) and setting your north star (Chapter 13) and those things apply here. Some examples of core values might be things like "customer obsession," "default to transparency," or "move fast and break things."

Once you've defined your core values, it's important to communicate them to your team and make sure everyone is on board. The best way to do this is to live and breathe your values every day. Be authentic. Set an example for your team by modeling the behavior you want them to emulate. It's not just words on a page. You can't just create a company culture checklist and check these items off like something on your to-do list. Telling people that you value something, and then showing over and again with your actions that you don't, will deliver a clear message to everyone about what your real priorities are. They say "actions speak louder than words" for a reason. It's not just about having a ping-pong table and a beer at 4 PM on Friday. What values are you showing your team the rest of the week?

A product-focused culture is essential for any business that wants to be innovative, responsive to customers, and grow revenue. This focus on product drives growth, allows for better communication across organizational stakeholders, and keeps the best people happy. Implementing a product-focused culture does not happen overnight, but it is possible with the right strategy and execution.

Here are six steps to take to build a product-focused culture in your company:

1. Put the customer at the center of your business decisions.
2. Drive toward product-led growth.
3. Invest in learning, research and new ideas.
4. Leverage organizational communication for clear narrative and transparency.
5. Use a "Business Agile" approach across internal stakeholder groups.
6. Keep the best people happy.

PFC #1: Putting Customers at the Center of Business Decision-Making

As we've discussed throughout this book, customers are the backbone of any business. In the long-term, no customers equal no company, which is why it's essential to prioritize their needs and desires. It's easy to forget sometimes that you don't have a job simply because there's a pile of work to be done. That pile of work exists because you're trying to meet customer needs. Companies that put customers at the center of decision-making are more likely to create sustainable, customer-centric cultures that drive innovation, growth, and profitability.

To truly embrace customer-centricity, businesses must go beyond treating customers as an afterthought or a source of revenue. They must develop a deep understanding of their customers, empathize with their challenges, and tailor products and services to meet their needs.

There are many examples of companies that prioritize their customers and have reaped the rewards. For instance, Amazon has built a reputation for being one of the most customer-centric companies in the world, with its obsession over the customer experience driving innovation and growth. Remember how they actually write the documents that describe the customer's experience with the launched product before they build it? Similarly, Zappos' success is rooted in its culture of WOWing customers through exceptional service and personalized experiences. By prioritizing their customers, these companies have created a loyal following that has propelled them to success.

Here are four practical tips and tactics for implementing a customer-centric approach within your business:

1. *Develop a deep understanding of your customer*
To create products and services that resonate with your customers, you must first understand their needs and desires. This requires more than just gathering data - it involves actively listening to customers, conducting user research, and gaining insight into their motivations and behaviors. You can do this by conducting customer interviews, surveys, and focus groups, as well as gathering data on their behavior through analytics tools. But most importantly, get out of your office and simply talk to them. See their environment and watch how they use your product.

2. *Use customer feedback to drive decision-making*
By asking for customer feedback and incorporating it into product development and decision-making, companies can create products and services that better meet customer needs and desires. This can be done through surveys, online reviews, or one-on-one interviews. It's essential to take this feedback seriously and use it to drive strategic decisions.

3. *Measure customer satisfaction and loyalty*
Remember, what gets measured gets managed. To gauge how well you're doing in prioritizing your customers, measure customer satisfaction and loyalty. As we mentioned, Net Promoter Score (NPS) is a popular metric used to assess customer loyalty. This metric measures the likelihood of customers to recommend your product or service to others. You can also look at things like churn rate and customer retention to measure loyalty. Additionally, satisfaction surveys are a great way to get direct feedback from customers. This will give you an insight into how well the customer experience is going and areas that need improvement. By regularly checking customer

satisfaction and loyalty metrics, companies can know if they're getting better (or worse) in their customer-centric efforts.

4. *Empower employees to prioritize the customer*

To create a customer-centric culture, businesses must empower their employees to prioritize the customer. This can be done by providing employees with the knowledge and tools they need to provide exceptional customer service, as well as incentivizing positive customer outcomes. Give them the ability to do the right thing for a customer, even if it's not always the easiest or most scalable path sometimes. By celebrating employees who go above and beyond for customers, you create a culture that puts the customer front and center.

PFC #2: Drive Towards Product-Led Growth

In recent years, there's been a lot of talk about "product-led growth" (PLG). But what is it? Simply put, PLG is a go-to-market strategy in which the product itself drives customer acquisition, retention and revenue expansion. By making the product engaging, quick-to-value and user-friendly, customers move as frictionlessly as possible from "just checking this out" to becoming paying customers.

Think about some of the most successful consumer tech companies out there today. Companies like Slack, Dropbox, and Grammarly all follow a PLG model. They offer free trials or freemium versions of their products with the hope that users will eventually upgrade to paid plans. And it works — Dropbox, for example, has more than 700 million registered users. Just over 2%, or 15 million, are paying customers generating almost $2 billion in annual revenue.

There are a few reasons why PLG is such an effective growth strategy. First off, it's a great way to acquire new customers. By offering a free trial or freemium version of your product, you're making it easy for potential customers to try out your offering without any risk. And if they like what they see, they're more likely to become paying customers down the road.

Secondly, PLG helps you retain existing customers. If your product is good enough, your customers will stick around—and maybe even pay more as they expand their usage over time. Again, Dropbox is a great example of this; as users store more and more files in their Dropbox accounts, they eventually need to upgrade to paid plans with more storage space.

Finally, PLG encourages customer advocacy. Word-of-mouth marketing is still one of the most powerful marketing tools out there—and it's something that you can't buy. If you have a great product that delivers value to your customers, they'll be happy to promote it for you by telling their friends and family about it. Slack, for example, has grown largely through customer referrals.

So how can you use PLG to build a successful business? Here are five tips on how to get started:

1. *Focus on user experience.*

A great user experience is essential for any product—but especially for those following a PLG strategy. As we just mentioned, this starts with an organizational obsession to understand customer needs and deliver customer value. Remember, with PLG, the product itself is responsible for acquiring and retaining customers. That means that if your product isn't easy and enjoyable to use, people aren't going to want to stick around—no matter how good your sales team is... or how much money you're spending on marketing campaigns.

2. *Figure out your core value proposition.*
What does your product do better than anything else on the market? Who are your power users and how do they get value from the product? Answering these questions is crucial for any go-to-market strategy—but especially for PLG. After all, if your product isn't delivering real value to users, they're not going to want to pay for it down the road.

3. *Take the friction out of your purchasing process.*
It'll be difficult to establish a product-led sales funnel if you've got complex pricing and it's not clear what people need to buy or how. Remember, as we've said previously, if it's confusing, the easiest thing for your customers to do is to just do nothing.

4. *Double-down on your onboarding process.*
Just like you did with the purchasing process, you want to remove as much friction as possible between the purchase and the customer getting back something that they value. Onboarding can either confirm that your newest user made a great choice or put them in a state of buyer's remorse that will likely lead to churn down the road. I'll say it again – frictionless and fastest path to value. Get them happy and engaged ASAP.

5. *Get feedback early and often.*
Feedback is essential for any product development process—but it's especially important when following a PLG strategy. Why? Because with PLG, the goal is for the product itself to drive growth . . . which means that if there are any issues with the product, they're going to show up pretty quickly. As such, you need to be prepared to listen to feedback and make changes accordingly. The best way to do this? Reach out to current potential users early and often ask them what they think about how they're using and liking products. You can also encourage feedback by making it easily accessible within the application

itself—for example, with an in-app chat feature or a form users can fill out within the app.

PFC #3: The Importance of Continuous Learning and Experimentation in Product-Focused Culture

In today's fast-paced business environment, companies that fail to adapt risk being left behind. To stay ahead of the competition, it's crucial for companies to invest in continuous learning, product and marketing research, and experimentation with new ideas. When companies take these investments, it creates a more sustainable product-driven business culture that brings value to both the company, its employees, and its customers.

There are many examples of companies that have invested in these areas and achieved great success as a result. For instance, Google places a significant emphasis on continuous learning and experimentation. The company offers its employees free, on-site classes and encourages employees to spend 20% of their time pursuing new ideas and projects. By doing this, Google has been able to remain on the cutting edge of technology and innovation.

Similarly, Procter & Gamble invests heavily in product research and development through a number of different paths, including its P&G Ventures Studio. Founded in 2015, the focus of this group is to find opportunities where P&G doesn't currently compete and come up with innovative new solutions. This has led to launching multiple new product brands, including the skin treatment Metaderm, and Zevo, a natural insecticide. P&G's investment in research and development allows them to stay ahead of the competition and deliver products that truly meet the needs of their customers.

If you want to create an environment for continuous learning and innovation, here are four practical tips and tactics for your business:

1. Invest in continuous learning.
Start here. Set a budget for this. Offer development and training programs. Attend conferences and workshops. Provide access to educational resources. Make time for it as a company-wide priority. Encouraging employees to learn and grow in their roles not only helps the individuals but also the company as a whole.

2. Conduct product and marketing research.
Learn about your customers. Investing in product and marketing research helps companies find potential opportunities and better understand customer needs and preferences. This can be done through surveys, focus groups, or user research.

3. Foster a culture of innovation.
We talked about innovation earlier. Encourage employees to innovate and experiment with new ideas. Create a culture that rewards risk-taking and encourages employees to pursue their ideas. Companies can do this by setting aside time and resources for experimentation and by creating an environment where ideas are welcomed and encouraged.

4. Learn from failures and successes.
This might be the most important thing. Some of the best work and greatest learning comes from failed projects. Companies that invest in experimentation and innovation must be willing to take risks and learn from any failures. Win or lose, find the lessons and make it productive. It's important to celebrate successes and to take the time to reflect on failures, identify lessons learned, and come up with new approaches.

PFC #4: Leverage Organizational Communications for Clear Narrative and Transparency

Good organizational communication is key to establishing and driving internal product understanding and transparency. For companies to ensure a successful product-centered culture, they must build a narrative around their products that resonates with their employees, customers, and stakeholders. By communicating clear and consistent messaging internally, companies can ensure that all teams are aligned and understand their role in creating products that meet customer needs.

However, crafting a narrative requires more than simply repeating product features and benefits. It requires understanding what motivates customers to use your products, what motivates your employees to do their best work and ensuring that all communication is transparent and honest. By doing so, companies can build trust with customers and employees, which can result in increased loyalty and a more engaged workforce.

In this section, we will explore the importance of organizational communication in a product-centered culture and provide practical tips and tactics for creating a clear narrative and fostering transparency within your company. Let's start by understanding the difference between the formal and informal communication flows in your organization.

> Formal Communications Flows

Formal communication is the official channel that a business uses to provide information to employees. These communications typically flow from the executive leadership to the rest of the company through things like memos, e-mails, reports, and company meetings. There are a few key things to keep in mind when setting up formal communications flows:

1. Define the purpose of the communication. What are you trying to achieve?

2. Consider the audience. Who are you trying to reach? What do they need to know? How can you best communicate with them?
3. Keep it as concise as possible. This can be a challenge, but it's important to remember that people are busy and likely won't have time to read a long, drawn-out message.
4. Use simple language. Unless you're confident that everyone in your audience understands any technical terms or acronyms, avoid them. Using jargon or complicated words will only serve to confuse them and turn them off from reading your message.
5. Communicate often. This is especially important in fast-moving organizations where things can change quickly. Keeping everyone up-to-date on the latest changes will help ensure that everyone is always on the same page. People will fill an information gap with their own narrative if they don't hear from you. Don't leave them guessing.
6. Make sure there is a clear structure and hierarchy in place. Who will be responsible for ensuring that the message is communicated effectively?
7. Ask questions about your communications before and after. Test the communication before roll-out. Once you've implemented the change, ask for feedback from employees on how well it worked. Don't let confusion linger.

> Informal Communications Flows

In contrast to formal communication, informal communication is unplanned and often happens spontaneously between co-workers. Think coffee, lunch, or happy hour. An office drop-by for a casual chat. Informal communications are often more important than formal communications when it comes to building a product-led culture because they are authentic and organic. They're not easily manipulated, and it can impact organizational trust if you try. But because of their power, it's important to understand what they are and how to participate in them.

Here are a few tips on how to build healthy informal communications within your organization:

1. Encourage open communication and transparency. Create an environment where employees feel comfortable speaking up and sharing their ideas freely.
2. Lead by example. If you want your employees to communicate openly, you need to set the tone by being open and communicative yourself.
3. Encourage feedback. Soliciting feedback is a great way to get employees involved in the decision-making process and ensure that everyone's voices are heard.
4. Be responsive to feedback. Once you've received feedback, take it seriously and act on it accordingly. This will show employees that their input is valued and appreciated.

One of the most important ways to foster positive informal communications is to identify the organization's informal leaders and influencers. Informal leaders and influencers are often the unsung heroes of an organization. They're the ones who navigate the waters of office politics, mediate interpersonal conflict, and generally keep the wheels of the organization turning. While they may not hold formal leadership positions, their influence is nonetheless significant. So how do you find these individuals? Here are a few tips:

1. Look for the connectors. These are the people who seem to know everyone in the organization and are always facilitating interactions and making introductions. If you need to know who can get something done, talk to these people.
2. Look for the ones who are always in the know. These are the people who always seem to be up on the latest organizational news and insider info. If something is going on in the organization, chances are they know about it before anyone else does.
3. Look for the ones who always have their finger on the pulse of employee morale. These are the people who can tell you how your employees feel about a situation or a decision that's been made. They're often seen as unofficial ambassadors for employee morale.
4. Look for the ones who are always willing to help. These are the people who are always quick to offer help or advice, whether it's asked for or not. If you need someone to lend a helping hand, these are the people you want to approach first.

Informal leaders and influencers play a crucial role in every organization, yet they often go unrecognized. By taking the time to know these individuals, you can develop relationships with them that will foster better communication and understanding within your organization as a whole. Once you have some of your influencers in mind, there's an important next step. Pair them with strong mentors to develop those relationships. This will give them a positive connection to the formal communication structure which hopefully results in less misinformation going out to the org and better feedback coming back to the leaders.

> Two Ideas for Creating and Managing Feedback

We've talked about how feedback loops are important for managing stakeholders and customers. But they are equally important parts of your company's communication flows. Feedback loops can be formal or informal, but they should always be consistent. Formal feedback loops might involve scheduled weekly or monthly meetings, while informal feedback loops might involve more spontaneous conversations. Either way, the goal is to create an environment where employees feel comfortable giving and receiving feedback regularly. As a part of providing a feedback-rich environment, I'm partial to two specific techniques — skip-level meetings and 360 performance reviews.

Skip-level meetings are meetings where lower-level employees have the opportunity to share their thoughts and suggestions with upper-level managers, skipping the manager levels in between. If your company is a little too hierarchical in its communications, a skip-level can establish healthy new dialogues between different levels of the org. Often, I've seen that a manager might be trying to control the information flow between their team and their boss and not presenting a realistic view of what's going on in the trenches. By having regular skip-levels, the boss can get a better handle on how things are really playing within the work teams and find issues that aren't being communicated that could be preventing teams from making progress.

I prefer these meetings to be one-on-one to get the best results, even if it means it takes longer to make the rounds. Skip-level group meetings tend to be dominated by a brave, confident vocal minority willing to speak up in front of the team. You'll get a higher level of quality input from a more diverse group if you take the time to do it one person at a time.

A *360 performance review* is another tool that can be used to create a culture of feedback at your company. In a 360 review, employees receive feedback from their peers, their managers, and their direct reports. This provides them with a well-rounded (or 360 degree) view of their performance and helps them determine areas where they can improve. We all think we're being perceived a particular way by the people we work with. Sometimes we're accurate, sometimes not. A 360 review can be an eye-opening experience. You might hear things you don't like, but wouldn't you rather know if people think you're micro-managing or (gulp!) you don't take feedback well? A little bit of other people's reality can help you do better.

> Managing Conflicts

As you work with formal and informal communications in a fast-paced business, you know that conflict and stress are inevitable. Having a strategy for managing these situations is a key part of resolving them with minimal impact.

First, don't take things personally. When someone is stressed or in conflict, they may say or do things that are not directed at you but are really a reaction to the situation. It's important to remember that when people are under stress, they may lash out in ways that are not productive or constructive. If you can, try to step back and see the situation from the other person's perspective. This can help you avoid taking things too personally and getting defensive.

Second, "seek first to understand, then to be understood." That's a quote from Stephen Covey's *The 7 Habits of Highly Effective People*. When you're in a conflict situation, it's natural to want to be heard and to have your point of view understood. But if you want to resolve the conflict, it's important to understand the other person's perspective first. Listen carefully to what they're saying and try to see the situation from their point of view. Once you've done that, then you can explain your own point of view in a way that is more likely to be heard and understood.

While conflict can be difficult and uncomfortable, it also creates an opportunity for growth and collaboration. One of the most important things to remember when conflict arises is to assume positive intent. In other words, rather than assuming that someone is trying to sabotage your work or deliberately make your life difficult, try to understand their perspective and what they are hoping to achieve. This doesn't mean that you have to agree with them, but it can help to diffuse the situation and open up a productive dialogue. By assuming positive intent, you can turn a potentially negative experience into an opportunity for growth and collaboration.

Next, be direct and honest with your communication. When you're communicating with someone who is stressed or in conflict, honesty and directness will matter. Avoid being passive-aggressive or making indirect comments that could be interpreted in multiple ways. It's important to be completely clear about what you're trying to say so that there is no misunderstanding. Don't make the situation worse by leaving things open-ended.

Finally, focus on the problem, not on the person. When you're in a conflict situation, it's easy to focus on the other person and what they did wrong from your perspective. But if you want to resolve the conflict, it's important to focus on the problem itself, not on the person. By focusing on the problem, you can come up with a solution that everyone can agree on. And if there really was a mistake made, try to use the situation as a learning opportunity for the person rather than playing the blame game. Removing the heat will keep a pot from boiling over and it works the same way here.

> Being Transparent

Before we move on from this discussion of organizational communications, let's briefly talk a little more about one area that can impact the product-centered culture — transparency. Transparency is often where formal and informal communications intersect because, if done well, it can be a cure for office gossip and negativity that arises from the informal channels by sharing actual information through the company's formal channels.

By making information as widely available as you can manage practically and securely, transparency has the power to create open communication channels, foster trust, encourage respect, and promote accountability. When information is readily available and accessible to all as part of your formal communications flow, there is less room for error and misunderstanding. Mistakes can be quickly found and corrected. Decisions can be made with the consensus of the team. And everyone can stay focused on the company's goals.

In addition, transparent communication can help build a positive product culture. A culture of transparency fosters trust and respect among employees. It also promotes accountability by making sure that everyone is aware of the company's goals and objectives. Finally, it helps ensure that information is shared as widely as possible so that all employees have access to the same data and resources.

PFC #5: Use a "Business Agile" Approach Across Stakeholder Groups

In recent years, the term "Agile" has become increasingly popular in the business world. Many organizations have turned to the Agile method to speed up their software development cycle and increase efficiency. However, what many don't realize is that the same principles that make Agile so effective in software development can also be applied to other areas of the business, such as organizational culture, to achieve similar benefits. This approach is often referred to as "business Agile."

In its simplest form, Agile is a philosophy that stresses the importance of collaboration, flexibility, and constant communication to get work done quickly and efficiently. When applied to an organization as a whole, this philosophy can help your business become more responsive to change, more customer-focused, and more profitable.

At the end of the day, almost any team that has deliverables and projects (marketing, HR, supply chain, legal, operations, etc.) can benefit from the structures and rhythms of Agile, such as:

- Daily team check-ins, often known as stand-ups because they're brief and people typically stand for the meeting.
- Project tracking boards
- Planning and estimations
- Sprints
- Demos

According to Dr. Jeff Sutherland, co-creator of Scrum, which is a specific Agile implementation framework, "We've found that Scrum can double the production of anything — it doesn't matter whether it's sales, marketing, software, finance — it works everywhere." Agile can be a useful approach wherever cross-department collaboration is frequent because it brings added visibility to the work being done.

Let's take a look at some of the key benefits of adopting a business Agile approach across your organization.

1. *Focus on the Most Important Work.*

    A key aspect of Agile is that business Agile teams are constantly evaluating the work backlog and business priorities, and they adjust the order of work accordingly. Typically, a business Agile sprint lasts two weeks and then a new set of prioritized work begins. This helps to ensure that the team is always focusing on the most important tasks. As a result, business Agile practices can help organizations to be more responsive to market changes and better able to compete in today's ever-changing business landscape.

2. *Better Understanding of Team Capacity and Increased Productivity.*
We've talked about making data-driven decisions in this book. One of the main benefits of a business Agile approach is that it can help to better understand a team's work capacity. This is because each project is estimated and measured, giving you the data that allows for more accurate forecasting of future workloads over time. You'll have a clearer view of the team's velocity and work volume, making it much more likely that you'll hit your deliverable dates.

In addition, because Agile helps focus on the most impactful work, productivity increases as unnecessary work is eliminated. With an Agile approach, most meetings are kept short and focused on specific topics. This reduces wasted time spent on tangents or discussing things that don't directly contribute to the task at hand. In addition, employees are encouraged to focus on tasks that will have the biggest impact, rather than getting bogged down in busy work. As a result, teams using an Agile approach tend to produce more impactful work than those using traditional methods.

3. *Faster Decision-Making.*
Another key benefit of business Agile is that it allows for faster decision-making and greater flexibility. This is because one of the hallmarks of Agile is empowered, self-managed teams. The time spent taking issues up the org chart to get approvals before an action can be taken is reduced if

not eliminated and teams move forward more quickly. By pushing the decisions to the teams that have the most information rather than taking a more hierarchical approach, decisions are made quickly and efficiently, based on team insights, data and customer feedback.

This level of flexibility allows businesses to adapt quickly to changing market conditions and customer needs. It also enables them to experiment with new ideas and strategies without being bogged down by red tape or bureaucracy.

4. *Reduced Project Drift.*

In a non-Agile environment, it can be easy to go days or weeks without making much progress on a particular project. This doesn't have to be intentional. It just happens sometimes. No one's tracking the work. No one has any data to set expectations on how long it should take. But in an Agile world, you're doing daily stand-ups and checking status. The work is visible, and progress is shared with everyone. The work tasks are short and focused so that they can be delivered in a two-week sprint. The team has estimated the level of effort needed to complete the work and knows if something's delayed. This added level of oversight and accountability makes it much less likely that a project is going to drift off course.

5. *Increased Employee Satisfaction.*

Another benefit of Agile is that it leads to increased employee satisfaction. This is because Agile teams are typically more collaborative and communicate more often than traditional teams. In addition, empowered employees are given more ownership and autonomy over their work and are encouraged to think creatively about how to solve problems. As a result, they tend to be more engaged and motivated at work. In addition, studies have shown that employees who are given more freedom and flexibility tend to be happier and less stressed than those who feel like they're stuck in a rut or don't have any autonomy over their work environment.

6. *Greater Transparency and Communication.*
Lastly, business Agile increases transparency and communication among employees. We just talked about how important this is earlier in this chapter. Agile helps deliver it. In an Agile organization, everyone understands the goals and objectives of the company—and they know how their work contributes to those goals. Progress is tracked in sharable public methods where everyone has visibility into what's happening, who's on point to deliver, and what's on time or behind schedule. As a result, there's greater transparency and communication between employees and managers. This also results in more trust between people or teams, which can significantly improve team culture.

PFC #6: Keep Your Best People Happy

It's a myth to suggest that people can give 110% effort - mathematically speaking, there is no giving 110% - and most people comfortably work in the 80% effort range. Beyond that range, there are discretionary levels of effort that someone can choose to give, just like you might choose to run a car's engine in the red zone for short periods. But if you run that engine in the red for too long, the engine will blow up. The same can happen with the people on your team if you're not careful.

How do you tap into that discretionary effort? For one, it helps to have a clear mission that people believe in. If people are passionate about the work they're doing, it feels less like work. The Chinese philosopher Confucius has been attributed with saying "Choose a job you love, and you will never have to work a day in your life." If you can inspire that kind of passion or give people the opportunity to do meaningful work that they enjoy, you'll tap that extra energy.

There are a few other things that help people to want to go over and above the call of duty. First, likeability is a big thing. If people like the person they're working for and there's a good relationship there, they'll pitch in to help out in a pinch. They also want to be able to trust that manager and know that the extra work is valued. No one wants to put in the hard work and feel like it was unnoticed or not appreciated. Acknowledge it. Say thank you.

It should also feel like a team effort. If someone's going to have to eat a shit sandwich, spread it around. Everyone gets a bite, including you. Make sure that it's not the same person over and over again just because they don't complain about it.

Make sure that it's not forever. If the short-term crisis becomes a constant state of affairs, eventually even the best people will run out of steam.

Using fear or coercion to motivate people rarely helps sustain their energy in the long run. People perform best when they are intrinsically motivated and feel a sense of autonomy in their actions. You might get away with using fear for short periods every once in a while. But once people realize that it's going to be used more frequently or for extended periods, the best case scenario is they'll figure out other ways to take back the energy by working slower or only doing the minimum viable effort — AKA "quiet quitting." More likely is that they'll bail out as soon as they can get another job lined up.

> When Good People Leave

Churn's impact on a business's customer base is well-established. But what about employee churn? Keeping good people happy costs less than finding new ones and getting them up to the same level of productivity as the person they replaced. When top performers start to leave, often what's left behind is a whole lot of "meh." And unfortunately, there's no way to reclaim the lost energy and experience that disappeared with those who have departed.

If you've got a bunch of mostly average to mediocre performers who are left after your best people bail, it could be because those folks are either already quietly quitting, too low-effort to find another job, or worse, actively looking but no one else wants them. Once you end up here, it can be almost impossible to reset expectations without going through a full team rebuild.

Addressing underperformance and making the low performers accountable is critical to keeping top performers around. Why? Your best people are putting in their best or max effort. They're delivering consistently and on-time. Maintaining a high standard of quality. They also might feel like they're carrying more than their share of the workload. But if no one else seems to care about workload, quality or performance, why should they? Setting high expectations for *everyone* on your team is a good start. But they can't just be blah, blah, blah words. Managing the day-to-day to those standards will show what your real intentions and priorities are. Again, actions speak.

Prioritize your team's workload ruthlessly. Put your best people in high-leverage situations, like a closer in baseball or a quarterback in football. But do it in a balanced way. Overloading their work queue isn't the answer here either. Just make sure that they're always working on interesting, important, and engaging work and once their plate is full, move on to the next plate.

> Some Truths About Burnout

Be careful not to burn out your team. According to the book *The Truth About Job Burnout,* by authors Christina Maslach and Michael P. Leiter, "Burnout is shown to be a sign of a major dysfunction within an organization and says more about the workplace than it does about the employees." It's not them. It's you, because as their manager, you are part of "the workplace" for them.

How do you know if you've got a potential burnout situation? Here are several indicators:

- Lack of engagement
- Poor morale
- Other people have left already
- Negativity and cynicism
- Missed deadlines and low-quality work
- Interpersonal conflicts
- Late to work/early to leave

Another research report, this time from Gallup, suggests that one of the best leading indicators of an at-risk employee is sick days. Per this report, "Burned-out employees are 63% more likely to take a sick day and 2.6 times as likely to be actively seeking a different job." Last-minute, unplanned days off could be the result of a bug going around, taking a mental health day, or someone having a job interview.

Either way, it's an opportunity to do a little introspection. How are you doing as a leader? Are you demonstrating the same habits you expect from your team? Or is there a little bit of "Do as I say, not as I do" going on? Are you hiring the right people? Giving them clear roles? Making sure that they have the resources to execute? Removing any blockers? Creating alignment between the work being done and the company's goals?

Are you dealing with the perfect storm of "Ugh"? Too much poorly-defined work. Unreasonable deadlines. Insufficient resources. A general lack of daily support from leaders or other work teams. If this sounds too familiar, is it any wonder that good smart people would eventually end up frustrated and leave? In fact, why are you still there? If you stay, what can you do to make it better?

> Building A Team

If you're in the position to do it, start by bringing in the right people in the first place. Hire for culture and fit. When you're building a product-focused business culture, it's important to surround yourself with people who share your vision—people who will buy into your mission and help you achieve your goals. That means when you're hiring new team members, the fit should be just as important as the skillset. I would argue that it's even more important.

The best way to hire for fit is to develop a clear understanding of your company culture and then use that as a guide when conducting interviews. When I hire people, once I've established their basic ability to do the needed work, I'm looking for intelligence and grit. I define grit as passion plus resilience. If you hire smart, self-starting, and persistent people, your team can weather almost anything the world throws at you. Ask behavioral questions that will allow candidates to show whether or not they share your company's values. And don't be afraid to dig deep—you want to make sure they believe what they're saying and that they would be comfortable working in an environment where those values are held in high regard.

You're building a team and the pieces have to fit. If you were building a house and threw windows, doors, walls, and floors together without a care for the overall design and aesthetic, how well would that work? If it did manage to look ok, it would just be dumb luck and that's no way to succeed consistently. There are a lot of people who can do the work. The right person can do the work well in the work environment that you're trying to create. The wrong person can not only fail at their job but also make your team less productive. Remember, you're trying to optimize across the entire team and not just individuals.

We talked earlier about the importance of learning in a product-centered culture. It's also relevant as we talk about how to keep people happy. If you want to build a deep bench of talented people, a continuous learning and training plan has to be a part of it. Make sure to cross-train your team so that they have exposure to a broad range of projects and platforms. As I mentioned, there's a tendency to go to the same people all the time because they've delivered for you in the past. But it's a balancing act to get work done efficiently while developing your people. If you wear out a path taking projects to the same members of your team, you could be pushing them out the door.

Finding a path that allows for rapid experimentation with new ideas is critical for any company that wants to stay ahead of the competition. However, it can be difficult to encourage employees to experiment when they're worried about making mistakes. One way to overcome this is to create a culture of where mistakes are seen as opportunities for learning rather than failures. Additionally, you can provide employees with the resources they need to experiment quickly and efficiently. Finally, make sure that employees understand that experimentation is valued and encouraged at all levels of the organization.

An important part here is giving your team autonomy and trust. One of my former bosses, Brian Smith, used to say, "There aren't enough people here that I trust that I can disagree with." He was hoping to have diverse viewpoints shared in an atmosphere of trust where disagreement was healthy and could lead to better overall solutions. If there's a sense of psychological safety in your workplace, it can foster the collaboration and creativity that most organizations crave. What is psychological safety? It's the idea that you can share thoughts, ideas, and feelings without feeling like you're making a possible career-limiting move in the process. Research has shown that improving psychological safety has several benefits beyond collaboration and creativity, such as improved employee engagement and morale, reduced turnover, and better team performance.

Because product-focused cultures are built on this trust between team members and trust between leaders and their employees, make time for it. As I've been writing this book, my cat Reggie likes to make me take an occasional break by jumping up in my lap. Once he's there, he'll push against my leg in such a way that he knows he's going to fall off backward unless I catch or cradle him. Essentially, he's doing trust falls and knows that I'll keep him from going splat on the floor. While HR might frown on the idea of jumping in each other's lap, your team can still do trust falls or other team-bonding activities like volunteer work. Build team trust. Let them know that you're there to keep them from going splat. On one of my teams, we had a monthly lunch outing, and we rotated the choice of restaurant to a different team member each month. Whether it's going out for drinks after work, doing volunteer work or playing softball on Saturdays, bonding activities help break down barriers and create an environment where people feel comfortable being themselves—an environment where creativity can thrive.

> Only You Can Practice Your Self-Care

Keeping your team happy is a critical part of a team leader's job. But there's an even more important person to keep happy every day.

You.

Anyone who's ever had a job knows that it's not always easy to maintain a healthy work-life balance. It can be downright difficult at times. That's why it's important to make self-care a priority and to set boundaries to avoid job burnout. Here are four tactics that can help you do just that.

1. *Unplug after work.* It can be tempting to stay glued to your laptop after clocking out for the day, but it's important to

unplug and take a break. Whether you use that time to relax, exercise or spend time with loved ones, make sure you're taking some time for yourself. Otherwise, you run the risk of burning out. To this day, I have a rule to never check my work email after 8 PM. This came as a result of too many sleepless nights after a last check of email right before going to bed. It'll be there in the morning. You'll be better able to deal with it if you're fully rested.

2. *Set limits on work hours.* One of the best ways to avoid job burnout is to set limits on how many hours you're willing to work each week. This is especially important as work-from-home and other remote work options increase. Of course, there will be times when you have to put in extra hours, but try to stick to your limit as much as possible. If you have to consistently work more than fifty hours a week, you're subsidizing the business with free work. Draw a line. If adding a full-time person is out of the picture, bring in a part-timer to offload some of those extra hours. Or go through the time budgeting process we outlined earlier in this book and stick to the results. You'll be glad you did when you have more free time to enjoy your life outside of work.

3. *Take your vacation days.* Vacation days are there for a reason, so use them! Even if you can't take a long trip, use your vacation days to take mini-breaks throughout the year. And when you're away, be away. Don't take your work with you and just set up a satellite office from your Airbnb. Be present where you are and gather new experiences away from your office. Those real-life interactions will make you a better product manager. You'll be a little more empathic and come back from your vacations feeling refreshed and ready to tackle whatever challenges come your way.

4. *Practice self-care.* Last but not least, make sure you're taking care of yourself both physically and mentally. This means eating right, getting enough sleep, and exercising regularly.

Be a part of a community. Stay connected with friends and loved ones. It also means taking time for activities that make you happy and reduce stress levels. When you practice self-care, you'll be better equipped to handle whatever comes your way both at work and at home.

This last point is really important to keep in mind. Being a product leader is a great job and a great career. I love doing product work. But always remember that your job is not who you are. This can be tough. Think about when you introduce yourself to someone new. One of the first things people will ask about or that you'll offer up is where you work and what you do there. And the more you love your job, the easier it is to think that this job you love defines who you are. It can be easy to get so plugged into a job that you forget the other aspects of your life that are important to you.

But your job is not who you are.

Think about it this way. As a productive person, you're always going to have a lot on your plate. It's also rare that you won't have several other things you think you could be doing if you had more time. While I'm not here to say that how you prioritize your life and the choices you make won't have consequences, they're still your choices to make. You get to draw the lines and set the boundaries.

Back during my Sprint days, I had taken over managing an established product and the first week on the job, I found myself in the middle of renegotiating a contract with the vendor from the current pay-per-usage price to a volume-based tiered pricing model. This was a critical issue for us as we were delivering serious scale to this vendor and a new deal was expected to save us around $200M over the three-year life of the contract.

A couple of weeks into the job, my new boss stopped by to see how things were going with the deal. I told him I thought we were making good progress and that my only real concern was that we might be squeezing them so tightly that ultimately they wouldn't be able to stay profitable and we'd lose them as a partner as a result. This was not unrealistic, as Sprint had a reputation for grinding down partners and then flipping them out for someone else without a thought towards the customer impacts.

My boss's response was something that's stuck with me ever since. "Jeff, we're going to push them. We have to trust that they know how to run their business and how to set boundaries so that we don't force them into a situation they can't support long-term."

This made sense. I agreed with him. Then I went out and over the next couple of weeks, we closed the revised deal with them.

A little more time passed, and my boss was checking in again. This time, he wanted to know how I thought things were going in the new job. Generally OK, I said and then outlined a couple of areas of concern to which my boss replied...

"Well, I'm gonna push ya..."

And even though he didn't say the rest, my mind connected back to his original words, but now paraphrasing them for me: "And I'm gonna trust that you know how to run your business and set boundaries, so that I don't force you into a situation you can't support long-term."

Only you can know where to draw your boundaries. Only you know if you're getting pushed into a situation that you can't support long-term. If you say you've got it, your boss is going to reasonably expect that you've got it. If you need help, ask. Sooner is always better than later. And remember, you're the reason it's called **self**-care, so please take good care of yourself. If you don't, who will?

Final Thoughts

That's it. That's the book. Thanks for taking the time to read it. But hopefully, while this is the end of the book, it's just the start of our conversation. If you found the information here useful, please drop me a note or connect with me on LinkedIn.

My email is jc@tyghtwyre.com. There's a blog on the Tyghtwyre website (www.tyghtwyre.com) where I drop other interesting nuggets from time to time. The book's website can be found at www.whatmakesgreatproductsgreat.com. Scan the QR codes to get all the links. You'll also be able to sign up for a newsletter and download a set of templates for the forms and diagrams in the book. If the time and space work out, I'm always up for a Zoom call, a coffee or a happy hour – I love to connect with product people, so please don't be shy.

Let's build great products and make a better world.

Together.

JC

CHAPTER NOTES

COMMUNITY

If you're interested in connecting with other product people who have read this book, head on over to our community page where you'll find the links to join our groups.

FUTURE CHAPTERS

If you'd like to get updates when we revise the chapters in this book or see early versions of chapters that may appear in future editions of this book, scan this QR code.

DOWNLOADS

If you'd like to get copies of the templates and diagrams in the book, scan this QR code

ACKNOWLEDGEMENTS

Since this is my first (but hopefully not my only) book, these acknowledgements may end up a bit longer and more inclusive but there have been a lot of people who have helped me get to this point and I don't want to leave anyone out.

First, I'd like to thank you, my reader. When you spend a couple years pouring what you know into a manuscript, you wonder if anyone will care when it's done. The fact that you're here reading it will always be something that fills me with gratitude.

To my early readers Lise Keeney, Michael Hoeschele and Claire Cooper, who read some pretty rough drafts, saw chapters that were a mess and gave me quality feedback that made this a far better book. I thank you and the readers also thank you.

To my allies Rick Morton, Anne Schoofs, and Vanessa Suwak, it's been more than six years since we've officially worked together, and we still have recurring one-on-one meetings on our calendars. I think that says a lot. I'm glad to have you as part of my trusted inner circle and hope that we'll have a great reason to work together again someday.

To Jessica Best (BetterAve), you patiently listened to all the stories as I was on this journey, shared great insights, gave me a great quote and provided endless support. I hope I can be there to do the same when you write the book that I know you have in you. Thanks for everything you do.

To Jason "Delk" Delker and Brian Smith. We've fought a lot of battles together and won more than our share. Thanks for always pushing me to do better. I hope I did justice to our stories. Delk, my first Kansas City friend and eventual best man, can you believe it's been twenty-five years? Thanks for being there, brother.

To John-Paul "JP" Cargnelli and Asif Alamgir, this wasn't the path we started on, but I'm glad we're here. Proud of the work you've done with your EdTech product and hope to see it reach the scale it deserves. Looking forward to the path forward from here and thank you for all your support and encouragement along the way.

I talk to a lot of people over coffee as well as work with and coach a lot of people and start-ups. Time to out myself here. They've all been my test market for this book. Their questions and reactions helped refine the stories in this book. Nearly everything in this book was said to at least one of them before it showed up here. I'd like to thank them for their curiosity and enthusiasm. They give me energy. Thanks to Kaitlyn Brennan, Mike Gugliuzza, Karen Smecher, Kaius Vu, Rafael Cardenas, Asami Wright, Vanessa Saunders, Matt Lace, Ifeoluwa Damilola Ayeni, Anna Bradsher, Allison Daley, Pravin Kancherla, Sarah Schumacher, Carey Rich, Julie Hall, John Coler, Rachel Cohen, Tamantha Means, Ted Grothe, Kirk Lakebrink, Stephanie Shelton, Jay Austin, Jack Blake, Betty Jones, Brandon Fuhr, Cambrian (Joel Teply, Heather Spalding), Epigraph (Bruno Guerreiro, Caleb Dermyer, Jasper Mullarney), Stenovate (Lauren Lawrence, Lee Zuvanich), The Beacon (Kelsey Ryan), Boddle (Clarence Tan), Heavy Tech (Matt Atkins, Steve Condon), Taurio (Julie Jackson), Course Cubby (Laura Patten), QMocha (Arvind Baliga), Clara Biotech (Jim West III), EB Systems (Jonathan Ruiz, Brendan Waters), and Canine Solutions (Emily Coleman).

To Malvina Velia, thanks for the QR codes idea. Looks pretty good, don't you think? To Geoff Tolsdorf, thanks for sharing your insights about the publishing process and patiently answering my questions. It always helps to know someone. To Alana Muller, thanks for the coffee meetup. I tried to follow your advice, both for networking (Coffee Lunch Coffee) and book publishing (own your own ISBNs) and here we are. Thanks!

During the pandemic, I discovered LunchClub as an outlet to meet and network with people online. Those connections were a lifeline for my quarantined sanity and many of those relationships have extended well beyond our initial conversation. Again, they became the test market for the stories told here. I'd like to thank all of them but especially Brian Monthie, Troy Winfrey, Brandon Badgett, David Caha, LA Walker, Robb Cheeks, Svetlana Kurilova, Kellan Fluckiger, Mark Herre, Juliette Zhang, Ben Guttmann, Mike Verret, Isabel Restrepo and Sandy Liu for all your thoughtful insights, support and encouragement.

One of the LunchClub folks that deserves a special shout out is Eric Burgess. When I first talked to Eric, I was really struggling to get this book done. Eric told me about something called London Writers' Salon and Writers' Hour where I could show up in a Zoom room for an hour four times a day and write in silence with as many as a couple hundred fellow writers. I started showing up May 10th, 2022, and haven't missed a weekday since. Thanks Eric more than you'll ever know.

To Matt Trinetti and Parul Bavishi, the founders of The London Writers' Salon, thanks for the community you've created. Thanks also to the members of that community. I'd estimate that I've spent more than 600 hours online with all of you. Over 600 daily words of wisdom later, I know this book wouldn't be done without the support of this group. Thank you.

To my teams throughout my career: Sprint ION, Sprint ID, Sprint Navigation, Softbank, Pinsight, Cincinnati Bell, thanks for the collaboration and the lessons learned that turned into wisdom shared in this book. Thanks especially to the ID and Pinsight teams where I think we did some of the very best work I've seen during my career: Jeff Contino, Abhik Barua, Mike Gailloux, Tom Anderson, Samuel Golomeke, Sowmya Kamaraju, Richard Dysinger, Danny Cates, Kenn Raaf, Bonnie Shakib, Katie Monsees, Jay Indurkar, Anand Arivukkarasu, Dan Dryden and Jen Walsh.

Thanks to all the people who helped me, collaborated with me, corrected me, counseled me or inspired me while I was at Sprint or Pinsight Media and have stayed connected in the post-Sprint days: Gil Gilliam, Jeff Luther, Jenny Tarwater, Ben Jones, Rob Burcham, Gooch Denice, Ashley Ivkovic (Have A F*cking Point!) Jon Ochenas, Jenn Brockman, Serge Bushman, Bryan Gorman, Donnelle Weller, Harry Lai, Jennifer Schafer, John Swiecicki, Brooke Bobe, JP Brocket, Charnsin Tulyasathien, Kristen Miller, Beth Gorzney, Brian Burchfield, Clyde Heppner, Cindy Sullivan, Charles Stunson, Scott Gibson, Alison Hill, Kristin Simeroth, Bob Winebrenner, and Monique Faros. Let's grab coffee or a drink sometime soon so I can thank you again personally.

At one company early in my career, I worked with eight different bosses over a two-year period. Then I came to Sprint and started to hit my stride working with a series of senior leaders including Jerry Adriano, Paul Sapenaro, Doug Dickerson, Evan Conway, Prag Shah, Ashwin Shashindranath, Joe Dudley, Mark Bolar and Nathan Stout. Thanks for your leadership and your example.

When I left Sprint/Pinsight and started up my product management consulting company Tyghtwyre, one of the first things I realized was that my network from Sprint was all over the globe and not really in Kansas City. I started to explore the KC start-up community and found it vibrant and welcoming. There are so many people to thank for making Kansas City a great business ecosystem. I'm sure I'm going to miss some key groups and leave out key people but they include Ewing Marion Kaufman Foundation, Kansas City Business Journal, Startland News, InnovateHER KC (Lauren Conaway), the Start-up Hustle podcast (the Matts - DeCoursey and Watson and Lauren), 1 Million Cups, KCRise Fund (Darcy Howe), UMKC Innovation Center/Technology Ventures Studio/SourceLink/Digital Sandbox KC (Maria Meyers, Jill Meyer, Chris Rehkamp, Charlotte Clark), Novel Capital (Carlos Antequera), Flyover Capital (Thad Langford), Keystone Innovation District (Kevin McGinnis), Pipeline Entrepreneurs (Melissa Vincent), Mid-America Angels, Digital Health KC (Maria Flynn), Seck & Associates (Sheila Seck), Larissa Uredi, Donald Hawkins, Eze Redwood, Toby Rush, Lesa Mitchell, T-Mobile Accelerator (Ari DeGrote, Tina Peterson), Erik Wullschleger, Mike and Gale McRoberts, Full Scale (The Matts, Jessica Powell), PROOF (Grant Gooding, Courtney Chapman), Crema (George Brooks) and so many more. If I missed you, my only excuse is that I relied heavily on my LinkedIn connections as a prompt. Please send me a note so I can include you in future versions of the book.

One of my greatest discoveries in the last six years working in the KC startup community has been finding and participating in mentoring teams through the Enterprise Center in Johnson County. The team mentoring approach is not only great for the startups but gives me a chance to learn from other wiser souls who are giving back to their community. Thanks to all of them but especially to the recent teams that had to listen to me talk about this project for so long and always asked for updates on my progress.

Thanks to all the Growth Mentoring Service mentors including Gary Gilson, Bruce Reed, Adi Walavalkar, John Christy, Taylor Clark, Garet King, Dan O'Reilly, Mickey Parker, Shawn Kinkade, John Hanson, David Larrabee, Elizabeth Usovicz, Becky Johnston, Tracy Nice, Bill Johnston, Matthew Mellor, Kip Wiggins, Cheryl Wright, Ken Millman and Pat Keplinger. Your contributions and wisdom show up in these pages and your support helped keep me motivated to see this project completed. Thanks also to the ECJC team -- Jeff Shackelford, Rebecca Gubbels, and Jenn Hackett along with former teammates Melissa Roberts Chapman, Wayne Morgan and Kathryn Golden for all your energy to make the program happen day-to-day.

To the memory of a couple people who may be gone but who still have an impact on me today, Jack Diemer and Steve Weadock. Jack was one of the first people I ever chose to be on my team working on Sprint ION. He was a great product manager, a fantasy baseball buddy and a loyal friend. Steve was my high school civics teacher who became a trusted friend and always encouraged me to reach my potential. I know he would have been proud to see this book on one of his many bookshelves. Miss you Diemer and Wead.

To Mark Winegardner, my college roommate (also a fantasy baseball champion and very accomplished author) who encouraged me to write my first published pieces for The Miami Student back at Miami University. I think that was the first time that anyone besides a teacher ever read something I wrote, and it changed how I thought of myself. Thanks Mark.

To my brothers, Marc and Scott, two of the most innovative minds I've ever known, thank you for sharing your unique perspectives and imaginative ideas. Your ability to envision and create your art and music is a constant inspiration that drives me to push my boundaries and think outside the box. Thank you for this invaluable lesson.

To my Mom, a champion debater in high school, thanks for teaching me how to put together words in a persuasive way. I hope it showed up in these pages. You encouraged my academic pursuits and also let me make a mess in the kitchen trying to learn to cook. I think that helped start my love of making things.

To my Dad, a coach and teacher, thanks for teaching me that how you win is just as important as winning itself. You showed me how to make hard choices that are aligned with values and integrity. Thanks for always believing in me and encouraging me to take risks. Your example of hard work and dedication has been an inspiration. Mom and Dad, I'll always appreciate your unquestioned love and support.

Thanks to my boys, Reggie and Myles, along with the angels that came before them. I grew up a dog person, but now realize as I get older that cats are more my vibe. YMMV. But no matter what animals you decide to love, our pets love us back and remind us to stay in the moment. Their presence in our life is one of the greatest gifts we can experience. They deserve the best lives we can give to them. Always.

And finally, thanks to my wife Laurie. There are no words sufficient, but I'll try. When you came into my life, everything changed for the better. It hasn't always been easy getting to this point, but I never felt your support waver. This is OUR book. You were the inspiration, the first reader, the trusted editor. Thank you for telling me I could do it on the days I had doubts and for showing up for me when it was hard and I needed a bit of a push. This book wouldn't exist without you. Period. We did it. Together. I love you.

About The Author

Author and Tyghtwyre CEO Jeff Callan has more than 25 years in various product management and strategy leadership roles working with everyone from startups to Fortune 100 companies. As a growth-focused product leader and mentor, he's established a proven track record of taking innovative new ideas and building them into mobile and data products with 10+ million customers, not once but multiple times. Over the past decade, his teams have generated in excess of 1 billion dollars in new bottom line value for his partners and customers through a variety of cost savings, strategic partnerships and revenue growth activities.

Jeff lives with his wife, Laurie, in Overland Park, Kansas where he's best known for his annual Christmas and Halloween lights, his candy-making prowess and his internet radio station, Musical Justice.

Author's Recommended Reading List

People always ask me for book recommendations. These are some of the books I aspired to be worthy of sitting next to on the same shelf when I wrote this one. They've all impacted the words on these pages and I'd highly recommend each of them. You can find an updated list of these recommendations along with my recs for apps, movies, games and other content by using the QR code at the end of the list.

Atomic Habits: An Easy & Proven Way to Build Good Habits & Break Bad Ones - James Clear
Be Obsessed or Be Average - Grant Cardone
Building a Storybrand: Clarify Your Message So Customers Will Listen - Donald Miller
Coffee Lunch Coffee: A Practical Field Guide for Master Networking - Alana Mueller
Competing With Luck: The Story of Innovation and Customer Choice - Clayton Christensen
Effortless: Make It Easier to Do What Matters Most - Greg McKeown
Empowered: Ordinary People, Extraordinary Products - Marty Cagan, Chris Jones
Epic Content Marketing: How to Tell a Different Story, Break Through the Clutter, and Win More Customers by Marketing Less - Joe Pulizzi
Essentialism: The Disciplined Pursuit of Less - Greg McKeown
Fix This Next: Make the Vital Change That Will Level Up Your Business - Mike Michalowicz
Growth Hacker Marketing: A Primer on the Future of PR, Marketing and Advertising - Ryan Holiday
Hooked: How To Build Habit-Forming Products - Nir Eyal, Ryan Hoover
How To Win at The Sport of Business - Mark Cuban

Inspired: How to Create Tech Products Customers Love - Marty Cagan

Measure What Matters: How Google, Bono and the Gates Foundation Rock the World with OKRs - John Doerr

One Small Step Can Change Your Life: The Kaizen Way to Success - Dr. Robert Maurer

Product-Led Growth: How to Build a Product That Sells Itself - Wes Bush

Quit: The Power of Knowing When To Walk Away - Annie Duke

Scrum: The Art of Doing Twice The Work in Half the Time - Jeff Sutherland, J.J. Sutherland

Sprint: How to Solve Big Problems and Test New Ideas in Just Five Days - Jake Knapp with John Zeratsky and Braden Kowitz

Start With Why: How Great Leaders Inspire Everyone to Take Action - Simon Sinek

Superfans: The Easy Way to Stand Out, Grow Your Tribe, and Build a Successful Business - Pat Flynn

The Cold Start Problem: How to Start and Scale Network Effects - Andrew Chen

The Creative Act: A Way of Being - Rick Ruben

The Design of Everyday Things - Don Norman

The E-Myth Revisited: Why Most Small Businesses Don't Work and What to Do About It - Michael E. Gerber

The Hard Thing About Hard Things: Building a Business When There Are No Easy Answers - Ben Horowitz

The Infinite Game - Simon Sinek

The Lean Product Playbook: How to Innovate with Minimum Viable Products and Rapid Customer Feedback - Dan Olsen

The Lean Startup: How Today's Entrepreneurs Use Continuous Innovation to Create Radically Successful Businesses - Eric Ries

The Making of a Manager: What to Do When Everyone Looks to You - Julie Zhuo

The Obstacle is the Way: The Timeless Art of Turning Trials into Triumph - Ryan Holiday

The Signal and the Noise: Why So Many Predictions Fail - But Some Don't - Nate Silver

The 6 Types of Working Genius: A Better Way to Understand Your Gifts, Your Frustrations and Your Team - Patrick Lencioni

The Upside of Stress: Why Stress is Good for You and How to Get Good at It - Kelly McGonigal

Think Again: The Power of Knowing What You Don't Know - Adam Grant

Thinking, Fast and Slow - Daniel Kahneman

This is Marketing: You Can't Be Seen Until You Learn to See - Seth Godin

Tools of Titans: The Tactics, Routines and Habits of Billionaires, Icons and World-Class Performers - Tim Ferriss

Traction: Get a Grip on Your Business - Gino Wickman

Who Not How: The Formula to Achieve Bigger Goals Through Accelerating Teamwork - Dan Sullivan, Dr. Benjamin Hardy

Updated Recommendations List

INDEX

20/50 brainstorming 387, 388

300-year plan 70
360 performance review 403, 404
80/20 rule (Pareto Principle)
  .... 60, 64, 190, 354

A
Acceptance criteria 226, 227, 228, 232, 318
Ad/data subsidized 366, 388
Advertising .. 43, 151, 152, 330, 331, 343, 430
AFC Championship 67
Agile ....17, 106, 216, 236, 254, 391, 406 - 210
Aha! 216, 242, 245
Amazon .30, 96, 99, 216, 230, 231, 232, 336, 380, 392
American Customer Satisfaction Index 300
Analytics.... 46, 102, 106, 107, 110, 111, 117, 123, 174, 229, 322, 393
Andreessen Horowitz ... 286, 292
Andresessen, Marc...... 286, 292, 296
Android 42, 151, 292, 350
Apophenia 117, 118, 119, 132
Artificial intelligence (AI)...... 48, 373, 382
Assembly line ...361, 362, 364, 387
Automation bias 105, 131
Awareness 152, 170, 176, 198, 199, 326, 328, 330, 331, 332, 343, 344

B
Bain & Company 173
Balfour, Brian......... 294, 296, 297
Bardeen, John.......................... 148
Barksdale, Jim 116
Beepi 368
Belichick, Bill .... 66 - 68
Bell Labs 148
Bellur, Saraswathi 348
Benz, Carl 361
Bernstein, Leonard 72
Berra, Yogi 54, 178
Big F-ckin' Guy (BFG) ...... 12 - 14
Big Mac 92, 96
Black Keys, The 12
Blizzard Entertainment 247
Blockbuster.......................364, 365
Blockchain 48, 266
Bounce rate..............................277
Brainstorming.... 63, 83, 324, 362, 363, 387, 388
Brattain, Walter...................... 148

Brazil 217
Broadcast.com 87
Budget ... 73, 74, 121, 144, 146, 157, 170, 190, 192, 254, 256, 275, 302, 355, 398
Buffalo Bills 67
Bunyan, Paul 13
Burnout 353, 358, 412, 413
Business case ...... 19, 32, 144, 200, 205 - 214, 315, 385
Business Hierarchy of Needs .. 30
Business model ..... 80, 81, 85, 190, 200, 211, 275, 290, 294 - 297, 315, 334, 343, 362 - 371, 387, 388
Business model innovation .. 362, 365, 366, 371, 387
Business Plan 73, 76, 142, 192, 267

C

Callan Curve 377, 378, 380, 382, 388, 389
Callan Data Cycle 108, 112, 131
Capacity plan 317
CB Insights 260
Champ De Mars 178, 179
ChatGPT 48, 266
Checklist .... 7, 143, 151, 213, 310 - 315, 322, 323, 324, 391
Chen, Andrew 292, 431
Chicken Boy 13
Christensen, Clayton 93, 98, 430

Churn rate 278, 279, 283, 291, 292, 393
Cincinnati 66, 382
Cincinnati Bengals 66
Cirillo, Francesco 353, 359
Cisco 383
Clark, Dorie 53
Cohort retention 291
Collaboration ..... 38, 44 - 46, 122, 199, 268, 363, 405, 407, 415, 425
Communication ..... 15, 18, 24, 25, 38, 44, 45, 73, 78, 85, 134, 167, 179, 216, 217, 231, 235, 242, 255, 258, 268, 303, 308, 311, 324, 336, 344, 350, 382, 391, 398 - 407, 410
Competing Against Luck . 94, 98
Competition ..... 6, 31, 74, 81, 87 - 92, 97, 98, 119, 123, 152, 168, 188, 190, 193, 197, 219, 265, 293, 355, 362, 365, 371, 372, 377 - 379, 381, 388, 397, 415
Competitive analysis 315
Computer Reseller News 87
Confirmation bias 105
Confucius 410
Consideration 306, 323, 328, 333, 334, 343
Contract .. 208, 242, 310, 311, 320, 324, 335, 418
Costco 294
Covey, Stephen 404

CRM (Customer relationship management) 110, 282
C-suite 8, 10, 40, 73, 263
Cuban, Mark 87, 88, 97, 98, 430
Customer acquisition cost 32, 342
Customer feedback .... 37, 42, 43, 51, 152 - 154, 162, 169 - 176, 263, 266, 270, 279, 393, 409
Customer interviews 161, 169, 170, 175, 176, 393
Customer journey .... 326 - 343
Customer lifetime value 275, 338
Customer satisfaction score (CSAT) 280, 281, 284
Customer touchpoints ... 327, 343

D

Daily Active Users (DAU) 180, 276, 277, 284
Daily Average Users 42
Dallas Mavericks 87
Data ... 6, 37, 43, 46, 47, 51, 52, 62, 78, 96, 99 - 120, 133, 144, 145, 155, 159, 161, 175, 229, 262, 269, 273, 275, 280 - 284, 299, 317, 319, 322, 337, 360, 370, 371, 380, 383, 393, 406, 408, 409, 429
Data bias 131
Data collection . 105, 110, 114, 124, 126, 133, 282, 317

Data Science 102
Data strategy .... 122 - 124, 132
Data validation plan 317
Dayton 92
Delker, Jason 12, 416
Deming Wheel .... 106 - 108
Deming, W. Edwards 106
Design thinking 268
Digital Wellbeing 350
Disney 95, 234
Do This First 352
Dollar Shave Club 370
Doyle, Arthur Conan 108
Dropbox 269, 394, 395
Drucker, Peter 128, 260, 269, 270
Dykes, Brent 102

E

Edison, Thomas 387
Eiffel Tower 178, 179
Einstein, Albert 36, 79, 189
Eisenhower Matrix 55, 57, 64, 65, 251, 252, 258
Eisenhower, Dwight D. 55
El Pollo Rey 29
Electric Daisy Carnival 22
Elevator Pitch .... 6, 78 - 83, 85
Elliott, Jane 103
Ellis, Sean 292, 297
Esrey, Bill 299
Essential Scrum 216
Essentialism 59, 64, 430

Exploring Data
  An Introduction to Data
  Analysis for Social
  Scientists 103
Exponential innovation 362, 373, 374, 388
Exponential Innovation Mashup Matrix 374, 375, 389

F
Facebook .. 103, 104, 286, 288, 371
Fail fast 289
Fast Food Nation 95
Feature team 40
Ferriss, Tim 60, 432
Fierce Wireless 300
Fix This Next 30, 430
Flat rate pricing 366, 367, 388
Forbes 102
Ford 31, 217, 361, 362, 364
Ford Pinto 31, 217
Ford, Henry 361, 387
Formal communication 399, 400, 402, 406
Franklin, Benjamin 346
Freemium 295, 366, 369, 370, 388, 394, 395
Frequently Asked Questions (FAQ) 230, 320, 329
Frito-Lay 27
Fulfillment 200, 255, 328, 336, 337, 343, 344, 353, 358, 368
Future of Work 78

G
Gemini Giant 13
Gillette 370
Gladwell, Malcolm 119
Goals ..... 19, 20, 36, 37, 39, 41, 45, 47-49, 51, 52, 54, 57, 58, 61, 67, 68, 70-76, 83-85, 96 -98, 110, 112, 120, 123, 126, 128, 132, 136 - 139, 143, 146, 163-165, 176, 180 - 189, 194 - 204, 226, 230, 235 - 237, 240, 244, 250 - 255, 257 - 359, 269, 272 - 275, 281 - 284, 299 - 312, 342, 351, 354, 362, 363, 368, 382, 396, 406, 410, 413, 414, 432
GOAT (Greatest of All Time) 6, 66, 286
Good Mythical Morning 376
Google 30, 160, 174, 175, 177, 178, 273, 282, 332, 350, 371, 373, 380, 397, 431
Google Analytics 174, 175, 177
Go-to-market plan 61, 200
Grammarly 394

H
Happy Meal 95, 96
Harvard Business Review. 53, 172
HBO 248
Hesse, Dan 299, 300
Hewlett-Packard 286
HiPPO 163
Historical bias 105, 131
Hoffman, Reid 60

Holmes, Sherlock 108
Hull, Kyle 348

I
Ideation 15, 141, 142, 146, 362
Incremental innovation 373, 374, 388
Influencers 163, 176, 225, 401, 402
Informal communication ... 399 - 401, 404, 406
Innovation . 7, 43, 44, 59, 93, 108, 205, 334, 361 - 365, 372 - 374, 386 - 388, 392, 397, 398, 426, 430, 431
Instagram 225, 226, 375
Intellectual property 211, 322
International Fiberglass 13, 24
Interpersonal Skills . 17, 18, 24, 25
Interruption culture 346, 350, 352, 358
Interruptions . 346, 349 - 353, 358, 359
Invoicing 318
iPhone 148
iPod 148

J
Japan 151, 216
JD Power 300
Job burnout 89, 416, 417
Jobs To Be Done 88, 94, 98
Jobs, Steve 59, 101, 131, 148
Juicero 260

K
Kahneman, Daniel ... 62, 347, 432
Kanban board 140
Kansas City 12, 23, 29, 423, 426
Kawasaki, Guy 120
Kelly, Jim 67
Key Performance Indicators (KPI) .... 73, 272 - 275, 283
Kickstarter 374
Killedbygoogle.com 380
King, Stephen 129
Knapp, Jake 216, 431
Kurzweil, Ray ... 373, 377, 382, 385

L
La Whiskeria 234
Lagging indicators 113, 131
Lao-Tzu 56
Las Vegas 22, 67
Le Petit Prince 187
Lead generation 321
Leading indicators 113, 131, 413
Leiter, Michael P. 412
Lencioni, Patrick 55, 432
Light bulbs 21
LinkedIn 60, 317, 420, 426
Location bias 105
Lockheed Martin 215
Lofton, James 67
London Writers' Salon 272, 352, 425
Lord Kelvin 127, 128

Loyalty ..... 173, 176, 193, 278, 280, 281, 326 - 328, 336, 338, 340 - 344, 367, 372, 393, 399

M

Market opportunity .15, 80, 81, 85
Market research 188, 202, 219, 282
Marketing 8, 15, 18, 19, 24, 25, 28, 30, 33, 40, 61, 62, 69, 71, 73, 76, 94, 111, 112, 127, 143, 151, 152, 158, 163, 167, 170, 176, 189, 192, 198, 200, 219, 230 - 232, 241, 255, 258, 262, 269, 270, 275, 276, 294, 314 - 321, 331 - 342, 365, 370, 371, 395 - 398, 407, 430, 432
Marketing Plan ... 73, 76, 200, 317
Marketplace .80, 94, 97, 330, 366, 368, 388
Mars Climate Orbiter 215
Marsh, Catherine 103
Maslach, Christina 412
McClure, Dave 290
McKeown, Greg 59, 64, 430
McLaughlin, Rhett 375
Meta 248
Metaderm 397
Michalowicz, Mike 30, 430
Michigan State 349
Microsoft 78, 85, 247
MicroSolutions 87
Minimum Sellable Product 263 - 267, 270

Minimum Viable Product (MVP) .... 7, 260 - 270, 431
Minimum Viable Prototype 7, 150, 158, 220, 260, 270
Model-T 361, 364, 387
Monday 9, 62, 216, 242, 245
Monthly active users 277
Monthly recurring revenue ... 275
MOS transistor 148
MoSCoW 255, 256, 258
Muffler men 13, 14, 23, 24
Multitasking ... 346 - 348, 358, 359

N

Nadella, Satya 78, 85
Narrative ..... 79, 84, 101, 102, 111, 129 - 132, 179, 184, 202, 212, 235, 241, 248, 255, 301, 308, 391, 398 - 400
NASA 215
National Football League (NFL) 66, 67
National Hockey League (NHL) 119, 120
Naughty Dog 248
Neal, Link 375
Net Promoter Score 173, 176, 195, 275, 280, 284, 291, 297, 393
Netflix 364, 366, 388
Netscape 116, 286
New England Patriots 66
New York Giants 67
Nextel 205, 299
No Meeting Fridays 351

Nobel Prize 62, 148
North Star ..... 6, 178 - 188, 194, 201 - 203, 390
Novak, Kristine 348

O

Obama, Barack 50
Objective/Key Results (OKR) 73, 143, 194, 195, 198, 201, 203, 204, 211, 273, 304, 309, 322, 431
Oculus 286
Olestra 27, 28
Onboarding ...... 32 - 34, 124, 152, 158, 265, 318, 321, 336, 337, 344, 396
One-Page Product Plan . 187, 194, 203, 304, 309
Opsware 286
Outlier bias 105
Outliers 115, 119
Overland Park 3, 382, 429
Overwatch 247, 248

P

P&G Ventures Studio 397
Pareto Principle (80-20 Rule) 60, 64, 190, 354
Patents 12, 150, 211, 322
Picasa 380
Pirate Metric 290, 297
Planning .. 15, 24, 39, 48, 51, 60 - 76, 107, 121, 145, 189, 197 - 201, 234, 235, 244, 248, 256, 269, 317, 332, 407
Planning Fallacy .... 62 - 64
Pomodoro Technique ... 353, 354, 358, 359
Press release 201, 230, 317, 320
Pricing schedule 319
Pricing Strategy 200, 203
Prioritization .... 7, 54, 134, 141, 142, 146, 173, 247, 250, 257 - 259, 354, 364
Privacy compliance 317
Pro Football Hall of Fame 66
Problem solving 17, 18, 24
Problem statement 201, 207, 214, 232
Process .. 15, 24, 32, 38, 42, 44, 46, 52, 66, 68, 69, 72, 75, 76, 83, 85, 103 - 114, 120 - 125, 132 - 146, 149, 156, 158, 161, 162, 167, 168, 176, 187 - 189, 192, 199, 202, 213 - 218, 225 - 227, 230, 236, 240, 255 - 257, 261, 266, 268, 270, 276, 280, 289, 304, 311, 314, 330, 335 - 337, 343, 344, 348, 354, 355, 357, 362, 364, 365, 367, 372, 374, 379, 381, 386 - 388, 396, 401, 415, 417, 424
Process innovation 362, 364, 365, 388
Procter & Gamble 27, 28, 397
Product dashboard . 273, 281, 282, 284

Product data sheet 319
Product development ..... 40, 42, 44, 46, 141 - 146, 162, 167, 187, 189, 192, 243 - 245, 261, 263, 342, 393, 396
Product documentation . 318, 319, 329
Product Feature Tracking Template 220
Product features 219, 399
Product fulfillment 151, 318
Product innovation 362, 365, 372, 382, 388
Product life-cycle ..... 15, 149 - 152, 158, 159, 167, 274
Product manager ..... 10 - 24, 36, 40, 42, 49, 68, 75, 78, 85, 101, 111, 112, 116 - 122, 132, 134, 159, 161, 165 - 168, 174, 175, 216, 218, 234, 235, 243, 244, 262, 322, 327, 417, 427
Product marketing 10, 17
Product plan .. 6, 72 - 76, 187-189, 192, 194, 199 - 204, 230, 235
Product requirements 17, 215, 216, 217, 222, 223, 230, 231, 232
Product Requirements Doc (PRD) .... 216 - 232
Product roadmap ..... 40, 69, 234 - 236, 240, 242 - 244
Product support 31, 318

Product team ...... 37 - 49, 161, 163, 167 - 169, 175, 199, 223, 229, 255
Product test plan 317
Product training 320
Product vision 17, 179, 184, 235
Product-channel fit 294
Product-focused culture 11, 390, 391, 416
Productivity ...... 38, 50, 62, 346 - 359, 408, 411
Productivity Challenge Timer 353
Product-led growth 391, 394
Product-market fit (PMF) .. 286 - 298
Project management 15, 20, 24, 37, 49, 52, 192, 382
Project Plan 73, 76
Prototyping ... 141 - 143, 220, 266 - 271
Psychological safety 415
Purchase ... 30, 94, 96, 99, 115, 125, 143, 205, 261, 262, 276, 281, 326, 328, 333 -337, 343, 344, 380, 396

Q

Quality Assurance (QA) 139, 216, 227, 228, 232, 280, 318
Quettra 292
Quick reference guide 320
Quiet quitting 411

R

Rachleff, Andy.................286, 296
Reed, Andre...................................67
Reichheld, Fred..........................173
Render 380
Research ..... 13, 15, 26, 30, 42, 74, 76, 121, 141, 142, 146, 150, 171, 173, 187 - 189, 190, 192, 194, 201 - 204, 210, 213, 217, 218, 229, 314, 326, 328, 333, 334, 347, 348, 358, 385, 391, 393, 397, 398, 413, 415
Residential Gateway................383
Resource Plan...................200, 203
Retention .....38, 50, 107, 154, 172, 176, 275, 278, 279, 281, 284, 290 - 292, 297, 337, 338, 393, 394
Retention rate 275, 278, 279, 281, 291, 292, 338
Revenue churn...........................279
Rhett and Link..........................376
Ries, Eric 266, 267, 289, 431
Risk management plan............201
Roadside America........................13
Rock and Roll Hall of Fame .. 310
Rolling Stone.......................72, 310
Rolling Stones..............................72
Roth, David Lee................310, 323
Rubin, Kenneth.........................216
Rule of 40 ....290, 297
Ruthless prioritization 248, 249, 258

S

SaaS (Software-as-a-Service) 282, 291, 292, 369, 388
Saez, Andrea..............................237
Sales .... 8, 9, 12, 15, 18, 27 - 34, 40, 60, 61, 71, 111 - 113, 118, 125, 143, 148, 150 - 153, 158, 161, 163, 167, 170, 171, 175, 176, 180, 189, 192, 195 - 200, 217, 219, 229, 230, 241, 242, 245, 260, 262 - 264, 274 - 276, 279, 295, 307, 308, 314, 317, 319, 321, 331 - 341, 367, 377, 395, 396, 407
Sales contract 319, 336
Sales demo 321
Sales presentation 319
Sales training.............................319
San Francisco 49ers...................66
Sandberg, Sheryl.......................248
Scrum ..17, 73, 216, 223, 225, 407, 431
Scrum: The Art of Doing Twice the Work in Half the Time..................................216
Search Engine Optimiization (SEO)................................331, 332
Security compliance 317
Selection bias 105, 131
Self-care 88, 416, 417, 419
Service blueprint ... 328 - 330, 343
Serviceable Available Market (SAM)...................................81

Serviceable Obtainable Market (SOM) 81
Shark Tank 87
Shockley, William 148
Shyp..................368
Silicon Valley..................148, 260
Silver, Nate 104, 431
Sinek, Simon 90, 98, 272, 431
Singularity, The 373
Six Sigma..................361
Skarp Technologies 374
Skip-level meeting..................403
Skype..................286
Slack 394, 395
Smith, Brian 415, 423
Snapchat..................375
Social media....30, 61, 62, 151, 182, 199, 225, 317, 330 - 332, 338, 343, 350, 352, 375
Softbank..................70, 71, 425
Son, Masayoshi..................70
Sony..................148, 248
Sony Walkman 148
South by Southwest (SXSW) ..12
Spira, Jonathan..................349
Spotify 288, 366
Springsteen, Bruce 22
Sprint ION......299, 382, 385, 425, 427
Sprint Navigation....160, 173, 425
Stack ranking....253, 254, 357, 359
Stakeholder..24, 68, 70, 114, 161 - 169, 175 - 177, 192, 225, 227, 228, 391, 406

Starbucks 95
Start With Why How Great Leaders Inspire Everyone to Take Action 90, 431
Storytelling ....101 - 103, 130, 131
Strategic Thinking....20, 24, 25, 53, 64, 65
Strategy.....6, 7, 15 - 19, 24, 39, 40, 45, 53 - 59, 64, 67, 68, 71, 73, 75, 107, 108, 112, 120 - 129, 132, 139, 145, 151, 158, 165, 168, 179, 184, 189, 195 - 205, 210 - 214, 220, 230, 234 - 236, 240 - 245, 273, 293, 296 - 309, 317, 332, 380, 382, 388, 391, 394, 395, 396, 404, 429
Strategy alignment 139, 299
Strayer, David 348
Subscription..200, 275, 278, 291, 295, 366 - 370, 387
Sun Tzu 68
Super Bowl ....66 - 68
Support...4, 9, 15, 18, 32 - 34, 62, 63, 71, 108, 124, 125, 127, 139, 150 - 155, 160, 161, 163, 167, 170, 171, 173, 176, 192, 203, 212, 214, 229, 262, 264, 276, 279, 280, 284, 317, 318, 320, 326 - 329, 338 - 344, 364, 413, 419, 423 - 428
Surgical Safety Checklist 313, 324
Sutherland, Jeff 216, 407, 431
Swift, Taylor 288

SWOT analysis 188, 192, 193, 194, 203
System 1 347
System 2 347
Systemic bias 105, 120

T

Tactics...3, 58, 64, 69, 73, 109, 112, 120, 129, 131, 188, 189, 194, 195, 198 - 204, 234, 240, 244, 245, 294, 327, 330, 334, 343, 344, 392, 397, 399, 416, 432
Taleb, Nassim............................ 116
Technical understanding... 17, 18, 24
Test cases 227, 228, 232
Testing......9, 31, 43, 122, 139 - 143, 146, 174, 227, 228, 262, 267 - 269, 280, 289, 321
The 7 Habits of Highly Effective People.................................... 404
The Amazing Race................... 178
The Black Swan 116
The Economist 217, 349
The Emotional Why 93, 95, 99
The Four Whys...6, 87, 88, 93, 98
The Functional Why ... 93, 94, 99
The gambler's fallacy................ 117
The Infinite Game 90, 91, 431
The Last of Us.......................... 248
The Lean Startup.... 266, 289, 431
The Logical Why 93, 96
The Social Why 93, 94, 99
Thematic grouping 255

Thiel, Peter 290
Thinking Fast and Slow 62
Thomas, Thurman.................... 67
Thoreau, Henry David 103
TikTok.......................................375
Time audit 355, 359, 360
Time budget ... 355, 358 - 360, 417
Time Management20, 24, 25, 63, 346, 353, 354, 359
Timeboxing...................... 354, 359
Timeline....16, 73, 74, 76, 121, 132, 157, 198, 201, 203, 208, 213, 234, 237, 241, 256, 263, 354
T-Mobile Center....................... 23
Tools of Titans 60, 432
Total Addressable Market (TAM) 81
Total support calls................... 279
Tour de France 134, 145
Transparency ..122, 390, 391, 398, 399, 401, 406, 410
Tube man....................................14
Tversky, Amos 62
Twitter 175, 286, 375
Twyman, Tony 104, 131
Tyghtwyre 2, 3, 420, 426, 429

U

Uber 292, 368
Unique selling proposition 79
University of California - Irvine 349
User experience UX 43

User trial..................150, 320

V

Value proposition....79, 293, 296, 297, 334, 388, 396
Van Halen 7, 310, 323
Vine.. 375
Vision..... 6, 16, 18, 49, 69 - 71, 75, 101, 164, 179, 182 - 189, 194, 195, 200 - 203, 230, 234, 235, 243, 287, 296, 299, 304 - 308, 380, 414, 427
VOIP (Voice over internet protocol)..............................384
Vonage..384

W

Walsh, Bill................................. 66
Watson, Jason 348
Web3 .... 48, 266
Webinar 321
Weighted scoring matrix.......256, 257

Weller, Edward 215
White paper.............................. 320
Whole Foods 380
Wi-Fi Alliance 383
Will It Taco 376
Word of mouth 331
Workflows 136, 139, 145, 156, 198, 318
World Health Organization..312, 324
WOW Chips............................... 27
WOW-NOW Matrix.............. 382

Y

Yankee Group.......................... 299
Yelp 30
YouTube 30, 90, 317, 375, 376, 380

Z

Zappos...................................... 392
Zevo 397
Zync.. 380

Made in the USA
Las Vegas, NV
01 April 2025

20411202R00246